P9-DXL-116

AUNT WINNIE

The memory is sometimes so retentive, so serviceable, so obedient; at others, so bewildered and so weak; and at others again, so tyrannic, so beyond control!

— Jane Austen, *Mansfield Park*

AUNT WINNIE

ELSPETH CAMERON

The publisher gratefully acknowledges the support of the Canada Council for the Arts and the Ontario Arts Council for its publishing program. We acknowledge the financial support of the Government of Canada through the Canada Book Fund (CBF) for our publishing activities, and the Government of Ontario through the Ontario Media Development Corporation, an agency of the Ontario Ministry of Culture, and the Ontario Book Publishing Tax Credit Program.

LIBRARY AND ARCHIVES CANADA CATALOGUING IN PUBLICATION

Cameron, Elspeth, 1943–, author
Aunt Winnie / Elspeth Cameron.

Issued in print and electronic formats.
ISBN 978-1-77086-290-6 (bound).— ISBN 978-1-77086-292-0 (mobi). —
ISBN 978-1-77086-291-3 (epub)

1. Cameron, Winnie. 2. Cameron, Elspeth, 1943– —Family.
3. Aunts — Ontario — Toronto — Biography. 4. Socialites — Ontario — Toronto — Biography. 5. Debutantes — Ontario — Toronto — Biography. 6. Toronto (Ont.) — Social life and customs — 20th century. 7. Toronto (Ont.) — Biography. I. Title.

FC3097.26.C34C34 2013   971.3'54103092   C2013-903664-4
                                               C2013-903665-2

Cover photo: Winnie Cameron, 1937. Photo by Dorothy Wilding.
Cover design: Angel Guerra/Archetype
Text design: Tannice Goddard, Soul Oasis Networking
Printer: Friesens

Printed and bound in Canada.

MIX
Paper from
responsible sources
FSC® C016245

The interior of this book is printed on 100% post-consumer waste recycled paper.

CORMORANT BOOKS INC.
10 ST. MARY STREET, SUITE 615, TORONTO, ONTARIO, M4Y 1P9
www.cormorantbooks.com

For Hugo Donald Cameron

CONTENTS

1   OF SILVER SPOONS AND GROUNDHOGS   1

2   SEVERAL WINIFREDS   3

3   PORT ELGIN   6

4   THE CANADIAN BANK OF COMMERCE IN DAWSON CITY   11

5   THE CAMERONS IN DAWSON CITY   18

6   GENTLEMAN HUNTERS   24

7   BACK TO DAWSON CITY WITH AUNT PUSSY, 1907   30

8   TORONTO, 1908   33

9   D.A. CLIMBS   40

10   ANOTHER DONALD   45

11   BISHOP STRACHAN SCHOOL   48

12   A VISIT FROM SCOTLAND, 1913   54

13   PARKLANDS: A SCOTTISH IDYLL   58

14   THE DEBUTANTE   65

15   AN IDEAL DANCE PARTY, 1920   75

16   THE BEAUX   80

17   MARRIAGES   91

18   THE QUESTION   96

19   YOUNG DONALD   104

20   AN UNTIMELY DEATH   107

21   A MILITARY FUNERAL, 1925   112

22   A WATERSHED   114

23   RETURN TO APPLEBY SCHOOL   119

24   THE UNIVERSITY OF TORONTO   124

25   THE HEIRESS   128

26   A BREAKDOWN   136

27   "FOR ONCE I FELT LIKE A DUCHESS"   139

28   CONFEDERATION LIFE   144

29   COLLISIONS   151

30   A WAR BABY   157

31   28 DUNDONALD STREET, BARRIE   160

32   128 HUNTLEY STREET, TORONTO   165

33   ROYALTY   170

34 VISITS TO WINNIE 174

35 ANOTHER DEATH 177

36 "OUR BRAVE LITTLE QUEENIE" 182

37 THE ROYAL WEDDING 185

38 THE CABIN 187

39 "SEE THE BROAD HIGHWAY IN YOUR CHEVROLET" 194

40 AUNTNESS, AUNTISM, AUNTDOM 200

41 MORE VISITS TO WINNIE 205

42 MEN 218

43 ANOTHER VISIT FROM SCOTLAND, 1957 221

44 *THAT* CHAIR 224

45 MERRY CHRISTMAS 230

46 MY MOVE TO TORONTO, 1961 239

47 MY MOVE BACK TO TORONTO, 1965 242

48 THE BANKRUPT, 1966 247

49 THE CASTLE 255

50 A VISIT TO THE CASTLE 260

51 A LAST VISIT TO WINNIE 262

52 THE MAUSOLEUM, PORT ELGIN 264

ACKNOWLEDGEMENTS 269

I

OF SILVER SPOONS
AND GROUNDHOGS

Aunt Winnie was born twelve days after the death of Queen Victoria, on 2 February 1901. Mother used to say that though she was born after Victoria's reign she remained Victorian all her life. That was wrong. If anything, Winnie was Edwardian. She was born with a silver spoon in her mouth. Not just the proverbial spoon, but a real one. I still have it. It is ornate, inscribed with her initials in whirls: *W.M.S.C,* for Winifred May Stuart Cameron. My sister and I each received a special spoon as children, and I got this one. My father called it the Pidgie Spoon, since he had nicknamed me Pidge soon after I was born, a ploy meant to unnerve my mother. Winnie also had a silver christening cup engraved with her name and the date: *2nd Feb. 1903.* I have that too. It sits on my mantel, full of matches used to light the fire.

Winnie's father had been posted to Seattle, Washington for a year as relieving manager of the Canadian Bank of Commerce when she was born. He was known there as "the Englishman." Mother liked to remind Winnie that she was an American. When she did, Aunt Winnie

blustered and denied it. She said she was a loyal subject of the King or
Queen, depending. As far as I know, no one but her parents ever saw
her birth certificate. She was always determined to hide her age. Later,
my sister and I went through her purse, her desk, and her drawers, but
we could find no evidence of her age, not even a driver's licence.

The 2nd of February was also Groundhog Day. Winnie did not like
sharing her birthday with groundhogs any more than she liked being
American. She spoke of this every birthday. She was a stout woman
accustomed to wearing her old patchy opossum coat and fur hat
inside as well as outside in winter. From a distance she looked rather
groundhoggish in the snow. Inside, her furs caused some controversy.
Father insisted the thermostat be turned down; Winnie insisted it be
turned up; my mother rolled her eyes.

SEVERAL
WINIFREDS

Among the scattered, frayed, mouldy papers Winnie left behind is a pink envelope labelled *Rapeljé* in her large round handwriting. Inside, on matching pink paper, she traced back how many Winifreds had preceded her. She was the sixth. They descended from the only branch of the family that was not Scottish. They were French Huguenot. In the early eighteenth century a Jeromus Rapeljé married Wyntie Winifred Went. Their daughter was Winifred Rapeljé. She went to Nova Scotia with her husband Henry Van Allen in 1784. Their daughter, Winifred Van Allen, married William Weir and named *their* daughter Winifred. The name skipped a generation, then reappeared in their granddaughter, Winifred Ireland. This was Aunt Winnie's mother (and my grandmother): Winifred Edith Hamilton Ireland. Then came my Aunt Winnie. There was one other Winifred, whom my family never mentioned. She was Aunt Winnie's cousin, the daughter of her mother's youngest brother, Lindsay Ireland.

I met this other Winifred in 1967 in San Francisco, where I had run off to with one of my professors, who was visiting Berkeley for a year, to take part in the Summer of Love. By then her father, an accountant, had died. She was a spinster in her sixties living with her mother, Helen Blumberg, in an apartment stuffed with shabby Victorian trappings high over a city turbulent with anti-Vietnam War demonstrations and hippies exploring drugs. Both women were dressed in 1920s clothing: dropped waists, lace collars, and pale stockings. They still had a wooden icebox cooled with ice that was delivered weekly. Winifred talked incessantly about Robert McNamara, secretary of defense under Presidents Kennedy and Johnson, whom she had met once. I think she showed me one of his books which he had signed for her. They served me tea and ice cream. This delicacy, they assured me, was a rare treat. I recall that Winifred looked wistfully down at the traffic below and wondered what it might be like to ride in a motor car.

It wasn't just this odd San Francisco branch of the family that wasn't mentioned. Lindsay had had a respectable job, and his wife's Jewishness would not have upset my parents, though it might have upset my grandparents. My family rarely mentioned anything about family at all, even those who were living not far away. My father wanted to distance himself from his past. He hated Toronto, where he had grown up. His miserable memories were lightened only by the time he was allowed to raise pigeons in the garage at 162 Isabella Street in Rosedale. He was astonished, he said, at the rapidity with which pigeons reproduced. He did not maintain contact with any of the men he had attended Appleby School with, though he was extraordinarily fond of his faded, moth-eaten turquoise-and-navy school toque, which he wore in winter until he died. Whenever my mother threw it into the garbage in one of her cleaning frenzies, he rummaged around and pulled it out, mumbling something about its "seeing me out." He did not regale us with stories of his family or ancestors. He was not one to regale anyone with anything. There are only three memories of my father's childhood that I recall being told about, and I think it was my mother who relayed them to me: he would hide for a long time when he was called in by his governess; he was fascinated with his "pusher," a flat square implement with a round handle like a baby spoon that was used to navigate food onto a fork; and he hated the day when he sat underneath a pine tree with his father, who shot straight up to kill the crows that tumbled and thudded one by one into a black heap around them.

My mother did not want to revisit her past either, but that was for entirely different reasons.

Because of my father's silence on most matters relating to his past, the boxes of papers, scrapbooks, and photo albums that my mother gave me, which she found one day while cleaning out the attic some time after Winnie died, offered me a series of discoveries. Mother also gave me the family tree that my father had put together on several huge sheets of paper, and which went back to 1773. I think I remember seeing the sheets laid out on the mahogany dining room table in Barrie, where I grew up, but I had no interest then in the family's past. It has taken me three decades to open these boxes, though they followed me to at least a dozen different addresses during that time. Now I have been astonished by revelation after revelation.

3

PORT
ELGIN

I knew that my Cameron grandfather, Donald Alexander, or "D.A.", had worked for the Canadian Bank of Commerce. That was long before that bank merged with The Imperial Bank of Canada in 1961 to become the Canadian Imperial Bank of Commerce we know today. Vague images about his career float around in my memory. Something about Dawson City, a mausoleum in Port Elgin, his fatal walk to the bank one Toronto winter. Aunt Winnie's boxes of hoardings and my father's disjointed family tree, with a few scribblings in pencil, have yielded letters and photographs — some labelled, some merely dated, some blank — and a flurry of facts, errors, or semi-facts. Ordering these like a borderless jigsaw puzzle with missing pieces, faded pieces, or pieces from some other puzzle, has given me an imperfect narrative, a hazardous assurance of continuity.

Donald Alexander was the eldest of William Cameron and Johanna Stark's nine children: five boys, then four girls. His father, William (born 1834), was from Ross-shire in the mountainous central Scottish

Highlands; his mother, Johanna (born 1837), was from Muirkirk, Ayrshire, an iron-manufacturing Lowland town. They left the large city of Fort William, where the Scottish Highlands rise north from the Lowlands, for Port Elgin, Ontario sometime before Donald Alexander was born in 1864, for he was born in that scenic haven for American tourists on the shore of Lake Huron. At that time Port Elgin had a woolen mill, a few tradesmen, and one doctor. I imagine the young couple leaving behind the financial city in Scotland for better prospects in Canada. William must have known someone in Port Elgin, possibly a banker or businessman. He may have had ready introductions to the business community and to whatever society Port Elgin offered at the time. He started his eldest son off in the Bank of Canada at age seventeen. In 1881, young Donald Alexander began as a junior clerk in what was then Berlin — now Kitchener — a large industrial centre just over a hundred miles south and slightly east of Port Elgin. He continued as a junior the following year in St. Catharines, just as the third Welland canal was being built, then became a ledger keeper in Windsor and, eventually, Chatham.

He arrived in the small town of Chatham in 1884 at age twenty, where William Ireland was manager of the bank, and stayed for six years, apart from a brief stint in the largely Methodist community of Blenheim. During D.A.'s time in Chatham the gregarious William favoured him, inviting him to his home on many occasions. There he met William's only daughter, Winifred. The seventeen-year-old was exquisitely pretty in a stern Victorian way, her heavy dark eyebrows a severe contrast to her thick fair hair and pale blue eyes. During this time, D.A.'s work and general character impressed her father, as he rose from ledger keeper to teller, then to accountant. After a long courtship, young Donald Alexander Cameron married Winifred Ireland in 1893, when she was twenty-six and he twenty-nine.

Because of her striking beauty and compliant nature, Winifred was known as Dollie. But pretty though Dollie was, she had had a difficult childhood that is reflected in the joyless expression she wears in every photograph. Her mother, Mary Alice (née Forsyth), had died at the age of thirty-five. This loss thrust the fifteen-year-old Dollie too early into the role of caring for her father and four younger brothers. She became — or perhaps had already been — a fragile and anxious young woman, fearful of life and of men in particular. She dutifully followed her new husband to Windsor and Walkerville, a town founded by Hiram Walker, who had opened a distillery on the Detroit River, but she refused to go with him to the wild new town of Greenwood, BC in 1898. There her energetic husband was thought just the man to set up and manage the first bank in a shambles of a town that had sprung up when copper was discovered. I still have the large silver punch bowl decorated with clusters of silver grapes that was given to him as a farewell present. It is inscribed:

Donald A. Cameron

FROM A FEW FRIENDS IN

WALKERVILLE & WINDSOR, ONTARIO,

UPON HIS DEPARTURE FOR

British Columbia.

November, 1898

First Canadian Bank of Commerce in Greenwood, BC, where D.A. got his reputation as a "frontier" banker, 1898–1900.

Perhaps it was his marriage that prompted D.A. to try to find out about his Scottish roots. Winnie kept the few letters he sent to and from the old country in 1890. He had begun by writing the Heraldic Office in London from Chatham asking about *Mackenzie's Clan Cameron* and the village "Dochnessie." The reply offered him a copy of this book for three pounds, but the office knew nothing of the supposed village. Perhaps, they thought, it might be the name of a farm. One of his relatives in Dingwall put him onto a Dr. Stewart, who was known for his knowledge of Scottish genealogy. In an excruciatingly detailed reply in tiny handwriting, Dr. Stewart surmised that the branch of the Clan Cameron that D.A.'s father came from was probably — though not certainly — the MacMartins of Letterfinlay. One of D.A.'s uncles, Colin, bore such a striking resemblance to Sir Ewen Cameron of Lochiel, a famous chieftain in the 1870s, that he was chosen to represent the Clan Cameron for the portrait that was painted for Queen Victoria (and that now hangs in Balmoral Castle).

In 1899, enthralled with the rough and ready year in Greenwood and inspired by a little knowledge of his background, D.A. bought an island in the Magnetawan River for \$32.52 and named it Cameron Island. He established a hunting club there with business friends he had made from his positions in the bank: Ernest Gardner Swift and John Gowie of Windsor, C. Clayton Ambrey and A.V. Spencer of Toronto, and Wilker Collins. They hired a local, John Broderick, to build the log cabin, which — in an updated version — still stands there today. No mention of this island or my grandfather's exploits there was ever made in my family. Only much later did I understand why. My father, who was not at all like his adventurous father, dreaded travel. The very thought of visiting Cameron Island would have been anathema to a man whose sensitivities precluded any sort of travel except by car, and then only to nearby places. Even in these cases he was uncomfortable, and would fortify himself from a flask of rye.

The year in Greenwood not only set Donald Alexander up financially with an income far beyond his previous salaries, it secured his reputation as a "pioneer banker." He was sent from there to manage the Seattle, Washington branch of the bank for the following year, and this time his now-pregnant wife went with him. The tone of voice in which Winnie's birth in Seattle was mentioned in my family implied that it was a horror for Dollie. Far from home, riddled with the anxieties of displacement, ill-prepared for the paroxysms of childbirth, she underwent what to her was trauma. Then her fate worsened. Having proved himself as an enterprising pioneer manager in Greenwood, her husband was sent on to an even more remote place. Little Winifred was only a year old when D.A. took up the position of manager in Dawson City, Yukon, in March 1902.

4

✦

THE CANADIAN BANK OF COMMERCE IN DAWSON CITY

In Dawson City, it was six short years since the Gold Rush had begun in 1896. The mass influx of prospectors and those who hoped to separate them from their gold numbered about 40,000 by 1898, when the Yukon Territory was founded. This greed-dazed, ragtag crowd usurped what was the ancient harvesting, fishing, and hunting area used by the Hän-speaking Tr'ochëk at the juncture of the Klondike and Yukon Rivers, not that anyone cared then. (The Tr'ochëk successfully asserted their ownership of the site in 1998, and it was designated a National Historic Site of Canada in 2002.)

News of the fabulous Klondike was widespread by 1897. It became obvious to the Dominion of Canada government that there would be large profits if royalties for their gold could be collected from the miners. The minister of the interior, Clifford Sifton, famed for his encouragement of immigration to settle the West, commissioned the Canadian Bank of Commerce to set up operations in Dawson to collect these royalties and also to act as the banker for the Dominion government in the Yukon Territory. The first wave of bank staff — the real pioneer bankers — set the stage for D.A. Cameron.

On 11 April 1898, the first of two groups of experienced, fit, and excited staff left Toronto. It would take them almost two months to reach Dawson City. That any of them survived the trip was remarkable. With six tons of supplies and equipment — including cash, bank stationery, and large Peterborough birchbark canoes — they somehow crossed the White Pass, moved through treacherous, half-melted ice on Lakes Bennett, Tagish, Marsh, and Laberge, then continued by scow down the Yukon river to Dawson. The second group crossed the Chilkoot Pass, a fourteen-mile journey over an altitude of 3,500 feet. Famous images of the Chilkoot show what looks like a tiny string of black ants in the snow, as thousands of men with their horses and mules and dogs made their fevered climb towards prosperity. Close up the reality was disturbing. Dead men and animals — or, worse, men fallen and moaning — were passed by others bent on making a fortune. Unscrupulous robbers — some white, some Indian — waited to dupe the exhausted men. Everywhere along the route they were driven nearly mad by hordes of mosquitoes that could not be evaded, even in sleep.

Elaborate precautions had been taken to conceal the cash they would need in Dawson. There were North West Mounted Police posts along the way at which they routinely stopped. The bills they carried were specially marked for identification if stolen. These were stashed in the middle of each man's kit bag of personal belongings. The boxes labelled CASH were filled with the displaced clothes. The second group stored their cash with the famous Superintendent Sam Steele — policeman, magistrate, and controller of rations — at Lake Bennett, where the two parties joined. Lake Bennett, the starting point of their river journey to Dawson, teemed with thousands of people and flimsy tent camps.

The Canadian Bank of Commerce was not the only bank to target the profitable Klondike. That same spring, the Bank of British North America in London, England also sent a party from their Toronto branch to set up a bank. They had made an earlier start, and reached Dawson about a week before the Commerce men. They opened their bank at once, but the unpredictable Dawson River flooded the city, forcing them to close down. The Commerce staff arrived, exhausted, just as the flood subsided, and were able to open in more secure premises while their rivals had to slowly rebuild. Since the Commerce staff had planned their venture more carefully and had included in their baggage an assay plant to weigh and measure gold dust, they were able to begin operations at once. Their foresight allowed them to attract clients and make lasting business connections in ways the British North America group, who lacked an assay plant, could not. By the end of the 1898 season when the Yukon River froze for the winter, the Canadian Bank of Commerce had made four large shipments of gold out of Dawson; the Bank of British North America had made only one.

The shack housing the Commerce was ready for business on 15 June 1898, with a crude canvas sign reading THE CANADIAN BANK OF COMMERCE, CAPITAL PAID UP SIX MILLION DOLLARS. It was a sign that prompted one drunken man to throw a stone through it, shouting, "I'm from Missouri, and you have to show me where they have six million dollars in that bum little shack!" The bank paid fourteen dollars an ounce for gold dust, melted it down into bricks, and packaged it for export to "the outside." Royalties of ten percent on the gross output of mines were charged. Except for the manager, the staff slept on the floor in the filthy garret upstairs. An NWMP guard stood duty on the office floor. Normal banking procedures were jettisoned, since miners could show up at any hour of the day or night to deposit their gold. Though the Bank's outlay to set up this primitive bank was around $50,000, by the end of that first summer the Canadian Bank of Commerce had sent out $2,300,000 worth of gold.

Many during that summer of 1898 — and the following winter — lived on the boats or scows they arrived in, or in rough little log cabins or makeshift tents onshore. Around-the-clock daylight encouraged crowds of men of many nationalities, and the dance hall girls who were the only women yet to arrive, to flit in and out of the dance halls, saloons, and gambling joints. Hangers-on, burglars, confidence men, prostitutes, fake doctors (who "cured" typhoid and dysentery), and outright criminals were everywhere. Convicts could be seen sawing, hauling, or chopping wood for Her Majesty under escorts of NWMP officers in short buffalo coats. There were no children. Paths were muddy quagmires. Dogs fought up and down the streets. There was no running water or electricity. Since everything arrived in Dawson at great expense, and successful claims like those along the Bonanza and Eldorado creeks made prospectors delirious with unimaginable wealth, prices soared. Seven months' rent for a twenty-five-by-forty-foot saloon on the first floor was $10,000. A man with a team of horses charged $100 a day. Two young lawyers registering claims made over $20,000 in their first two months. A banquet for the newly arrived Commerce men of moose steak, fried eggs, and champagne at the opening of the Tammany Dance Hall cost their miner host nearly all of the $1,500 he took that day in one of his claims. Lunches at what passed for a restaurant cost the bankers $7.50 for an indifferent meal of fatty bacon, fried eggs, bread and butter, and a strong cup of boiled coffee.

Chances are Donald Alexander Cameron did not tell Dollie much of this seedy Dawson history before they set out from Seattle. Even though the city had come a long way since its crude beginnings, it would still have seemed godforsaken to Dollie. Dawson officially became a city in 1902, the year D.A. and Dollie arrived, and it was no longer the raw, chaotic place it had been when the first Bank employees landed in 1898. The Rush had subsided, and many had given up and left after large-scale hydraulic mining replaced the original sourdoughs panning for gold and staking their claims anywhere and everywhere. Robert Service, in a poem that shows the horror of the old prospectors at seeing the dredges of the Canadian Klondyke Mining Company, wrote, "Ah old-time miner, here's your doom!" The population had dropped to about 5,000. The civilized community that had in those five years replaced the chaos of the late '90s was manifest in several public buildings put up between 1901 and 1902 that established Canadian sovereignty: the Territorial Administration Building, the Courthouse, the NWMP Commander's house, the large, elegant Commissioner's residence, and St. Paul's Anglican Church. The "bum little shack" that housed the Canadian Bank of Commerce had been replaced by a larger log building downtown. Yet some signs of the place's disreputable past remained. The Yukon Hotel, with its false front, still stood where it had been built in 1898. It was impossible not to notice the Orpheum vaudeville and burlesque theatre that Alexander Pantages built with his racy business partner and lover, the salon- and brothel-keeper "Klondike Kate" Rockwell.

D.A. Cameron thus arrived in 1902 at a newly incorporated city, in a territory that had now been official for four years. He would be joining a less hectic community than that of the first rush for gold, though it was still by any standard a tough, somewhat wild environment. In any case it would have been a place of terror for a young mother like Dollie, forced to care for her year-old baby in a fierce climate with few traces of civilization. The elaborate Edwardian clothes she wears in a photo of the two of them arriving in Dawson show this complete mismatch of person to place. It was the sixth move she had made with her husband in as many years, all moves that were unforeseen. She had expected her life to be lived in southwest Ontario where D.A. had worked before marrying her, not a place like this.

Dollie (RT) and friends, Dawson City, 1903–04.

D.A. loved Dawson City as much as Dollie

D.A. and trophy moose, possibly on his hunting trip with F.C. Selous in 1904.

hated it. He relished the challenge of banking in such adverse conditions. It was a chance to use the skills he had acquired in Greenwood. He loved the extreme landscape and the extreme temperature, which could fall to forty below in the winter. He loved the bleak, untamed landscape, full of wildlife he could hunt and fish he could snag.

As part of the second wave of Commerce employees, D.A. and Dollie did not find the boozy, disorderly place that featured wild, intoxicated dance hall girls like "Diamond Tooth Gertie" Lovejoy. "Diamond Tooth Gertie" was still in town, but she had married C.W. Taber, a respectable lawyer and prominent Conservative. Gambling was abolished, restrictions were placed on the infamous dance halls, and women could no longer be served a drink anywhere. Schools had appeared. A reliable water supply and sanitation system were in place, as well as a telephone and electrical service. In five short years, Dawson had taken shape as a place to which men brought their wives and children. Donald Cameron, as manager, and his assistant manager could live in their

Canadian Bank of Commerce staff, Dawson City, Yukon Territory, 1903–04. D.A. is in back row, centred under porch.

own houses or cabins apart from the other eighteen bank staff, who made do in the cramped apartments above the bank building.

After over twenty years' experience with the Commerce, D.A. was considered an authority on banks. He wrote an eight-chapter article on banking — almost a book — for the 23 June 1905 issue of the *Dawson Weekly News*. In this article he argued that the Canadian banking system was superior to the American one because it was based on the Scottish system. He explained at length that the instability of banking "panics" in the United States could be avoided by adopting the Canadian system. "Would that I had the ability to arouse the American people to the importance of a banking system!" he wrote. Though the English was quaint, the sentiment is eerily contemporary.

5

THE CAMERONS
IN DAWSON CITY

The daily life of the Camerons in Dawson City can be deduced from a few of the clippings and photos in Aunt Winnie's scrapbooks. It appears that they did their best to transplant the Victorian way of life they had known in Chatham to the utterly incompatible setting of Dawson City. A photo of the interior of their cabin shows a boxy living room with a full bookcase, landscape paintings (one gilt-framed) on the wall, lace curtains, leather chairs, and a white wicker table supporting a large, ornate Chinoiserie punch bowl. I remember that big bowl, with its pink and green stripes and quasi-Chinese decorations against a white background, from my parents' home. The occasion for this photograph is a visit from a moustached friend — possibly a bank employee or client — who sits smoking a curved meerschaum pipe in a tweed jacket. Across from him sits D.A. with little Winnie, aged about two in a white pinafore, sitting on his lap "smoking" his pipe. To one side is Dollie in a high-collared Edwardian white blouse with leg-of-mutton sleeves tucked into a floor-length dark skirt, a long

Interior of Cameron home in Dawson City: Dollie, Winnie on D.A.'s knee, and a guest.

string of pearls falling into her lap. Her thick hair is done up in such a way as to create a cushion of hair beneath elaborate coils.

It seems unlikely that Dollie had live-in servants in that small cabin. Yet no doubt she had help from somewhere. As with most marriages at the time, she and her husband would have spent their lives mainly apart, she visiting or walking with the wives of other suitable professionals, he gathering with other men to drink and dine, or hunt and fish, when his bank work was done.

D.A. loved socializing with his friends. Men's clubs were his natural milieu. The professional men in Dawson City — lawyers, doctors, ship captains, French-Canadian officials — had formed a branch of the Canadian Club, which held elaborate six-course dinners with speeches and sing-songs. My grandfather was treasurer of this club of almost a hundred members — mostly Scots. A programme from one of their luncheons, kept by Winnie in her scrapbooks, lists the songs they sang. All were British, patriotic; one was French-Canadian ("Vive la Canadienne"). The ten speeches on that occasion were also patriotic, from one lauding the imperialism popular at the time with men like Stephen Leacock and Colonel Denison, to "Canada's Soldier Police (RCNWMP)," to "Canada's Future." (This occasion must have been in 1904 or later, as the addition of "Royal" to the NWMP was not bestowed by the King until that date.) The five-course menu was elaborate and British, including three meats and a lettuce salad, which must have been difficult to obtain in the Yukon. There were many jovial toasts to King Edward VII and others.

In his spare weekends, D.A. was off with friends camping, stalking the big game that was so plentiful. In an 18 May 1907 article called "Sport in the Yukon Region," saved in one of Winnie's scrapbooks, he is featured, along with two photos. One of these is of an arrangement of skulls (three moose, eight bighorn mountain sheep, and three smaller ones, perhaps female mountain sheep or caribou) mounted on the outside wall of the Canadian Bank of Commerce. The other shows him behind a dog sled in a tasselled toque and a coat tied with a woven *habitant* belt. There are four huskies behind the lead dog, a half-breed

D.A.'s dog sled, with Winnie in furs, used as illustration in Robert Service's *Songs of a Sourdough* (1907).

Close-up of Winnie in furs with D.A., 1903.

Scotch collie — a dog he touted because it was Scottish. On the sled, bundled up in a white fur "envelope" that I used much later for my own children on their sled in Montreal, is little Winifred about age two.

This last photo was used by Robert Service in the original copy of his collection of poems *Songs of a Sourdough* (1907). We were always told that Service was a teller in my grandfather's bank, but the four-volume *A History of the Canadian Bank of Commerce* indicates that he worked at the Whitehorse branch that opened in 1900. Not until 1909 did Service move to Dawson City, where he did work in "my grandfather's bank" — but by then D.A. and his family had moved to Toronto. Yet, since travel between the two banks was common, it is possible that Service took the photo himself.

Judging by the few photos of Winnie at the time, she was a daddy's girl. It seems that at every place he took her — even to events like the first annual Dawson City Dog Sled Show — she was the only child. She not only rode on his dog sled, but he also gave her a husky pup to play with outside. She had her own toboggan to which she could hitch her pup. Like her mother, she was always dressed fashionably. In one photo when she was about four years old, she is wearing a smart long wool coat with a thick fur collar and a large beret with ribbons down one side. She holds a toy shovel in her fur mitts — the very picture of a pampered Edwardian child, encouraged by her father to adventure in the frozen north.

Somehow, from somewhere — perhaps ordered in from Toronto — D.A. obtained the engraved silver mug for Winnie in February 1903, which implies she was christened at St. Paul's Anglican Church on her second birthday. No expense was spared, and why would it be? D.A. Cameron was earning a great deal of money during his years in the north. He loved fine things, beautiful things: furniture, silver, and china. He was also attracted to Indian arts. While travelling in

Winnie with snow shovel, Dawson City, 1904.

the north he would pick up a mahogany table here, a set of carved ivory seals there, a duck preserved by a taxidermist in a glass case, an Indian deerskin jacket embroidered with beads and fringe. These items were all in my parents' home in Barrie, though I did not know how they got there. I recall mention of Lake Athabasca and the Athabascan Indians. The duck was stored in the attic, then given to my first husband, who admired it. The two or three little ivory seals sat on the windowsill of my mother's sewing room. My second husband appropriated the Indian jacket in the late 1960s, when such items were highly valued as hippie gear. He wore it to the discotheques we frequented in Montreal in the '70s. Later, it went back to the attic. Later still, I believe my sister, by then director of Parks Canada, saw that it was donated to the Royal Ontario Museum in Toronto.

Wealth poured into Dawson City, and none profited from that wealth more than the banks who stored gold nuggets and gold dust. In D.A. Cameron's first two years as manager, the Canadian Bank of Commerce handled $12 million and $11 million in gold respectively. These years were the high point of Yukon gold production. By 1907, when the Cameron family left the Yukon for Toronto, profits had steadily declined to about $3 million — still an astonishing sum. By then, D.A. had made his fortune. His obituaries later would describe him as a man who had "a flair for making money." Certainly he had the good luck to be in the right place at the right time, and to be the right kind of man for his job.

6

GENTLEMAN HUNTERS

D.A.'s exploits with his friends in the Yukon are better documented than any other aspect of the time the Camerons spent in Dawson City. Later, the *Toronto Star* — with exaggeration — hailed him as an "ardent sportsman who knows Canada from coast to coast."

There are countless photos in Winnie's scrapbooks of his adventures. Several show D.A. and other burly men holding up the heads of mountain sheep or caribou or moose as trophies. Some show their filthy campsites and tents. One of these, a musty old canvas Arctic tent, ended up in our garden on Mulcaster Street in Barrie, where my sister and I occasionally slept in the summers. Others show the Indian snowshoes that we clumsily clomped around in on the winter snow after tying the stiff leather straps. I had no idea where these things came from or why they were special.

The licences, resembling official graduation certificates, that my grandfather obtained to hunt in the Yukon Territory are in Winnie's scrapbook as well. On 24 July 1906, for instance, the commissioner of the Yukon Territory, Clifford Sifton, gave him permission to shoot three mountain sheep and three caribou, which he did. He clearly spent much time canoeing or dog sledding in remote areas of the north to hunt for big game. At times he was in areas that had never been explored, even by native people.

A high point for him was the time he hunted for moose, caribou, sheep, and bear with Captain Frederick C. Selous. D.A. was thirty-nine at the time, and Selous was fifty-three. They travelled with eleven others up the Pelly River, a headstream of the Yukon River, and along the Macmillan River, one of the Pelly's tributaries. Selous was a British explorer and officer, arguably the best-known big-game hunter in the British Empire. A friend of Theodore Roosevelt and Cecil Rhodes, he was renowned in particular for hunting in Kenya and South Africa. This was his first foray into the north.

Selous describes the trip in his book *Recent Hunting Trips in British North America* (1907). His description of Dawson City in 1904 gives a clear idea of the town at the time Winnie was growing up there. "The romance of the Klondyke was short-lived," he writes. It was over by the time Selous saw Dawson, an attractive little frontier town with a population of "about three thousand five hundred souls," situated on the eastern bank of the Yukon just where the waters of the world-renowned Klondike River join the greater stream. "It boasts a Carnegie library," he wrote, "an up-to-date school, quite an imposing government house, extensive police barracks, and several hotels where good accommodation can be obtained at very moderate rates." Selous might have chosen Alaska instead, but no hunting was allowed there at that time.

Selous travelled the 7,500 miles from London, England in three weeks, via Vancouver, Skagway, and Whitehorse. He had been invited to hunt in the Yukon by his old friend J.B. Tyrrell, the famous Canadian geologist and cartographer, after whom the dinosaur museum in Drumheller, Alberta is named. Selous praises Tyrrell's book *Across the Sub-Arctics of Canada*, which had piqued his interest in the north. To his chagrin Tyrrell could not join the Yukon hunting party, nor could

F.T. Congdon, then governor of the Yukon Territory.

This expedition was typical of the era. At the time, naturalists, geologists, and cartographers were still exploring parts of the world that had not been charted. Often they took along photographers with their Kodaks, or artists who specialized in wildlife and their terrains. These explorer-naturalists followed the "Dr. Livingstone, I presume" tradition. Dressed in rough gear, they kept careful records of each day's weather and rhapsodized about the landscape and natural phenomena. They thought of the British sportsman's code as "aristocratic," distinguishing themselves from their moral, racial, and class inferiors who hunted for food. They deplored "passive" hunting — waiting on animal trails for their quarry to pass — claiming that their "active" stalking method and bans on killing females gave animals "a sporting chance." By such rationalizations, and by claiming that they were advancing natural history, they tried to legitimize what amounted to reckless slaughter and the acquisition of trophy heads for their personal aggrandizement. They did record details of their expeditions and took back specimens of animal and bird species for museums of science. Yet Selous's writings leave the impression that he saw the land in terms of its ability to provide him with game. The Yukon Territory, he wrote, was "a beautiful country for caribou" and "ideal moose country." Some of the men who made up this venture with Selous and D.A. were famous already for the fieldwork that "legitimized" the hunt.

The party of thirteen men who set out from Dawson City on 21 August 1904 with D.A. Cameron and Frederick Selous were a Mr. Patterson, Judge Aimé Dugas, and three Americans: Charles Sheldon, naturalist; Wilfred Osgood, of the American biological survey; and Carl Rungius, a German-American painter of big game. D.A., Patterson, and Dugas were simply experienced wildlife hunters from Dawson. The others were far more important. Charles Sheldon, a Yale graduate who had made a fortune developing the silver mines in San Luis Potosi, Mexico, had retired in 1902 at age thirty-five to pursue his passion: exploring the wilderness and adding to the scientific knowledge of

North American wildlife. His first book, *The Wilderness of the Upper Yukon: A Hunter's Explorations for Wild Sheep in Sub-Arctic Mountains* (1911), documented this very trip in diary form. Wilfred Osgood, at age thirty-three, was then working for the Biological Survey of North America, collecting specimens from the western and northern parts of the continent. He had begun his systematic review of various types of rodents, which in 1909 would earn him a position as curator in the relatively new Field Museum of Natural History in Chicago. Carl Rungius was already at thirty-five America's first career wildlife artist. His sketches and paintings in the European sporting art tradition represented a wide open and idyllic world where human life is invisible.

Each member of the expedition from Dawson had one man to assist him. The Canadians hired two French Canadians and a Nova Scotian; the Americans employed two fellow Americans experienced in the Canadian north; and Selous had engaged a Métis named Louis Cardinal.

This large party set out by steamboat — the *Emma Nott* — landing first at the small Indian village of Selkirk, which consisted of a church and mission station, a few trading stores, a telegraph office, and a North West Mounted Police post. Selous showed great interest in these Indians, as did D.A., who took a photo of them that would be printed in Selous's book and mistakenly credited to "D.S. Cameron." It is one of the few photos that does not capture the "splendour" of carcasses, but rather the humanity of — or the group's curiosity about — an Indian group. Perhaps the two little carved ivory seals on my mother's windowsill in Barrie came from these people.

After Selkirk it was upriver on the Pelly, and on into the Macmillan until the *Emma Nott* could go no farther. The party then broke into three groups. Osgood and Rungius went up Slate Creek; Sheldon and Selous took the north fork of the Macmillan River; D.A., Patterson, and Judge Dugas took the south fork of the same river. According to Selous, "we were in a country where in all probability the foot of a white man had never trodden before." He praised the Yukon — despite its short hunting season — as "splendidly health-giving … its mountain and river scenery superb … [where] there is still a fair quantity of game." They all marvelled at the construction of beaver dams (without shooting any beaver) and the vast shimmering luminescence of aurora borealis at night. D.A. Cameron returned in September after a month, flaunting better trophies than Selous.

It is only now that I am able to fit together two pieces of this puzzle. It must be due to Selous that there was an elephant gun in our attic in Barrie. D.A. could have acquired it from Selous, then passed it along to my father. (Photos of Selous from the 1880s show him holding a similar elephant gun.) I remember well my father opening the mouldy leather case and fitting together the parts of the gun with its huge barrel. Having taught shooting and orientation at Camp Borden during the Second World War he had an interest in guns, though he never hunted himself.

Because of expeditions like the one with Selous, and the extensive socializing D.A. did with his friends, Winnie would have spent much more time with her mother than with her father. Letters between the two women much later show that they were affectionate and close. Yet in all her photos Dollie looks brittle, crestfallen, even depressed. I imagine the Yukon years took their toll, turning her inward, making her more anxious and fearful — the very opposite of her husband. Little Winnie, encouraged by her father's bravado, more like him in temperament, and no doubt spoiled, emerged as a personality much stronger than her mother. There was no counterbalance at home to curb her pig-headedness. Her father could have exerted control over her, and he does appear to have laid down laws — laws she observed. Yet he was not around much to enforce them. With her meek mother, Winnie got her way.

In her early childhood in Dawson City, Winnie was adored by a father who was successful and fortunate as a banker in the early years of the Gold Rush. He was an adventurous outdoorsman, who, as the Dawson newspaper put it, risked "the more inaccessible portions of the northern mountain range, to bring back trophies to decorate his bank and his home." The ideas and values shaping Winnie as a small girl were those of many of the privileged in Canada at the time: passionately patriotic, both towards Britain and Canada, but especially towards Scotland; accustomed to luxuries; expected to be gregarious and sociable with others of her class; convinced of the superiority of strong men over passive women. By the time the family left Dawson City in March 1907, Winnie, aged five, was a bonny, strong-willed child, used to being the centre of attention.

7

BACK TO DAWSON CITY
WITH AUNT PUSSY, 1907

The Camerons left Dawson City for Toronto in March 1907. D.A. was needed at the Head Office as relieving manager. Any relief Dollie felt at returning to civilization in Toronto was soon shattered. A mere three months later, D.A. was back in the Yukon as manager for a year. Winnie, now six, would have been delighted. Returning to Dawson City meant more fun with the huskies, more time as the focus of attention, and an atmosphere of exciting unpredictability.

This time Dollie fortified herself against loneliness by taking along her young aunt Jean Forsyth, the youngest sister of her mother. As was often the case in large families, Dollie was actually older than her aunt, by fifteen years. The two were more like sisters than aunt and niece. This thrust Jean into the role of aunt to Winnie, who would always refer to her as her aunt, not her great-aunt. This year in Dawson City created a bond between Winnie and Aunt Pussy — as Jean was known in the family — that was to continue long after the year in the Yukon.

Jean was a vivacious, larger-than-life character, a dramatic soprano said to have "a very genius of personality" — quite the opposite of the meek Dollie. She had travelled to Europe twice, to train with Madame Mathilde Marchesi (a German mezzo-soprano who favoured the bel canto style) in classical and operatic singing in Paris, and with the Royal Shakespeare Company in London for dramatic performance. She had also studied voice training with George Sweet in New York. Her ambition had been to sing in light operas on the international scene, but she was reined in to become a respectable soloist in Winnipeg's Holy Trinity Church instead. Like Dollie she had been born in Chatham, to the family that established itself when her grandfather (Dollie's great-grandfather) Lieutenant Forsyth emigrated from Ireland and was given a military land grant in what was then the "West."

Jean was not only a gifted singer, she was also beautiful and funny.

As one story in the *Edmonton Journal* has it, a teamster in Winnipeg drove his horse and cart into a ditch when he passed Jean on her way to a garden party. When Jean became angry at him, he is said to have replied, "Well, lady, you look so fine, I just couldn't take my eyes off you, and that's the truth." As a young woman, Jean — like Dollie — attended social activities in Woodstock, Hamilton, London, Kingston, and Brockville, where so many of Canada's old families lived. At such events she was admired for her fashionable clothes, her cornflower blue eyes, and her fair hair, but mostly, it seems, for her sarcastic observations and witty remarks. A later 1923 article about her claims that she had the courage to be herself and was "utterly frank in the way she hurled out dynamic statements."

Aunt Pussy (Jean Forsyth).

Jean had taught singing in Winnipeg to support herself, and brought music with her to Dawson. During that year she trained singers and directed the orchestra herself for a production of Gilbert and Sullivan's operetta *Patience*. This operetta is an obscure satire on the aesthetic movement of the 1870s and '80s in England — an unlikely topic for a Yukon audience.

It is no wonder Winnie adored her Aunt Pussy. They were both strong-willed, gregarious lovers of life, unlike Winnie's melancholic mother. One of the few things Winnie could do was sing "I'm Called Little Buttercup," a tune from Gilbert and Sullivan's *HMS Pinafore*. She used to sing this for me in her strong soprano voice, accompanying herself on the piano, when I visited her and Dollie in Toronto many years later. Now I have no doubt that her Aunt Pussy taught her this song, and many others that she used to sing with pleasure — and on key. As Jean had no children of her own, I believe Winnie became a sort of daughter to her.

It is probable, too, that Aunt Pussy reinforced the love of animals in Winnie that was begun by her father's gift of the husky pup. Jean Forsyth had helped found a branch of the Humane Society in Winnipeg to care for what she referred to as the "little brothers." As the same article about her says, "Woe betide the person caught by her ill-treating a horse or a dog."

At the end of the year Aunt Pussy moved on to Vancouver, where she again taught singing. Winnie visited her there several times. She told me of only one memory she had of those visits. As she and Aunt Pussy were walking on one of Vancouver's beaches, they passed a man who exposed himself. The look of distress on Winnie's face when she told me this, much, much later, betrayed the dismay she and her aunt must have felt at this shocking sight.

8

TORONTO, 1908

Toronto in 1908 could not have differed more from Dawson City. Dawson had been remote and edgy, despite its slick veneer of civilization. Donald Alexander, Dollie, and their seven-year-old Winnie now found themselves in the second-largest city in Canada. Within a few years, it would overtake Montreal as the largest commercial centre in the country. Its heavy Victorian atmosphere and mainly Protestant morality had earned it the sobriquet "Toronto the Good." To leave behind a log frame bank, the enveloping fur coats needed to live and work there, travel by dog sled, and the thrill of wilderness forays would mean adjustments.

A debate over the city's first skyscraper characterizes this moment in Toronto's history. The Toronto City Council argued long and hard about whether or not to permit it. There were objections from the more conservative council members about sanitation, safety, and traffic. More important were objections about aesthetics. Tall buildings were thought "unsightly." Paris limited buildings to six storeys, and London disdained high buildings as well. The debate centred on whether or not Canadian cities should follow this British, European tradition or model themselves on New York City, which boasted 175 structures of fifteen-or-more storeys (the Woolworth Building having more than fifty). In approving the fifteen-storey Trader's Bank, designed by New York architects Carrère & Hastings, the city council opted for North America rather than Britain. Toronto would now evolve slowly in the direction of a North American identity.

The staunchly British Camerons arrived in a city on the cusp of this transformation. The population had exploded from about 200,000 in 1901 to about 350,000 only seven years later. The nature of that population was changing too, from an artificially imposed British class system to one that reflected those self-made men who had quickly won commercial and industrial power. These men — with names like Gooderham, Massey, and Eaton — had made money in such areas as, respectively, the whiskey trade, farm machinery, and retail stores. (Sir John Craig Eaton had just finished his year on the Commerce's board of directors shortly before D.A. arrived.) There was a large middle class, an only slightly smaller working class, and a truly destitute underclass. This underclass lived in dreadful conditions in two sections of the city: the Ward in the centre of the city, bounded by Queen, College, Yonge, and University; and the area that stretched east along Queen Street from the Don Valley and its river. In the absence of building regulations, many dubious suburbs, hodge-podges of buildings, sprang up outside city limits.

Forty-five percent of Toronto's workers were employed in manufacturing, many in the pork-packing industry that gave the city its nickname, Hogtown. Some mischievously said that "Hogtown" referred instead to the prosperous business owners and bankers, like D.A. Cameron, who made up the thirty percent in finance and commerce. Fourteen percent plied building trades, and twelve percent worked as domestic servants or menials.

Toronto then looked Dickensian. Downtown factories belched

smoke. The harbour was a grimy jumble before the Toronto Harbour Commission began in 1911. The area was dignified a little by the stately Queen's Hotel flying the Union Jack on Front Street, where visiting royalty and other dignitaries stayed. More typical were the churches that commanded the city's morality and the dives or taverns that undermined it. To anyone looking around its centre, the city spoke of Victorian and Edwardian England. The five square blocks of the downtown that had been decimated in the Great Fire of 1904 had been rebuilt. By the time the Camerons arrived, City Hall (now Old City Hall) at the top of Bay Street — an elegant Romanesque structure — had stood solidly in place since 1899. Even before that, University College (1850s), the Ontario Legislature at Queen's Park (1880s), and Osgoode Hall (1850s–80s) were focal points of the city. Government House, the residence of Ontario's lieutenant-governor, Sir John Gibson,

Dollie (left) in Monaco where D.A. was sent to scout possibilities for a bank in 1908.

whom D.A. had quickly befriended, stood at the southwest corner of King and Simcoe Streets. Its grandeur and huge gardens offered Toronto's elite the feel of British royalty at balls, receptions, and garden parties. The corner was famous, not just for Government House, termed "Legislation," but for the other three buildings known as "Education" (Upper Canada College), "Salvation" (St. Andrew's Presbyterian Church), and "Damnation" (The British Hotel and Tavern).

The Commerce had more tentacles now than it did when D.A. left for Dawson. In 1908 it had more than 350 branches across Canada, as well as several international offices. Yet it was not through with expanding. In his first year at the Head Office, D.A. was sent to scout possibilities in Monaco. There are photos of Dollie disconsolate beneath palm trees. In Toronto, there were two branches: the Head Office on the northeast corner of Yonge and Bloor, and another — the Market Branch — across from St. Lawrence Market at King and Jarvis. Perhaps there is symbolic significance in the fact that the Head Office (now demolished) was literally built on the backs of the poor. It was erected on Strangers' (or Potter's) Burying Ground, a cemetery for outcasts and suicides who were refused burial in St. James's and other religious cemeteries.

People got around the city by walking, a daily exercise the British praised. Bicycles were a common sight on such ample tree-lined boulevards as Jarvis Street and University Avenue. Massey-Harris, of farm machinery fame, had a bicycle division. The golden age of the bicycle in the 1890s had passed, but for many who could afford nothing else it was the only means of transportation. Horses drawing wagons, carts, and carriages made their way through the unpaved streets. Eaton's and Simpson's made twice-daily deliveries (except on Sundays) in small wagons pulled by one horse. Simpson's dappled greys were rivalled by the chestnuts that drew Eaton's wagons.

Public transportation was in disarray, and was widely criticized. The original large horse-drawn carts were gone, and the rail system was electrified in 1882. But ownership veered back and forth between public and private companies, and the city encountered difficulties coordinating separate systems as surrounding areas were annexed. In 1908, the Toronto Railway Company had inadequate lines in and out of the city to its boundaries at Bathurst Street to the west, Davenport Road to the north, and Parliament Street to the east. It would not be until 1910 with the Toronto Civic Railway that a city rail service would begin. A decade later the Toronto Transit Commission (TTC) would be created, in 1921.

Cars would not widely replace horse-drawn vehicles and bicycles until after the Great War. At the time the Camerons arrived in Toronto, there were only about 250 cars in all of Ontario. Torontonians might glimpse — or rather hear — a one-cylinder car chugging along the dirt road in High Park to the extreme west of the city. Such cars were not much bigger than golf carts, seated only two in the open, and bore three-number licence plates. They cost an exorbitant $1,000. More often, walkers and cyclists in High Park might see mounted police in uniforms like those of English Bobbies.

High Park was only one of the public spaces Toronto was opening up, partly as a result of the City Beautiful Movement. Playing fields for cricket and other games, pools and beaches, libraries, gardens, and parks sprang up around the city. Centre Island had long been a popular destination for Sunday afternoon strolls and picnics. Ferry service to the island had begun in 1883, and by 1908 more and more ferries were under construction.

Though the Camerons seemed uninterested in the arts, there was much available. The Grand Opera House, with its domed auditorium, private boxes, and plush seats, proclaimed its attachment to Britain with the Royal coat of arms on its tower. No reference to performances there or at the newly opened Royal Alexandra Theatre is made in Winnie's scrapbooks. I recall my father mentioning the British vaude-ville that was played in theatres along lower Yonge Street, but even the popular silent Hollywood movies that signalled the eventual influx of American entertainments were not mentioned.

Nor did the family become involved with the social events held by Toronto's churches. Winnie does not mention the bazaars, teas, picnics, and receptions that were the centre of social life for many Torontonians. St. Andrew's Presbyterian Church was the church of the 48th Highlanders, D.A.'s regiment. Probably the Camerons attended some services there. Yet it is more likely that they were among the 100 families who petitioned the Presbytery of Toronto for a new church to serve those who, like the Camerons, had moved north of Bloor Street. The Rosedale Presbyterian Church building at 127 Huntley Street (now Mount Pleasant Road) was not dedicated until 1910, but services had begun early in 1908. That same year, a remarkable four-teen-year-old named Ernest MacMillan was already organist at Knox Presbyterian Church.

Instead of arts performances and church gatherings, the Camerons regularly attended events at Government House, such as large garden parties. There, men in top hats and handlebar moustaches wandered about the lawn, their women in long, light trailing gowns of lace and silk, wearing hats decked with feathers or flowers and sheltering their complexions beneath frilly parasols.

The Camerons also attended the Woodbine Racetrack to watch "the sport of kings." Woodbine was then located at Queen Street East and Kingston Road. It had become a Canadian-British institution largely because Princess Louise, Queen Victoria's daughter, was the wife of the Marquis of Lorne, then governor general of Canada. The Queen had supported a Queen's Plate race since 1881, and the Marquis and Marchioness had attended a race there that spring. Many royals over time would attend.

The Protestant churches in Toronto were behind the vigorous Temperance movement. A few areas of the city were already "dry," though Prohibition would not begin until 1917. Middle class women, who were already pressing for the vote (which would not come to Ontario until 1917), rallied for reform on many fronts: social condi-tions, health, and morality. By then a few women had trickled into the universities. It is impossible to imagine Dollie being involved in the sometimes strident calls for reform. Certainly, her husband drank: my father inherited a few bottles of his 100-year-old whiskey and port after Dollie's death. It is doubtful she knew these were in his low, square mahogany liquor cabinet. She did not drink, except in rare and — for her — terrifying circumstances, such as thunderstorms. On those occasions, the servants carried her on her mattress to the basement, where she would sip a little brandy.

The whole Cameron family supported every aspect of old Toronto the Good. They were conservatives who were involved in the military, country clubs, the outdoor sports of hunting, fishing, golf, horse racing, and yachting, and were, of course, members of the Empire Club. They thought of themselves as loyal and true subjects of King Edward VII and, after his death in 1910, of George V. Already, as thoroughly Victorian and Edwardian citizens of Toronto, they were beginning to be out of date, though they could not know it. As Toronto moved slowly from being a British bastion to a North American metropolis like New York, they were typical of the wealthy old guard.

9

D.A. CLIMBS

The Camerons had rented a three-storey brick home at 162 Isabella Street, near Sherbourne, in the fashionable Rosedale area. It was an address that reflected D.A.'s promotion to inspector at the bank's Head Office, which was within walking distance. To Dollie's relief, he would stay in Toronto permanently.

D.A. set about becoming one of Toronto's elite with energy and shrewdness. He was already *en rapport* with the Commerce's new president, Byron Edmund Walker, who also thought the American banking system was unstable and a dangerous investment possibility. Walker had been general manager of the bank almost from its beginnings in 1867. He was an immensely important figure in Toronto, playing leading roles in promoting music and art, as well as helping the University of Toronto get on its feet. It was an era in which men's and women's worlds were quite different. D.A. joined as many of the men's clubs as possible. The 1920 *Blue Book* of Toronto Society shows that he belonged to more clubs than any other man in the city. In addition

Winnie at 162 Isabella Street (demolished) in Rosedale, Toronto, 1908.

to the regimental gatherings of the 48th Highlanders, where he was adjutant and lieutenant, he was active with the Caledon Mountain and Fishing Club, the Canadian Club, the Royal Canadian Institute, the Canadian Military Institute, the National Club, the Ontario Jockey Club (which owned Woodbine Racetrack), the Royal Canadian Yacht Club, the Toronto Club, the Toronto Golf Club, and the Toronto Hunt Club. Dollie belonged only to the Toronto Golf Club, though I believe it was for social reasons rather than to actually play the game. She saw the wives of D.A.'s friends for lunches, teas, or bridge, and accompanied him to receptions at Government House, where D.A.'s friend, Sir John Hendrie, had replaced another friend, Sir John Gibson, as lieutenant-governor of Ontario. Dollie took Winnie to dressmakers and the exclusive Toronto women's shops for the elaborate clothes and hats they both wore.

One of the guests they entertained at dinner parties was Vilhjalmur Stefansson, a Harvard-educated Icelander whose mission in life was to persuade the world — especially Canada — to value and settle the north. Interviewed for an article titled "Northward the Course of Empire is Moving" — which was run when one of his many books, *The Friendly Arctic* (1921), was published — he recalled a dinner conversation he had had at the Cameron's Isabella Street home. He had asked D.A. whether he preferred the winter climate of Toronto to that of Dawson. D.A. replied, "There are no two opinions in this family. My wife and daughter agree with me; we all prefer the climate of Dawson." D.A. went on to say that this was the general opinion of those who lived in Dawson, though they agreed one had to live there two or more years, long enough to get over the predisposition towards a summer climate they would have brought with them from a country where summer is longer than winter. Stefansson thought Cameron's views were typical of those hundreds of people he knew who had lived in the Arctic.

The Camerons settled in to Toronto with a new Auburn touring car and a chauffeur to drive it. They hired a maid, Kate, to cook, clean, and launder. That summer, D.A. rented a fifty-four-acre property on the north shore of Lake Simcoe just west of Shanty Bay. The property was owned by three Toronto friends: Senator Frederic Nicholls, John P. Northey, and James Brock O'Brian. At the turn of the century, Senator Nicholls had employed the famed Toronto architects Pearson & Darling to build a house on the property, which he named Wharton Grange. It was to be the "most pretentious [house] of any on Kempenfelt Bay or Lake Simcoe." Wharton Grange, built of stone and brick in the English bungalow style, had seventeen guest rooms and an annex to accommodate overflow guests. The senator had his own railway station just west of the village. After eight years, he formed the syndicate of three men who owned it when D.A first rented it. John P. Northey was head of Northey & Co., the steam pump business established in Hamilton by his father, Thomas Northey. James Brock O'Brian was a Toronto lawyer.

From then on, the Cameron family would spend summers on what was a magnificent estate that in many ways resembled country

Achnacarry Castle, 24 km. northeast of Fort William, Scotland.

manors in Britain, especially in the Highlands of Scotland. In fact, there was probably a specific Scottish property that D.A. had in mind: Achnacarry Castle.

Sometime between 1908 and 1912, D.A. visited the chief of the Clan Cameron in Scotland. Donald Cameron, the 25th chief of the Camerons, known as Cameron of Lochiel (or simply Lochiel), lived in Achnacarry Castle. He was knighted in 1934.

Achnacarry Castle was then, as it is now, the epitome of the romantic Scottish seat. On 100 acres, next to a stream rippling with salmon, the property at Spean Bridge lay in the heart of the Lochaber District, known as Cameron Country. The grand stone building with its crenellated walls had seen numerous raids and battles. (Later, in the Second World War, it was used for military exercises.) Lochiel took his role seriously and welcomed any Camerons who stopped by, greeting them in his kilt and sporran. To visit there, as D.A. did, in the early 1900s was like walking into another century — not the nineteenth so much as the eighteenth. It was 1776 when Bonnie Prince Charlie of the House of Stuart, the Jacobite pretender to the throne of Scotland, fought the British soldiers who marched north under the Duke of Cumberland. On the barren expanse of Culloden the British decimated the Scots in a short, brutish battle. The severed limbs, decapitations, and horrible wounds of soldiers on both sides are depicted in the brilliant film *Culloden* by Peter Watkins, famed BBC director. It was the Camerons who hid Bonnie Prince Charlie and protected him as he made his way from France to the north of Scotland, and more Camerons were killed in Culloden than any other clan. Watkins's cool, documentary-style recreation of the battle reveals a motley collection of Scottish men, scarcely emerged from the Middle Ages. Some were so ignorant that they believed Englishmen had tails, like the devil.

At Achnacarry Castle there are still several mementos of that catastrophic defeat, including two of Bonnie Prince Charlie's waistcoats and various weapons. All this D.A. would have seen and talked about when he visited Lochiel. This visit — during which, photos show, he climbed nearby Ben Nevis, the highest mountain in Scotland — spurred D.A.'s imagination, ensuring his passion for all things Scottish.

D.A.'s Scottish affectations served him well, too: far into the twentieth century, Canada imported bank clerks from Scotland believing they were exceptionally well trained in "the sternest frugality and industry" (Ken McGoogan, *How the Scots Invented Canada*, Harper-Collins, 2010.) Even now, Canadian banking has traces of nostalgia for its Scottish connection.

In 1918, D.A. would buy about half of the Parklands property for $10,000, taking a short-term mortgage for half that amount to be paid off a year later. (The other half of Parklands was bought by Mrs. John Holden, a friend from Toronto.) Later, in 1923, he added a small parcel of the property for $2,500.

10

ANOTHER DONALD

It was late in a hot, humid August that my father was born at Parklands. Dollie — terrified of the imminent pain — took to her bed six weeks before the birth. There she moaned and sobbed to the family and servants about what was to come. She had some cause for concern. The rate of death in childbirth at the time was between four and six per 1,000 births. These deaths occurred either from "puerperal fever" (caused by infections or excessive bleeding) and "accidents" (convulsions, coma, or exhaustion, for instance). Only around 1903 did these death rates begin to decline, and even then slowly. This was 1911, and, though chloroform had been used in Britain since 1847 and forceps were being used in hospital births, it is unlikely that a home birth in Canada would have involved their use. What was remarkable about Dollie's behaviour was not so much her worries as her taking to bed six weeks before the birth. Nowhere in the medical histories is there any suggestion that a woman ought to take to her bed before labour begins.

Winnie, aged ten and a half, saw and heard her mother's carryings-on. She was old enough to understand that childbirth was one of the worst things that could happen to a woman, yet too young to put her mother's dread into perspective. When her little brother finally appeared on 20 August 1911, she loved him on sight. He was a real doll for her to play with, another child in a house darkened by Dollie's mood, a sort of lasting present for a sociable little girl. True to the time, neither of her parents nor the servants would have explained childbirth to Winnie. Perhaps if they could have, her sense that a gruesome tragedy had occurred to her mother might have been dispelled — or at least mollified. As it was, somewhere in her memory that trauma would sit like a black shadow.

Just as Winnie had been named after her mother, the baby would be named after his father: Donald Stuart Forsyth Cameron. D.A. now had a son — someone he could raise to love the outdoors life, someone who in the future would move out into the far reaches of Canada to hunt and fish with him. Someone, too, whom he could raise to love Scottish traditions, and who could socialize with him in the men's clubs he adored. The chauffeur drove the family back to Toronto that September in the blue Auburn to begin another stage of their lives.

It seems that Dollie's sadness increased after her son's birth. Perhaps she suffered from what we today call postpartum depression. Perhaps she had been this way since the death of her mother. Perhaps a predisposition to melancholy was made worse by the displacements to inhospitable places occasioned by D.A.'s postings with the bank. The historical record also shows that the way girls were raised resulted in socialization that affected men and women in different ways. According to *Women, Health, and Medicine in America: A Historical Handbook* (1990), female patients at that time suffered more from melancholy or depression — or other forms of "nervousness" — than men, whose reactions to stress were more likely to be alcoholism and violence. Certainly Dollie viewed men with apprehension.

Once my father arrived, a series of governesses joined the household to care for him. One, I believe, was French. The little my father told me of his childhood was that he recalled hiding in the garden at Parklands listening to one of them call him, but refusing to answer her call or come in. Something about the baths he was given then affected him for life.

These governesses — no doubt under instructions — kept Donald in the immaculate white lacy dresses fashionable among the rich at the time. His golden hair would not be cut until he was about five or six, and even then it would be kept chin-length. Meanwhile, it was curled into ringlets. Anyone seeing photos of him at the time would swear he was a girl. Perhaps it was this regimen that resulted in his lifelong hatred of getting dressed up. My mother had to force him to buy a suit or jacket now and then. The outfit of his I remember most — apart from the business suits he reluctantly wore to work — was an old shirt, a sweater full of holes, and torn grey flannels with a broken fly, the gap held together by a large safety pin.

BISHOP STRACHAN
SCHOOL

Aunt Winnie did not believe in education. She would rather have stayed home where she was indulged by Dollie and the servants and could now pass her time playing with the new baby. Rigged out in lace and curls, he was a perfect plaything for his sister.

It was the fall after Donald was born that eleven-year-old Winnie was sent, against her will, to Bishop Strachan School, one of the four main girls' private schools (Havergal College, Branksome Hall, and Loretto Abbey were the others) that educated the daughters of Toronto's elite. (There were also a number of privately run girls' finishing schools in the city.) At BSS girls would learn the basics of literature, math, and history, but also the social skills and manners that as ladies they would need once they married: needlework; a smattering of French (for reading menus and throwing an occasional *bon mot* into conversation); the correct way to drink from a soup spoon; how to pass both salt and pepper when asked for either; how to plan menus, set tables, and oversee laundry; the principles of childcare — or rather how to instruct others in childcare. The school, Wykeham Hall — an elaborate Victorian building — was then located in downtown Toronto on the corner of College and Yonge Streets facing Buchanan Street, not on Lonsdale Road near Upper Canada College where it stands today. Winnie was driven from Isabella Street to school by the family's chauffeur. She used to arrive throwing her toast crusts out the window in front of the school, in somewhat the spirit with which Becky Sharp cavalierly tosses a dictionary out the coach window as she leaves her school in *Vanity Fair*.

Where Winnie learned to read, write, add, and subtract before she attended BSS is a mystery. Ontario law at the time required children between the ages of seven and twelve to attend school. Few girls remained in school after that; they helped at home or were sent out to work. Perhaps Winnie was taught at home by governesses; perhaps her Aunt Pussy taught her in Dawson City; perhaps she attended a small neighbourhood school. It is unlikely that Dollie had the force to instruct her. Yet Winnie had a smattering of these skills when she entered BSS.

The curriculum at BSS when Winnie began at age eleven in 1912 included the basic academic subjects: English grammar and composition, reading, writing, spelling, arithmetic and elementary geometry, Canadian history, and geography. The girls were also taught holy scripture and church catechism from an Anglican point of view. The "extras," intended to refine the girls into ladies, were recitation, brushwork, nature study, sewing, and class singing. All the students took part in military drill.

My mother — who had stood top of her matriculating class in Prince Albert, Saskatchewan — enjoyed saying that Winnie left BSS at age fifteen because she refused to read Thomas More's *Utopia*. Certainly Winnie rebelled at being sent to school at all. She regarded it with the same loathing as David Copperfield did the Murdstones, and consistently maintained she hated it. Anything that involved work of any kind — especially intellectual concentration — bored or distressed her. When I read *Utopia* in preparation for my Ph.D. general exams (a five-day ordeal covering everything from *Beowulf* to *Virginia Woolf*), I saw her point. It focuses on politics and religion in 1515, during the reign of Henry VIII. Maybe because the book was written in Latin, English versions are heavy, turgid, and numbing. Some sentences are fifteen lines long. Who prescribed it for the daughters of Toronto's elite? It could not have helped with small talk or planning dinner parties. When More was not much older than the adolescent Winnie he was studying law, wearing a hair shirt, using a log for a pillow, and whipping himself on Fridays. This lifestyle would never have appealed to Winnie. I'm certain she never understood what "utopia" meant, but had she been able to define her ideal society it would have involved playing at home with her baby brother, being waited on and driven anywhere she wanted by servants, and choosing and wearing beautiful clothes.

Records from the archives at BSS show that More's *Utopia* was not the only reason Winnie dropped out. Nor was she fifteen when she did. My parents had distilled a woeful school performance into one dramatic event. In truth, Winnie only attended BSS for three years, from 1912 to 1915. Even that is an exaggeration, for Winnie's records show that she had the worst attendance of any student in her years there. In that first fall term, she was in class less than half the time. Her name is stroked out for the entire winter term that year. In the 1913 fall term, she was present only forty-one of seventy days. In the winter term, she was there only fourteen of sixty-three days. She was absent for the entire 1914 spring term. On one attendance report, someone has speculated about her absences: "It is possible that she may have had health problems herself or was needed at home to help in some capacity, perhaps with an invalid." This was unlikely, since Winnie enjoyed excellent health all her life, and the Camerons had a maid and a chauffeur at the time to deal with whatever went on at home. For whatever reason — lack of parental discipline or her own bloody-mindedness — her education at BSS started at age eleven and consisted of only about a quarter of the material offered over the next three years. She ended that education at age thirteen.

Why was Winnie allowed to leave school so early? The answer, I suppose, was that as a girl in a wealthy family she did not need education. The main point of attending private school was to make the right friends and acquire good manners. It seems she was not disciplined at home, a job that would have fallen to her mother, who was too compliant — and possibly too depressed — to discipline anyone. Much, much later, when I asked my father if he had rebelled against his mother, he replied, laughing, "No, there was nothing to rebel against."

BSS did not even equip Aunt Winnie with good table manners, as one might expect. My father always properly seated her on his right as the guest of honour, the first served. Yet even my mother could not prevent her from "digging in," as Winnie called it, before the rest of us were served. In winter, she protested my father's heating economies — as we all did — by complaining and by wearing her old, moth-eaten opossum coat to the table. Towards the end of the meal, she was likely to burp, laugh, and exclaim, "Pardon me. Same trouble."

BSS, however, did provide her with suitable friends, and she kept them for life. We seldom met them, but we heard about them. Mildred Holden, the younger sister of Winnie's friend Barbara Northey, I came to know well much later. After Winnie died, my then-husband and I spent much time playing bridge with her and Winnie's cousin Don Ireland, a blustery widower who had recently retired as bursar of Trinity College. I knew Mildred as an avuncular widow resembling a friendly pug. The Holden family house on the east side of Queen's Park Circle eventually became the McLuhan Centre for Culture and Technology at the University of Toronto.

These and other friends of Winnie's were important to her. They represented correct views (conservative) and proper social protocol (regular overnight visits). She often inserted her friends — all daughters or wives of Toronto's Conservative, financial, and business elite

— into discussions with my mother. When they disagreed, which was most of the time, Aunt Winnie would say, "All my friends agree with me." This drove my mother into a fury. It reminded her that she was, in Winnie's view, only a prairie girl from Saskatchewan, who had been my father's secretary at Confederation Life in Toronto. In other words, she was an unsuitable wife for a Cameron, and far, far beneath Winnie.

I remember when *The Canadian Social Register* appeared in 1958. There was much discussion about it at home, since my family, including myself and my sister, had been listed among those "worthy families" described in the preface "[that] have contributed markedly to the social development of their nation." Father thought this was nonsense. Aunt Winnie treated it with more reverence than the Bible, often checking the alphabetical listing and showing our names and the names of her friends to us. Since invitations to be listed in the *Register* had been extended by a "Secret Committee," it was impossible to argue with those who had filtered out Canada's elite. Since both Aunt Winnie and my father had attended private schools, they were no doubt ensured a place — even if Winnie had not graduated from BSS. Father thought it was ridiculous, not least because Winnie had somehow qualified to be included.

When I was a graduate student, I tried to explain to Aunt Winnie what a Ph.D. was. She could not understand. Why philosophy? What *was* philosophy? Doctors in her world were medical men, and a bad lot. She avoided them. In her eighty-one years she never saw the inside of a hospital.

Her views on education for women were clear. "Stop studying!" she would order me and my sister. "Women," she said on other occasions, "should never talk about politics or money." When she saw us reading, she used to say, "If you girls don't stop reading, you'll ruin your looks!" These admonitions sent me and my sister into hysterical giggles. There were times when we rolled off our chairs at the dinner table from laughter. Both of us were devotees of the work ethic, thanks to both our parents, who — unlike Winnie, or perhaps *because of* Winnie — thought everyone should be educated and girls should be equipped to be economically independent if need be. (And "need be" later arose for both of us.) Winnie could not understand our seriousness about school, where we both usually headed our classes.

These — and Winnie's other views — never changed. Whenever I encounter the early nineteenth-century world of Jane Austen in books or movies, it seems to me the kind of world Winnie believed ought to exist, though her lack of manners and her eccentricities would never have been acceptable within it. In some ways, she seemed like a female Falstaff or Sir Toby Belch, without the drunkenness. Whoever had instructed her to take a walk every day, eat three square meals, avoid garlic or spices, and have no more than one alcoholic drink had made a lasting impression. That person was probably her father, who also instilled in her a Darwinian understanding of human nature that dated from the late nineteenth century. "The greatest instinct," she used to say, "is self-preservation. The second is preservation of the race." In other words, sex. She clearly understood the dangers of sexual behaviour, without understanding much of the mechanics of sex. To the best of my knowledge, she did not indulge — ever.

12

A VISIT FROM
SCOTLAND, 1913

Just before my father's second birthday in August 1913, the Cameron family were scurrying here and there, making preparations. I imagine young Donald's birthday was all but overlooked. That much more important Donald — Cameron of Lochiel, 25th clan chieftain of the Camerons — was making a cross-country tour of Canada to meet his colonial clan members.

By this time, D.A. had had five years to situate himself within Toronto society. He would entertain Cameron of Lochiel and his wife in Toronto — the largest city on their tour. D.A. was now almost fifty, a little more than a decade older than Lochiel. He set out to impress his visitor with the best Toronto had to offer. Isabella Street was scrubbed and dusted, its silver polished, its linen laundered and pressed into perfect creases by Kate. The blue Auburn would have been polished and pristine, and the chauffeur ready to ferry the guests about town.

Winnie was eleven, about to enter BSS, when the Lochiels visited. She would have been outfitted in finery, shown how to curtsey properly, expected to be a family adornment her father could show off. She used to speak of this event as a sort of royal visit. Had the King and Queen appeared in her home, no greater impression could have been made.

D.A. arranged not one but two formal entertainments for Lochiel: one at the York Club and, on 29 August 1913, a dinner at the Royal Canadian Yacht Club. D.A belonged to both organizations, and was by now fully at ease as a host to any group of men. Winnie kept both guest lists in her scrapbook.

There is much duplication in the lists of about fifty invited guests for the two events. There were leading politicians — all Conservative — such as Sir John M. Gibson, KCMG, KC, LLD, Lieutenant-Governor of Ontario. Through the bank D.A. had made many business contacts, some of whom he invited, such as Sir Edmund B. Osler, of the investment firm Osler & Hammond, one of Toronto's richest men. Naturally he included the top officials from the Canadian Bank of Commerce, such as Sir Edmund Walker (who had dropped his first name, Byron), the bank's president. D.A.'s rank as lieutenant and adjutant in the 48th Highlanders and his membership in the Military Institute led him to befriend military men such as Colonel George T. Denison, a Conservative civic politician and one of the founders of the short-lived Canada First movement. Naturally he invited senior officers of the 48th Highlanders, Toronto businessmen such as R.S. Gourlay of the piano-building firm Gourlay, Winter & Leeming; Lieutenant Colonel D.M. Robertson of Mackenzie and Mann, owners of the Toronto Suburban Railway Company; J.P. Northey of the Northey Hydraulic Works (the same John Northey who had once owned Parklands); and T.H. Plummer of the Plummer Machine Company. These two companies had recently merged into Northey-Plummer Ltd. He included a couple of relatives as well: his brother Archibald Cameron, his brother-in-law A.H. Ireland — both in the Canadian Bank of Commerce — and his uncle Colin S. Cameron, KC (later Conservative MPP for North Bruce in Owen Sound). The overall cast of this assembly of *bon vivants* was Scottish, conservative, and prosperous.

At the Royal Canadian Yacht Club dinner, where D.A. drew up a seating plan later kept by Winnie, he sat at the centre of the head table with Cameron of Lochiel on his right and Sir Edmund Walker on Lochiel's right. Sir John Gibson sat on D.A.'s left. D.A. would keep in touch with Lochiel after the visit, sending him and his wife, Hermione, daughter of the 5th Duke of Montrose, boxes of chocolates at Christmas.

A few months later, D.A. was among those members of the Canadian Club that attended the banquet for former US president William Howard Taft on 30 January 1914. D.A. would have agreed with the sentiments in Taft's "landmark" speech. Taft praised imperialism and asserted the supremacy of British institutions in all of North America.

Yet D.A. was not simply a capitalist with social flair. He also established himself in the city by donating money, and substantial amounts of it, to charitable causes. Dollie occasionally hosted events, such as thirty tables of bridge for the 48th Regiment, to raise money for the Imperial Order of the Daughters of the Empire (IODE). She also dealt with the money raised by the Women's Temperance Union to provide homes for 8,000 orphans displaced by the Ottoman Empire's bloody slaughter of 1.5 million Armenians during the Armenian Resistance of 1914–18.

Winnie had nothing to do with such causes, but her father gave often and generously, and he served on the boards of several committees. In 1914, he donated $1,000 towards the building of the new Toronto General Hospital at the corner of University Avenue and College Street. In time, he would serve as a member of the finance committee of the Toronto Red Cross, as treasurer for the American Committee for Armenian and Syrian Relief, as honorary treasurer for the China Famine Relief Committee of Canada (run by the Canadian Presbyterian Mission), as treasurer for the Toronto branch of the Canadian National Committee for Combatting Social Diseases, and, for a time, as honorary treasurer for Ontario. Though it was common in my childhood for parents to remind children at dinner about all the little

Chinese children who had no food, in my family such remarks might have been personal observations handed down by my grandfather to my father.

13

PARKLANDS:
A SCOTTISH IDYLL

It was not unusual for Torontonians to seek cool lakes and simple cottages in the hell that was summer. Even working class families without vehicles took the railroads that were laid from the city to resort areas for that purpose. What was unusual about the Cameron holidays at Parklands was their scope and scale. Leaving Isabella Street behind, its furniture draped in ghostly white sheets as if it had fallen into a coma, the family were driven in the blue Auburn up Yonge Street to Barrie, then along the narrow winding road over the rattling wooden Thunder Bridge that crossed the railway, in through the limestone-walled property, past the Gate House, and up to the Big House, as Wharton Grange came to be called.

The fact that D.A. owned an Auburn touring car in 1908 was extraordinary. Motor cars only began to replace horse-drawn vehicles after the war ended in 1918. The car would have cost over $1,000, a vast sum then that testified to D.A.'s financial success.

Parklands was a self-contained world, which lent a mythical aspect

D.A. (left), Dollie
(right), and
Dollie's nephew,
Don Ireland,
Parklands.

Parklands postcard, Shanty Bay, late 19th c. or early 20th c.

to the lives of the family. That myth was romantic and Scottish. D.A.'s visit to Scotland had inspired him to emulate Lochiel's life at Achnacarry at Parklands. While he could not change an English bungalow-style house into a crenellated castle, he could wear the kilt and sporran and play Chief of the Clan Cameron, Canadian-style. Parklands could not boast salmon fishing or deer hunting, but it had its own beauty. The property was, and still is, fenced with layers of flat limestone about three feet high. It had a gatehouse just to the right of the entrance where the gatekeeper and his family lived. Beyond was the tennis court, where much later I saw my father play with his friend Bill White, who rented the gatehouse one summer from the Holdens (the family of Winnie's friend Mildred). There were stables over to the left of the Big House, and a greenhouse. A broad sweep of road lined with fragrant lavender led down to the dock where there was a small lighthouse and a slip for boats. When I was an adolescent, the Shanty Bay Regatta, with its competitions in such Canadian skills as swimming, diving, and gunwale-bobbing took place there. I recall winning a diving competition with a dubious version of a swan dive. On an incline to one side of the dock area stood a gazebo from which some spectators watched in comfort, like theatre-goers in a box.

There was more than one postcard made of the place. Family photos feature Winnie at eighteen, poised on the brink of making her debut in Toronto the following year. She is pictured at Parklands with several friends, swimming, playing tennis or croquet, and simply enjoying the grounds at picnics in the middy dresses of that time.

Not only did D.A. wear Highland gear at Parklands, he hired a bagpiper, Alasdair MacPherson. MacPherson also wore full Highland regalia as he strode around the grounds. He played his pipes at seven a.m. on the lawn in front of the Big House to wake the family and staff — a sort of Scottish alarm clock. He piped around the dinner table, which must have made conversation impossible. On Sundays, he played in the open car that the chauffeur drove to St. Thomas Anglican Church in Shanty Bay. They were Presbyterian, insofar as they

Group around World War I cannon at Parklands: Dollie (left) Winnie (top centre), young Donald (bottom centre), Mary Hendrie (bottom right), and Don Ireland, Dollie's nephew (right), c. 1918.

Winnie with dog, and friends (Mary Hendrie, centre), on Victoria Day, c. 1910.

Winnie demonstrating the Highland Fling at Parklands. Her stance indicates that she did not know the dance.

Winnie (left), Bill Hendrie, and Mary Hendrie at "Gateside," the Hendrie estate in Hamilton, Ontario, 1912–13.

were anything, but the picturesque little church in the old lakeside village (where the famous painter Lucius O'Brien had been born in 1832) was the only one in the area. I don't think the Camerons could have realized that Shanty Bay was named after the shanties built by blacks that had escaped slavery via the Underground Railway. Had they known this they would have been taken aback, and would perhaps have even shunned the place.

One photo of Winnie when she was about eleven or twelve — around the time her little brother was born — shows her in a kilt, sporran, dancing shoes, and the Glengarry wedged cap with ribbons worn by Scottish marching bands. She is striking the pose taken when dancing the Highland Fling. Her pose suggests that she never actually learned to dance the Highland Fling, though she did love to dance. I learned to dance it (along with the Sword Dance), and performed both to the pipes at my elementary school along with a friend who was also named Elspeth. Winnie's taste was for the foxtrot, the waltz, and the two-step. Another photo around the same time shows

Winnie and young Donald, Parklands, c.1916.

Winnie and young Donald, Parklands, c. 1918. His kilt and sporran were worn by each of his grandsons in turn at New Year's *ceilidhs* in Barrie, Ontario.

her holding a puppy amid a group of children enthusiastically waving Union Jacks.

When my father was about six or seven, he was removed from the white, frilly Little Lord Fauntleroy outfits he wore as a toddler and was installed in a kilt and sporran like his father's. At the same time, his long golden curls were cut. He had his own pony, cared for by a groom in the stables. One photo shows him riding it with a big smile. Parklands also featured a little wicker pony cart drawn by a small pony so children could drive around the grounds. Somehow, this pony and cart were transferred from Toronto, or perhaps there were two ponies and two carts. Certainly Winnie and my father both recalled driving the cart around their Isabella Street neighbourhood. My mother relayed the information Father must have told her, that Winnie used to take him for rides around Bloor Street and St. Clair Avenue in this pony cart. To make sure he stayed seated, she jabbed him with her hatpin whenever he stood up. Now I wonder if this was where her nickname "Win Pin" came from. St. Clair was the northern limit of the city then, and was filled with orchards and etched with dirt roads. My mother told us that our father used to roller-skate on Jarvis Street and walk with his father from Isabella Street to chop down a Christmas tree in the woods north of St. Clair.

It is clear that there was much entertaining — especially of children — at Parklands. D.A. would have seen to that. His son Donald, however, was proving to be far less gregarious than his father and sister. One photo shows him sitting on a two-seater swing on the veranda of the Big House with his mother, quietly looking at a book. He disliked being fussed over by his governess. It was Winnie who loved the ambiance at Parklands. So it was that as an adolescent she was driven in an open car each summer to be "by the lake" — a phrase of annual entitlement that never left her vocabulary.

14

THE

DEBUTANTE

The Great War did not deeply affect the Camerons. Some 70,000 military-aged men left Toronto to serve between 1914 and 1918. This did not include D.A. Cameron. He was too old at forty to serve in any way except as a reservist with the 48th Highlanders, where he was an adjutant and, eventually, a major. Instead, D.A. continued his forays on behalf of the Commerce. In 1916 he was sizing up Santiago, Chile, Buenos Aires, Argentina, and Sao Paulo, Brazil as possible sites for branches of the bank. The young men who were Winnie's age were too young to enlist (she was thirteen to seventeen during the war). Neither the inflation and coal shortages that occurred towards the end of the war, nor the flu epidemic of 1918 (in which 1,300 Torontonians died) touched the Camerons.

When Winnie made her debut into Toronto society in 1919, the city — like the rest of the western world — had changed. The population was growing, despite the loss of 60,000 Canadian soldiers overseas, many of whom came from Toronto: it would more than double from

208,000 in 1901 to 522,000 by 1921. Many sections outside the city limits of 1908 had been annexed to the city. In 1919, Guglielmo Marconi set up the first radio station in Toronto, based on naval wireless technology. His first demonstration of the machine was at the Toronto Industrial Exhibition (now the CNE) in 1920. Soon the "wireless" would be installed in the homes of the wealthy, affording access to news broadcasts and music. Telephones were already in place, though not widely owned. The city's working class and underclass still lived in areas such as Cabbagetown or grim slums such as The Ward without running water or heat.

While the poor suffered, the lives of the rich were enhanced. The angry, insulting cries of "Bolshevism" that accompanied the Winnipeg General Strike of May 1919, which included about 22,000 tradesmen, would have been echoed heartily by the financiers and businessmen of Toronto. They would have pooh-poohed any notion that labour regulations, fair wages, and better working conditions — and eventually the socialist CCF party — were on the way. The stock market crash did not affect those, like D.A. Cameron and most of his friends, who were invested in financial institutions rather than stocks. The rich did not pay taxes on income, corporations, or goods and services, such as we know today. Nor did the poor, but they did not have corporations or much income. Federal taxes mainly came from customs duties. Provinces and cities like Toronto got most of their tax income from sales of property, rental of natural resources, and subsidies from the federal government. The adaptation of the inventions of the war industry to peacetime uses meant rapid technological progress had been made. Some Toronto industrialists focused their businesses on war-related production, such as munitions, parachutes, and airplanes, and made enormous profits. In some cases, typical of the time, they were recognized by Britain for their "contributions to the war effort" more than the soldiers themselves. Their children, who were Winnie's age, lived amidst wealth that would have been unimaginable to the pioneers who had settled the land a mere three or four generations before. Bankers like D.A., stockbrokers, and insurers made huge profits. Car ownership in the city grew from about 10,000 vehicles in 1916 to 80,000 by 1928. The paving of roads became a huge business. Planes had been refined from pre-war aircraft, and adventurous pilots began to cross the Atlantic, though air travel for most people was a thing of the future. Instead, travellers booked passage abroad on liners, such as the Cunard and White Star ships, which separated the classes. Prohibition, which took hold across Ontario from 1916 to 1927, ironically enriched distillers like Gooderham and Worts.

The consequences of this commercial wealth could be seen everywhere. Many multi-level buildings appeared in the city. The grand Union Station, interrupted by the war, was finished in 1920. Toronto's tallest building, the Royal York Hotel on Front Street, would be completed in 1929, defining the skyline of the city for many years.

The twenties was an exciting, hopeful decade, as Toronto surged into prosperity after the end of the Great War. Smart new streetcars similar to today's trolleys appeared at the beginning of 1921. Over eighty percent of Toronto's population of half a million was British. Prejudice against Asians was rampant; they were thought to be unfit for full citizenship. As for blacks, they were rare, frightening, and despised, unless, of course, they marched in the King's regiments from South Africa. Toronto's financial institutions and the men who ran them were on top of the world in Canada. The combination of wealth and postwar adulation for everything British meant that many wealthy Torontonians at the time would do all they could to imitate the rite of coming out that set apart those young women in Britain who were from the upper class. The emulation of this custom declared that a similar class system was viable in Canada. Though Toronto was gradually becoming more and more North American, the British garrison with their debutantes was centre stage for now, the stuff of newspaper reports on the social pages.

By 1919, D.A. was solidly established in Toronto society. He had befriended each succeeding lieutenant-governor. In addition to his service in the 48th Highlanders, he had been elected president of the St. Andrew's Society. He also held the important post of treasurer on two newsworthy charities: the All-India Relief Committee and the Armenian Relief Committee. Though Dollie was not much of a socialite, the couple appeared from time to time in the social pages of local newspapers at balls, teas, and concerts. In a speech D.A. made in May 1917 against the prospect of an election, he made his political position clear. At that time, Conservative prime minister Robert Borden was dealing with the conscription crisis. D.A. was pro-Borden and pro-conscription; he thought an election would be disloyal to Britain. He believed that Canada should devote all her energy to the current war. In any event, he added (wrongly) that there was no public support for an election.

So, for a time, Toronto's inevitable move towards an American rather than British identity was delayed. Postwar patriotism, a pro-British prime minister, and currents of anti-Americanism all played a role. To imagine Toronto's elite in 1920, think of Timothy Findley's *The Wars*.

Today it is hard to imagine making a social debut at eighteen. In England the ceremony used to culminate in a presentation to the King and Queen at court. A debutante "came out," leaving childhood behind, and was "presented" to society as a marriageable woman. The presentation of debutantes to the Queen ended in 1958. Yet the tradition continued in England, and in other parts of the British Empire and the U.S. These days debutantes hope not for husbands, but for contacts useful in future careers.

In Winnie's day, the operative word was "marriageable." Young women wore white dresses symbolizing their virginity for the Debutantes' Ball that launched the Season. There they would be on display to eligible and suitable young men at a round of social events. During the Season — from September through June — debutantes and their beaux attended dances, receptions, teas, plays, operas, and openings of art shows. In summer there were lavish garden parties. Other venues were the horse shows (with dinners afterwards) at Woodbine Racetrack, and events at clubs such as the Toronto Club at York and Wellington Streets, the Lambton Golf Club, the Royal Canadian Yacht Club, and the Toronto Golf Club on Kingston Road. To prepare for the Season, debutantes and young men took dancing lessons from the Toronto Dancing Club at the fashionable King Edward Hotel. The social events proper would begin in the fall. At these each girl would receive a small, tasselled dance card listing the dances, with a break for supper in the middle. Men engaged these dances, never taking two in a row from the same young woman. The names of partners for the one-step, the two-step, the foxtrot, and the waltz were filled in on the dance card before the dancing began. A special partner was selected for the mid-dance supper. Always chaperoned, young women were introduced to as many eligible men as possible and expected to dance or dine with all of them at some point. Winnie kept boxes of her dance cards, all filled out in her broad, round handwriting with the names of the partners she had danced with. On some there are signs of playful scuffles as one of her beaux (as she always called them) stroked out one name and replaced it with his own. One signed his name "Cupid." There are about a hundred of these cards, probably one for each dance she attended in the few years following her debut.

It was understood that the families of debutantes would coach them to find a husband from an appropriate family sometime during a year or two of such activities. It wasn't arranged marriage, but it had some things in common with it. Marriages often consolidated business alliances between families; others were based on land ownership or sheer wealth.

Winnie's scrapbook contains yellowed and worn clippings of newspaper accounts of these events from the social pages of the Toronto papers. Their glue has long since dried up, and the yellowed clippings slide free. One 1919 clipping announces that "the debutantes of the coming season are Miss B. Buntin, Miss Harriet Browse, Miss Ethel Kirkpatrick, Miss Marion Baillie, Miss Barbara Northey, Miss Winifred

Cameron, Miss Isabel [sic] Cawthra, Miss Raybelle George, Miss Sybil [sic] Lyon, and Miss Helen Gooderham." These debutantes came from the wealthiest and most prominent families in the city.

Four of these young women came from families that had made their fortunes in manufacturing. Their fathers were usually third-generation Canadians who profited from the labour of their fathers and, sometimes, their grandfathers. Handed control of well-established businesses, they brought the practices of corporate capitalism to the quickly growing economic and social life of Canada in the second-largest, most commercial centre in the country. It would be years before the government would take part in business ownership. During the war years, these businessmen profited even further from the stepped-up production triggered by war industries.

Luella Lois "Billee" Buntin's grandfather, Alexander Buntin, had been a Scottish immigrant who became the most advanced paper manufacturer in the industry. He made Hamilton — Ontario's indus-trial giant — the main distribution centre for office supplies to the north and west of early Upper Canada. One of his contemporaries told him he was "as rich as Croesus," to which he is said to have replied, "I don't know who Croesus is, but I will put up two dollars to his one." Eventually, Buntin added his son — also named Alexander, and Billee's father — to his business.

Barbara Northey, who was to become one of Winnie's lifelong friends, came from a family of engineers and inventors. Her grand-father, Thomas Northey, had invented the famous steam pump, which was widely used in the late nineteenth century. He incorpo-rated the Northey Company in 1878. In 1903 his son, and Barbara's father, John Pell Northey, patented an important modification to fog horns, changing them from the single siren to the diaphones (low, two-toned fog horns) we recognize today. In time John, in addition to owning Parklands, branched off to start his own company, Canadian Fog Signal Co., Ltd. At this point, the Northey Company merged with the Canadian Foundry Company in Toronto. The Northey family lived in a grand Italianate mansion at Elm Avenue and Sherbourne Street in Rosedale, named Guiseley House after the place in Yorkshire, England that old Thomas Northey came from.

Marion Baillie's father, Sir Frank Wilton Baillie, was a steel, munitions, and aircraft manufacturer. Starting with Hamilton Canada Steel Co., Ltd. (then Burlington Steel), Baillie led Canadian steel production. During the war, he had focused on producing brass cartridge cases and eighteen-pounder shell cases for Britain. Towards the end of the war, he had manufactured aircraft. He adroitly invested his profits in utilities and manufacturing projects, such as Dominion Coal, at a time when Toronto homes were heated by coal. He averted a worker's strike in Hamilton by giving the workers in his Canadian Cartridge Company a *reduction* of work time to nine hours a day. Britain rewarded him for his "war effort" by making him the first Canadian to be made a Knight Commander of the British Empire. When he died in 1921, two years after Marion came out, he was worth $2 million, a staggering amount for that time. Marion's mother, daughter of Aubrey White, Ontario's deputy minister of lands, forests, and mines, had thrown herself into public charities for the blind and for incurable children, among others.

As for Helen Gooderham, she hailed from the large and prosperous distillery family. The original William Gooderham had left England to join his brother-in-law, James Worts, in Toronto in 1831. In 1832 they opened their mill, and in 1837 their distillery, Gooderham & Worts. By 1861, they owned the largest distillery in Canada, capable of producing two million gallons of whiskey a year. The sprawling Gooderham family boasted lawyers, professors, bankers, and military officers. Helen's grandfather George Gooderham combined his management of the distillery with banking. His son, Helen's father, William Hargraft Gooderham, became a stockbroker.

The other debutantes mentioned with Winnie in the newsclip also stood at the top of Toronto's society, though for different reasons. Harriet Brouse's grandfather had been a doctor and Liberal member of the Canadian senate. Her father, William Brouse, was also a doctor and had married into the Gooderham family. His wife, and Harriet's mother, was Florence Gooderham, the sister of Sir Albert Edward Gooderham, a distiller who established the Connaught Laboratories. The Brouses belonged to the Thousand Islands Country Club, which, at that time, was thought a fairyland of unspoiled beauty.

Ethel Kirkpatrick's father was Lieutenant Colonel Arthur E. Kirkpatrick with the Argyll-Sutherland Highlanders. He was also president of the Skating Club and an officer in the Hunt Club. Sylvia Lyon's father, George Seymour Lyon, was a wealthy golfer who had won the gold medal in the 1904 Summer Olympics in St. Louis, Missouri. In Canada, he won the Amateur Championship eight times and the Senior Golf Association Championship ten times between 1918 and 1930.

Rachel — aka "Raybel," or "Ray Belle" — George was the granddaughter of a Scottish immigrant who was a scandalous minister and a professor of systematic theology at Queen's University in Kingston. (While he was principal at Queen's, he allegedly fathered an illegitimate daughter with the sister of his bitter enemy, Professor George Weir.) Her father, W.K. George, was a lawyer who was active in the National Club, home of the Canada First Party. This short-lived, ultra-conservative, Ontario-based party viewed Confederation as a political transaction among elites like themselves. The party campaigned for exclusively British immigration and saw Canada as a future white, Anglo-Saxon, Protestant (WASP) stronghold of economic wealth equal to — or even surpassing — Britain.

The arrogant Cawthras were known as the "Astors of Upper Canada." Isobel Cawthra's mother, Ada Austin, was among the representatives of twenty or so families who formed the United Empire Loyalists' Association of Ontario. Her Irish Austin ancestors, wildly successful businesspeople, built the grand Spadina House, which is now Spadina Museum. She was the daughter of the Honourable Samuel Mills, a Conservative senator. Isobel's father, H. Victor (aka Victor H.)

inherited some of the wealth amassed by his grandfather William, a businessman and financier reported to be Toronto's richest man in the 1880s. Victor Cawthra, a barrister, built a grand mansion at 163 St. George Street (now the Phi Kappa Sigma Fraternity house). The Cawthras, with their official coat of arms from England, were widely thought to have gone "mad from snobbery," according to contemporary descendent, Anthony Adamson. Adamson scoffs at his family's past in his memoir *Wasps in the Attic*, thought them all "lunatic snobs and bloodsuckers." Isobel — whose parents fiercely believed in their tradition — arranged for the foremost portraitist of the time, E. Wyly Grier, RCA, to paint her portrait at about the time she made her debut.

Each of these debutantes' families would host a party for their daughter's coming out, at astounding expense. The party for Winnie was enormous. According to the two newspaper clippings she saved, there were more than 300 guests. It was held at the most popular spot for such entertainments, Jenkins' Antiques and Art Galleries (popularly called Jenkins' or simply JG). Jenkins' at 25 Grenville Street stood east of Queen's Park, a block north of College Street, near Bay Street. (Today a condo named The Gallery stands on this site.) According to a long account in the newspaper, Winnie's was the first event there to feature "the skirl of the pipes." The gallery was decorated with palms, ferns, and flowers. Jardine's orchestra provided the music for alternations of the one-step, the two-step, the foxtrot, and the waltz, which would make up the dances after dinner. But before supper, the pipes "merrily" accompanied a Scottish reel during which, according to one newsclip, "the Highland blood warmed to the music as it raced with the dancers' feet."

Winnie and her parents formally received the guests. By this time, D.A. was president of the St. Andrew's Society, a captain in the 48th Highlanders, and an active member of about a dozen of the best men's clubs. Newspaper accounts spared no details. "Mrs. Cameron [was] wearing a becoming gown of black charmeuse and net, blue ostrich tips trimming it effectively. Her ornaments were a necklace of diamonds and aquamarines, and she carried a black feather fan." The contrast between Dollie and her debutante daughter must have been striking. "Miss Winifred Cameron [was] wearing a lovely frock of white net, the bodice and part of the skirt being of opalescent sequins. Silver shoes and stockings, a blue feather fan and an armful of roses made the pretty toilette complete." From then on, Winnie would no longer be included in invitations to her parents. Now she would receive her own invitations. And many, many invitations there were.

15

AN IDEAL
DANCE PARTY, 1920

On one of the little gold-tasselled dance cards kept by Winnie is an inscription in her round, upright handwriting: "My Ideal Programme for a Dance." It is the only dance programme labelled in this way. The formal invitation was to an At Home (the hostess would be "at home" for her guests, even if the location was not her actual home) held by Winnie and her mother.

My Ideal Programme for a dance.

W. Cameron

JANUARY 23RD, 1920

Mrs. Donald Cameron
Miss Winifred Cameron
At Home
on Friday, January Twenty-third
at nine o'clock
Jenkin's Art Gallery

R.S.V.P.
162 Isabella Street

This invitation card bears the somewhat ferocious Cameron family crest, a raised arm in metal armour grasping a dirk. The motto beneath is "Pro Rege et Patria." The King was George V; the country was England (or, in the Camerons' minds, Scotland).

What made this dance programme ideal? Since every detail resembled all Winnie's other dance programmes, it must have been the seven young men who had signed Winnie's card. These young men had all been educated at one of the five private schools for boys in Ontario: Upper Canada College and St. Andrew's College in Toronto, Bishop Ridley College in St. Catharines, Trinity College School in Port Hope, or Appleby School (later College) in Oakville. This education already marked such young men as coming from wealthy families and having important futures, for the fees then (as now) were even higher than university tuition fees. These schools did their best to emulate boys' schools in England, such as Eton and Harrow.

Two of Winnie's partners, Lieutenant Paul Greey and Lieutenant John "Jack" Boyd, had recently returned from the Great War. Greey had survived six battles with the Canadian Field Artillery. Before leaving for the war, he had worked in the Canadian Bank of Commerce, where — no doubt — he'd known D.A. Now that he was back in Toronto, he took up manufacturing in his father's highly successful firm, Fibreglass Co., Ltd. Greey was a member of the Toronto Hunt Club and played on the Toronto Argonauts Football Club, who later that same year would win the Interprovincial Rugby Football Union championship. Jack Boyd was the grandson of Sir John Alexander Boyd, an intense Anglophile who, as president of the High Court, was the second-highest-ranking judge in Ontario. Jack's father was a surgeon, head of the otolaryngology department at the Hospital for Sick Children. Nancy, Jack's sister, became one of Winnie's best friends.

Peter Campbell and Hollis Blake were also headed for careers in law. Campbell was a member of the 48th Highlanders, and had been awarded the Military Cross. He had been an excellent hockey and football captain at Trinity College School (a rink there is named after him), and he would continue to be involved in sports throughout his life. He was captain and quarterback for the Varsity (U of T) team. After the war he joined R.C. Matthews and Co., after which he formed a brokerage firm with his TCS friend George Stratton, Stratton & Co. He was one of the key figures in building Maple Leaf Gardens in Toronto when he worked as manager of the financial advertising section of *The Globe and Mail*. At Winnie's "ideal" dance he danced the Scottish reel with her, the Reel O'Tulloch. Hollis Blake's great-grandfather, son of the Rector of the Church of England in Ireland, emigrated in 1832. He became an outstanding jurist. One of his sons, Edward Blake, was leader of the Liberal Party and became premier of Ontario. Edward's brother, Samuel Hume Blake, was Hollis's grand-father. A pioneer in legal education and an irascible evangelist, he was a leading business lawyer of his time. His wealth was acquired through investments in Brazil, where Canada had begun the intro-duction of hydro and electric power. Hollis's father, Major Hume Blake, Jr., was a partner in the family law firm Blake and Blake, which became Blake, Cassels and Graydon. (It eventually became Blakes, still an outstanding international law firm today.) Hollis, also headed for law, claimed Winnie for both the romantic waltzes that concluded the two sections of the programme.

Cecil "Cess" Cowan was the son of a businessman; Hugh McCul-lough's father was Dr. J.W.S. McCullough, chief medical officer for Ontario, whose job it had been to tally and report on casualties resulting from the Spanish Flu epidemic of 1918.

Winnie's most frequent dance partner that evening, as well as her companion for the supper halfway through the programme, was Strathearn "Stratty" Hay. He and his twin brother Robert (Bob) were about to go to the Olympics in Antwerp as two of the team of four Canadian rowers from the Argonaut Rowing Club, the most successful team in Canada during the '20s and '30s. There they made it to the semi-finals. Stratty and Bob would both dance often with Winnie over the next three years. So would the other six young men on her "ideal" dance programme that night.

I picture the couples that cold January Friday — the debs, who were eighteen or nineteen, and their partners a few years older — dancing around the smooth floor at Jenkins' Antiques and Art Galleries, past the landscape paintings and portraits on the wall, past the expensive, ornate antiques that furnished the large room, past the other couples laughing and chatting. These young women no longer wore the Edwardian long skirts and high-necked blouses their mothers had worn. Skirts shortened to avoid stains from the dust and horse droppings in the streets had reached what was then the almost scandalous length of twelve inches above ground, giving an erotic edge to fashion. Legs were now clad in flesh-coloured, white, or silver stockings, held up by garters attached to much less restrained corsets than the breathtaking cinches their mothers had worn. Shoes, which had formerly been hidden, emerged as high fashion. Shaped heels of about two inches supported pumps, ankle-strapped Mary Janes, or T-straps in openwork leather, brocade, or silk. The toes were pointed, and the shoes were decorated with diamante clips, bows, or beaded buckles.

Pastel dresses in charmeuse, crepe, satin, silk, or chiffon, with geometric art deco-inspired drapery or elaborate beading, fell straight from sleeveless shoulders. The boyish silhouettes with dropped waists, made possible by strapping the breasts flat, gave an impression of girlish immaturity. The long, intricately dressed hair their mothers took such pride in was cut into straight bobs or Marcelled waves. Jewels of all kinds glittered on necks, ears, and hands. The physical freedom made possible by these new fashions must have been exhilarating. Though south of the border the flapper had begun to make her appearance dancing the Charleston in knee-length dresses, the more conservative version of women's fashion emancipation and dancing held sway in Canada.

Men, too, dressed less formally than their fathers, apart from those who chose to wear military uniform. The dinner jacket had appeared, and black tie replaced the white tie that accompanied tails. The longer hair and thick moustaches of their fathers had been trimmed back into sleeker styles. They still had moustaches, but these were trimmed and neat, and their shorter hair was parted on the side and slicked back with the aid of hair oil. Everything money could buy in the way of clothes and grooming made evenings such as this as aristocratic and British as possible.

These young people — carefree after a war that had cast a shadow over pleasure — exuded the confidence of being British and best. Some affected mid-Atlantic accents, and peppered their remarks with expressions like "By Jove!" or "I say!" Skilled from the dancing lessons they'd all received, they moved smartly to the foxtrot played by the small band at one end of the room, or dipped and swayed to the waltz, shimmering in their silks and jewels.

16

THE
BEAUX

$\int$ome of Winnie's dance partners were destined for fame. I remember her telling me with a faraway look about how she danced with HRH, the Prince of Wales, at the York Club on St. George Street in 1924. On that occasion Leslie McCullough, brother of her friend Barbara and her frequent partner Hugh, was her supper date. At this time, David, as HRH was known, had not yet met Wallis Simpson, though he was rumoured to have been interested chiefly in married women. Newspaper accounts confirm that most of his dance partners in Toronto were married. From her comment in a letter written ten years later Winnie seems not to have liked HRH much, finding him "too fidgety." Yet I can't help wondering what might have happened had Winnie struck his fancy.

The future King Edward VIII was on his third trip to Canada to, as he said, "learn more of the gallant Canadians who had rallied round the standard at the first call from the Mother Country in 1914." After his first trip in 1919, he had bought a ranch sixty miles outside Calgary.

Returning in 1923 and 1924, he sought the privacy and novelty this ranch afforded him. Photos show him out west looking ridiculous as he rides British-style in a western saddle.

Interested, like all the Royal Family, in horses, HRH was not only entertained at the York Club ball during his 1924 visit, he was also invited that October to ride with the hounds hunting foxes at the Toronto Hunt Club. On a crisp autumn day, HRH rode out west of Aurora near Sir John and Lady Eaton's farm. Like many wealthy Torontonians, the Eatons owned a large estate outside the city. In fact, it was then possible to ride around the city's outskirts without leaving the ample estates of Toronto's "country gentry." The prince fell off his horse, Alter Fire, on that occasion, as did several of the members of the Hunt Club, since they had chosen "the toughest country" (up Yonge Street, halfway between Aurora and Newmarket) for the royal hunt. Several of the families of Winnie's dance partners were avid riders, taking part in competitions both in Canada and the United States. Though several women from the families the Camerons knew rode to hounds, Winnie never did.

The fascination of the British royalty and aristocracy with horse-racing offered a parallel with aristocratic breeding. Just as the patriarchal divine right of kings determined the rules of succession to the British throne, well-bred gentlemen were understood to have come from good bloodlines. He (or she) was a "blueblood" (hence the title of the *Blue Book* that listed Toronto socialites). Similarly, the bloodlines of horses were all-absorbing for horse breeders. Thorough-bred horses were those descended from the outstanding lines shown on their pedigrees. For this reason, the Toronto Hunt Club and the Royal Woodbine Racetrack, where horses competed for the Queen's Plate, were strong connectors between Toronto and Britain. To belong to the Toronto Hunt Club, to race at Woodbine — or even to attend those races, as Winnie did, in the finery of the day — asserted that there was an aristocracy in Canada linked to that in Britain and, ultimately, to the Royal Family. One of the main purposes of the rite of coming out was to flaunt a debutante's pedigree, to breed the best with the best.

The young British businessman and banker Hugh Kindersley, 2nd Baron Kindersley, met Winnie at debutantes' gatherings held during the few years he studied at the University of Toronto. Later he became a director of the Bank of England (1947–67), chairman of Royal Exchange Assurance in London, and chairman of Rolls-Royce (1956–68). Winnie liked Hugh and kept in touch with him, and later visited him and Lady Kindersley, her "great friend" Nancy Boyd, in England. I recall her returning from these visits surprisingly full of complaints. "It was not only damp, it was *dank!*" she'd say, as if taken aback that all was not perfect. She would also joke about the fact that "W.C.," the British euphemism for water closet, or toilet, were her initials.

Eric Haldenby, a lieutenant in the 48th Highlanders who had won the Military Cross for his deeds at Vimy Ridge, had entered the degree program in architecture at the University of Toronto. He, too, danced with Winnie, and his was a name she often mentioned to me. In 1921 he formed the firm Mathers and Haldenby. It was a firm that would build many of Toronto's landmarks: the Bank of Nova Scotia at King and Bay, the United States Consulate on University Avenue, the David Dunlap Observatory, and many buildings on the University of Toronto campus.

Winnie also danced with George Drew, who later founded a Conservative dynasty in Ontario that lasted forty-two years. He would be Ontario's premier from 1943 to 1948. Like several of Winnie's dance partners, Drew was a lawyer who had served in the Great War as an officer in the Canadian Field Artillery. Winnie also danced with Timothy Eaton, the son of Sir John and Lady Eaton, and the grandson of the Timothy Eaton who established the famous department store in what is today the location of the Eaton Centre. One of the Masseys — probably Denton Massey, who became an Anglican priest and politician — was also a partner. He was descended from the original

Daniel Massey, a blacksmith and producer of farm implements, via Hart Massey, the Canadian businessman and philanthropist who built Massey-Harris. Hart House at the University of Toronto was erected in his name.

Winnie danced with these young men on the brink of fame only once or twice. Most of the beaux who were courting her came from the established business, banking, military, medical, and legal families in Toronto. Though social occasions often took place at Jenkins' Art Galleries, they were also held at Government House, the King Edward Hotel, the York Club, and in the large mansions these families owned.

One such mansion was Chudleigh at 139 Beverley Street, opposite the Art Gallery of Toronto (now the Art Gallery of Ontario). The mansion was built by George L. Beardmore, known as "the leather king." A prosperous tanner who made saddles, harnesses, and shoes, he named it after his home village in Devon, England. His son, George W., who took over the house and the business in the Beardmore Building (still there, including the sculpted name) on Front Street, threw an annual fancy dress New Year's ball for his son, also George, his two daughters, Elizabeth and Helen, and their young friends. Young George danced with Winnie more often than any of her beaux, and she was a guest at these costume parties each year. (Later, Chudleigh would become the Italian Consulate, apart from one year during the Second World War when it would serve as a barracks for the RCMP.) Costumes for these balls were often idyllic — shepherd-esses, French ladies, peasant maids, Prince Charmings, ballet dancers, Pierrots or Pierrettes, and flower girls — or they reflected a fascina-tion with ethnicities other than WASP, such as Arabian dancers or harem girls, gypsies, Spanish dancers, Russian courtiers, Chinese coolies, Indians like Pocahontas, and hurdy-gurdy men. At one Chud-leigh party there were two Methodist ministers — satires, given this Presbyterian or Anglican group. There were a few novel costumes that defy the imagination, such as a powder puff, bubbles, and a rainbow. Huntley Christie cross-dressed once as a tennis girl. Winnie tended to the idyllic, playing up her blue eyes and fair hair by dressing as a Dutch girl for one of these parties. She would have appreciated, too, the "braw Hieland laddies" who played the pipes on such occasions. The saddle-maker Beardmores were enthusiastic riders at the Toronto Hunt Club. George W. had been president and master of hounds in the early days. He had made an extravagant gift to the club of an old hotel at Steeles Corners near Thornhill that he'd renovated, enlarged with stables, and named Green Bush Lodge. It was, he said, "near to tales and prints of English hunting life."

William "Bill" Christie, the brother of Catherine Christie, who made her debut the same year as Winnie, appears often on Winnie's dance cards. He, too, had served in the Great War with the Royal Canadian Artillery and the Royal Canadian Infantry. He began as a stockbroker, then took over as president of the biscuit company founded by his grandfather when it merged with National Biscuit Co., Ltd. (Nabisco) in 1928. He, too, was an active member of the Toronto Hunt Club. Another steeplechaser at the Hunt Club was Colonel William Hendrie of Hamilton, a true gentleman of the sport of racing, and his son, later Sir John Strathearn Hendrie, who became lieutenant-governor of Ontario from 1914 to 1919. Both William and William, Jr. in turn were presidents of the Ontario Jockey Club. The Hendries had made their money in the moving business with their company Hendrie Cartage Co., Ltd. (then Hendrie and Co.) Before becoming lieutenant-governor, John was involved in other businesses as well, such as the Hamilton Bridge Works and the Hamilton Tool Works, later combined as the Hamilton Bridge and Tool Company, and the Bank of Commerce. In the Great War he commanded the 2nd brigade of the Canadian Field Artillery and was knighted in 1915. His son Bill danced often with Winnie. She was also good friends with Bill's sister, Mary Hendrie, and visited often at Gateside, the family estate in Hamilton.

There were two other dance partners that appear often on Winnie's dance cards: William "Bill" Duggan and Walter G. Cassels.

Bill's grandfather, George Duggan, was a lawyer, judge, and Tory politician who had opposed the 1837 rebellion. His son, Bill's father, was also a lawyer. Walter Cassels's grandfather, Richard S. Cassels, had been the first member of the Toronto Stock Exchange. His father, W. Gibson Cassels, was founder of the distinguished law firm Cassels, Son & Co., Ltd.

Other beaux who appear less often in Winnie's dance cards came from the same kinds of backgrounds. Typically, the tradesman grandfather had emigrated from England, Scotland, or, occasionally, Ireland. He had started a business or a legal firm or had worked in a bank like D.A. With no competition at that initial stage of Canada's economic history, this generation had established companies such as Hamilton Steel, Christie Biscuits, or Cassels, Son & Co. The money they made was frequently invested in various business ventures, stocks, and banks, with huge returns. They founded clubs and associations that directly imitated those of the aristocracy in Britain. They built mansions with names glamorizing their usually humble British roots. Their sons had often joined their fathers in expanding those companies and firms, sometimes absorbing competing new companies in mergers. This generation, too, invested money. It was the third generation of these original families who were Winnie's beaux. Some were the idle sons of rich fathers, lacking self-discipline or a talent for business. Their mothers had not "come out." Their fathers, however, had often inherited substantial wealth as well as continuing to make large profits working in the businesses and legal firms their fathers had established. Those who were from Scotland usually joined St. Andrew's Presbyterian Church. Others, including some former Presbyterians, associated themselves with St. James's Anglican Church, the church of the elite because it was English, the church of the Royal Family. None of Winnie's dance partners came from Roman Catholic families.

Not surprisingly, given D.A.'s profession, two of Winnie's other beaux were connected to the Canadian Bank of Commerce or other financial institutions. Eric White's father, the Right Honourable Sir William Thomas White, had been finance minister in Sir Robert Borden's government. In 1919 he began to practise law, and in 1920 became a director and vice president of the Bank of Commerce. Wilfred W. "Gamey" Stratton had been quarterback in the University of Toronto Grey Cup team that was beaten by the Toronto Argonauts in 1914. During the war, he was a lieutenant with the 3rd Canadian Division of the Royal Flying Corps. Now that the war was over, he had become an investment broker and member of the Toronto Stock Exchange. Like many of Winnie's beaux, he belonged to several clubs, including the Toronto Hunt Club.

The Toronto Hunt Club was a main nexus for another of Winnie's dance partners, Edward F. Seagram. His grandfather Joseph E. Seagram was a distiller, as was his father, E.F.S. Seagram, who had served as mayor of Waterloo, Ontario in 1906–07. Seagram Stables, established by Edward's grandfather, was internationally renowned for horses that competed all over North America. The Seagrams were also famous for their wealth. An American at the Hialeah racetrack near Miami, Florida was heard to comment of the Seagram contender Solace, "Oh, he's a real good horse. I was told he belongs to a big liquor - man up in Canada, who is worth a hundred million dollars." It was Joseph E. Seagram and Sons, Ltd. that would merge with the Montreal Bronfman distillers during U.S. Prohibition in 1924 to form the largest distillery in the world. This distillery was vastly enriched by running illegal liquor across the border. George E. Leishman's father was president of William H. Leishman and Co., Ltd. George would have met D.A. when he joined the Canadian Bank of Commerce in 1915. Almost immediately, he went overseas to serve as a lieutenant in the RCAF. By 1919, he was back in Toronto, a hero who had narrowly escaped death by a head wound in 1917.

Winnie's beau Eric Clarke was the son of Dr. Charles Kirk Clarke, after whom today's Clarke Institute of Psychiatry is named. Dr. Clarke had founded the Canadian National Committee for Mental Hygiene (now the Canadian Mental Health Association) with another doctor in 1914. Clarke was an early proponent of eugenics, a movement aimed at limiting immigration to whites and preventing the marriage and reproduction of the "mentally defective." (He would later disagree with this extreme philosophy that, among other things, endorsed sterilization of the "defective.") By 1911, having served at the Hamilton asylum, the Kingston asylum, and the asylum in Toronto known by its address, 999 Queen Street, he had become superintendent of the Toronto General Hospital. Eric, his son, would also become a doctor. John Phippen, another of Winnie's suitors, was the son of the Honourable Frank H. Phippen, KC.

The dance partner of Winnie's who was closest to his lower class roots was Murray Fleming. The Fleming fortune had been made in only one generation. Murray's grandfather had been a poor Methodist Irish immigrant who settled in the working class area of Cabbagetown. His son Robert quickly made a fortune as a real estate investor and financier. This charismatic man — known as "The People's Bob" when he was mayor of Toronto from 1892–93 and 1896–97 — had been the manager of the privately owned Toronto Street Railway Company. He established himself among Toronto's elite by joining the country gentry associated with the Toronto Hunt Club. His 1,000-acre farm, called Donlands, on the outskirts of the city ensured social acceptance. Now his son Murray was among those young men courting Toronto's debutantes.

Another somewhat unlikely contender for Winnie was Jan Strachan, whose father was the Reverend Daniel Strachan, minster at St. Andrew's Presbyterian Church from 1893–97, and the first minister of Rosedale Presbyterian Church, from 1909–17. Strachan was hired as assistant to the president on industrial relations at Imperial Oil, where he was accused of trying to "usurp unionization." It seems improbable that Winnie could have fit in to a religious family, or become Mrs. Strachan, given her experience at Bishop Strachan School.

More typical was Arnold Ivey, whose father was one of the original members of the Toronto Hunt Club. He was head of the family business, John D. Ivey Co., a millinery wholesale business. Ivey was also associated with the 48th Highlanders. He was active on the executives of many clubs, as well as in St. Paul's Anglican Church and the Canadian Institute of the Blind.

These were by no means all of Winnie's dance partners. There were many others who danced with her only once or twice, including the fathers of the young men and women who were hosting and chaperoning the parties.

This social elite did not include any of the artists who were already well known in Toronto. The Group of Seven had held shows at the Arts and Letters Club as early as 1916. J.E.H. MacDonald had designed the club's crest, and members of the Group of Seven met there often for lunch. Their controversial and widely publicized show at the Art Gallery of Toronto opened in 1920. Sir Edmund Walker, president of the Canadian Bank of Commerce during D.A.'s time with the bank, was by far the most active patron of the arts in the city. He had helped found Appleby School in Oakville in 1911, the Royal Ontario Museum in 1912, and the Art Museum of Toronto (later the Art Gallery of Toronto and now the AGO) in 1913, and he had helped in amalgamating the University of Toronto over the same time period. He patronized artists in the Group of Seven, and steered commissions in the direction of sculptors Frances Loring and Florence Wyle. In 1915 he was knighted for his contribution to business and the arts. Yet Walker's high-profile enthusiasm for the arts did not influence his friend D.A. at all.

Sculptors Frances Loring and Florence Wyle bought their "Church" studio in Moore Park in 1920. This place was almost at once the centre of an active social life for other sculptors like Emanuel Hahn and Elizabeth Wyn Wood, artists like A.Y. Jackson and Arthur Lismer, professors like Barker Fairley, and doctors like Frederick Banting. Perhaps because Loring and Wyle were American, this group was decidedly bohemian and intellectual compared to the pseudo-British world of the Toronto Hunt Club, or that of the debutantes and their military men.

There is no sign among Winnie's papers, or in my memory of things she told me, indicating that she was aware of the suffragette movement or the many social causes, such as the pasteurization of milk, that some other wealthy Toronto women were canvassing for. Had it been mentioned, she probably would have exclaimed "Hog-wash!" or "Bilge-water!" She never mentioned her father's extensive charity work for India, China, and Armenia. Nor was she aware that women were already practising as doctors in the late nineteenth century, and if she had been, she never would have visited one. Nor does she seem to have been influenced by her free-wheeling aunt, Jean Forsyth, whose Edmonton friend Emily Murphy (coincidentally an alumna of BSS) had become the first woman judge in the British Empire in 1916. It is doubtful Winnie, busy with her dances as a debutante, heard of Agnes Macphail from Kingston, who became the first female Member of Parliament in 1921. Doctors, lawyers, bankers, business owners, MPs, even bus drivers, were men, and that was that.

Winnie's beliefs were closer to those of Queen Victoria, who stated,

I am most anxious to enlist everyone who can speak or write to join in checking this mad, wicked folly of "Women's Rights," with all its attendant horrors, on which her poor feeble sex is bent, forgetting every sense of womanly feelings and propriety. Feminists ought to get a good whipping. Were women to "unsex" themselves by claiming equality with men, they would surely perish without male protection.

I heard Winnie proclaim often, "Women should never discuss money or politics." This is not surprising, considering books of eti-quette at the time instructed women not to talk about money or speak rudely to servants. When money or politics came up — and they increasingly did as the decades passed — she would get up and leave the room.

By the time Winnie made her debut, the Women's Art Association, established in 1886, had been thriving on the Toronto scene for over thirty years. The Heliconian Club (established 1909), which was intended to offer a forum for Toronto women to discuss arts and letters, had been active for ten years. While never belonging to either of these clubs, Winnie was a member of both the League of Honour for Women and Girls of the Empire and the Imperial Order of the Daughters of the Empire. The League was a religious group dedicated to prayer, purity, and temperance. The IODE, founded during the Boer War in 1900, was intended "to stimulate and give expression to the sentiment of patriotism which binds the women and children of the Empire around the throne and person of their gracious and beloved Sovereign." For Winnie, this came down to cutting photos of royalty from the newspapers for her scrapbooks and knitting socks for the soldiers in both World Wars, a skill she would have learned in needlework classes at BSS.

17

~♦~

MARRIAGES

Winnie's dance cards and invitations are most plentiful from 1919 to 1922; after that, her attendance would mostly be limited to the St. Andrew's Ball, the 48th Highlanders' Ball, and a few other social events. The flood of invitations to teas, balls, At Homes, and other events that had welcomed her as a new debutante rapidly subsided, as wave upon wave of new debutantes came out each Season. Even so, Winnie held teas and dinners for the younger sisters of her friends, such as Marjorie Northey, Barbara's sister, when they made their debuts.

It would have been just after the Great War ended that Winnie was taken up in a plane over Toronto by famous daredevil flying ace Billy Bishop, though he was not one of her beaux. He was seven years older than Winnie and by this time had married old Timothy Eaton's granddaughter, Margaret Burdon, when he was on medical leave in 1917. After the war, Bishop and fellow war pilot William Barker had started up a passenger airline company called Bishop-Barker Aeroplanes, Ltd. It was probably in this context that he treated friends like Winnie to the novelty of seeing Toronto from the air. This commercial venture was beset by legal and financial problems, which were compounded by a serious crash on an Orillia-Toronto flight in September 1920. Soon after, another crash occurred in which Bishop's knee broke his passenger's back with a horrifying crunch. This near-fatal event induced Bishop to abandon Bishop-Barker and move to London, where he dabbled in various businesses including Loblaws. There and in France the Bishops became Roaring Twenties celebrities. Winnie's flight would have occurred sometime just before Bishop's two startling accidents. Yet she said she felt "perfectly safe" with him on this exciting excursion. It would be the only time she ever went up in an airplane. As for the commercial airliners that took over international passenger travel by the 1950s, she would have nothing to do with them. She thought they were too dangerous. When she travelled in future it was always by car, by train, or on ships that were named after the Royal Family.

Winnie should have married by the late '20s, or at least become engaged. Jane Austen's *Persuasion* suggests that a woman's chances of marriage were almost nil after age twenty-seven, and assumptions hadn't changed much by Winnie's era. Certainly she was no stranger to weddings, having been decked out like a young Marie Antoinette at fourteen to be a bridesmaid at the Sears-Jackson wedding in Brockville. One by one, the debs and beaux she had supped with, danced with, chatted with, and hosted since she came out in 1919 settled down, taking their places in Toronto's retrograde Anglophile establishment.

Her beau Bill Hendrie, son of Sir John and Lady Hendrie, married a Hamilton girl, Frances Holton, in June 1920. Later that year, Winnie's fellow deb, Lucille "Billee" Buntin, married another of Winnie's suitors, William Phillips. Hugh McCullough's cousin, Jacqueline, daughter of Dr. J.W.S. McCullough, married a young doctor, Charles Fenwick, in 1921. Another of her dance partners, Hugh Aird, son of Sir John and Lady Aird, married May Black in 1922. That same year, Hugh McCullough himself married Winnie's "great friend," as she always called her,

Winnie as
bridesmaid
at the
Sears-Jackson
wedding in
Brockville,
December 27,
1915.

Barbara Northey. At that wedding Winnie was maid of honour, one
of the three bridesmaids who wore — *The Globe and Mail* reported —
"blue crêpe and georgette over silver with wreaths of silver lace and
blue forget-me-nots in their hair" and carried bouquets of pink roses,
sweet peas, and maidenhair ferns, interspersed with forget-me-nots.
By 1924, the marriage stakes for debutantes from 1919 were getting higher.

Three more married that year: Phyllis White, sister of Winnie's beau Eric White, and daughter of William White, KC, married James Beatty. Another of Winnie's suitors, Peter Campbell, was best man at that wedding. Winnie's "great friend" Marjorie Scott married Allen Boothe, and Margaret Phippen, sister of her dance partner John Phippen, married John McKee, another of Winnie's beaux. At the 1924 wedding of James Beatty and Phyllis White, *The Globe and Mail* reported, "Winifred Cameron caught the wedding bouquet," which could only have raised everyone's expectations for Winnie. That same year Helen Hall, daughter of one of the guests at Winnie's coming-out party, married John Joseph Cawthra. The following year, her dancing partner Stratty Hay married Marion Beck, daughter of Sir Adam Beck of hydro-electric power fame. Another of her beaux, Paul Greey, married Margaret Campbell, one of the Gooderhams, in 1926. That same year another of the debs who came out when Winnie did, Helen Gooderham, married John Maitland, a Scottish lawyer; Barbara Northey's younger sister, Marjory, married the son of the late Sir Alexander Mackenzie, William Mackenzie; and Winnie's suitor Robert Hay married Lallie Watson. In 1927 Gwynneth Broughall, who had been a guest at Winnie's coming-out dance, married Donald Bethune.

The most impressive wedding at the time was that of Winnie's childhood friend Mary Hendrie. Mary married a wealthy Scot in a splendid wedding in Hamilton on 29 December 1925. Ronald Stuart Cumming was the son of the wealthy John Fleetwood Cumming who had built the mansion The Dowans in Aberlour, Banffshire. In the long write-up of the wedding in the *Toronto Star*, which Winnie kept in her scrapbook, much was made of the bride's return to "the land of her forebears." Her father, Colonel William Hendrie of the 48th Highlanders, had recently died. Her brother Bill, one of Winnie's main dance partners, gave Mary away. Two of Winnie's other partners, Bill's brother George and Robert Hay, were ushers. Elizabeth "Libby" Boyd, sister of Winnie's friend Nancy and her beau Jack, was the maid of honour.

According to one newspaper account in Winnie's scrapbook, Mary, "the most beautiful bride in many decades," was wearing a medieval ivory moiré dress that was the exact duplicate of the dress worn by the Duchess of York (later Queen Elizabeth, and, later still, the Queen Mother) at her wedding two and a half years earlier. Even the flower girl, little Mary Bankier, was dressed in a miniature version of the same dress. The groom, and all the men in the wedding party, wore the kilt. The bride and groom were piped from Central Presbyterian Church to Gateside House for a reception of 200 guests. The couple spent their honeymoon in Florida, Cuba, and Jamaica. They would live in London, England for a few years, before settling in Kinloss, Scotland.

Winnie could have had a wedding very like this, though unlike Mary she did not have cousins in England, Scotland, or the United States. Such lavish weddings were the expected culmination of all the social events that she and her contemporaries took part in at such great expense when they came out. Certainly by 1928 she ought to have married one of the wealthy beaux who had courted her for five years. Instead, she was one of ten unmarried models in a Creeds' fashion show sponsored by the Junior League of Toronto that year.

18

THE

QUESTION

Later, my sister and I pestered Winnie about why she never married. With the sixth sense of children, we knew something didn't add up and that this was a touchy subject. She always answered the same thing: that all the young men of her generation were killed off during the war. Since Winnie would have been thirty-eight, far past the usual marrying age, when the Second World War broke out, and was middle-aged when it ended, she could not have meant that war.

I now see that she couldn't have meant the First World War either. Several of her dance partners had survived it. Her favourites — Jack Boyd, Paul Greey, Peter Campbell, and Bill Christie — had all returned from active duty overseas. So had George Drew, "Gamey" Stratton, George Leishman, and Eric Haldenby. In fact, the C.M. Haldenbys had held a surprise party to celebrate their three recently returned sons in May 1919, at which Winnie was one of sixty guests. It was true that Lieutenant Colonel George Denison, Jr., the eldest son of Police Magistrate Denison, had died at the front in 1917. Even with the war dead, though, the 1921 census showed thirty more men per 1,000 than women in Canada. Winnie's later claims about the loss of young men of her generation probably reflected remarks her father made at home. Of the 1,863 Canadian Bank of Commerce employees who served in the war, 360 died and 367 were wounded or missing.

The hundreds of invitations Winnie received, the dazzling number of social events she attended, and the dozens of more-than-suitable young men who danced or supped with her make it clear that she had ample opportunity to marry. Yet even catching Phyllis White's wedding bouquet in 1924 hadn't done the trick.

When asked, my father would keep a determined silence on the subject. My mother's answer to this question was that Winnie was "too difficult" for any man to put up with. Mother was certain that Cyril Backhouse, a frequent dance partner, had proposed to her. He was heading off to Brazil to work for Brazilian Traction, Light and Power Co., Ltd. This company, whose president was Sir William Mackenzie, had been incorporated in Toronto in 1912. It was only one of Canada's imperialist moves to profit from setting up hydroelectric power in developing countries. Similar to how the "gentleman hunters" rationalized their plunder of Canadian big

Two of Winnie's beaux at Parklands.

game, Toronto capitalists legitimized their investments (including loans from the Canadian Bank of Commerce) in electric railways and utilities in Brazil — and in other countries in which there were often no regulations or tariffs — by emphasizing their satisfaction in bringing jobs and better living conditions to the countries they were helping to develop. Since Rio de Janeiro was a far-off place Winnie had probably never heard of, and therefore disliked, she declined the proposal.

Winnie and one of her beaux, Hans Selwye, Parklands.

The Camerons did all they could to foster a marriage for Winnie, hosting dances, teas, and At Homes at 162 Isabella. They had provided her with all the finery money could buy — I inherited a watch they gave her for her twentieth birthday, a small rectangular art nouveau platinum piece encrusted with dozens of tiny diamonds and inscribed *Winifred Cameron, 1921.* Even during the summers the Camerons had hosted parties of her friends at Parklands and occasionally at Cameron Island. They had seen her off to the house parties of a dozen or so friends, such as the McCulloughs in Galt. Photos show these young people in tennis garb (white flannels and shirts with black bow ties for the men and long white dresses or skirts for the women, as well as the headbands fashionable at the time), playing on the courts of

Winnie (front) and friends in some association at a picnic on Cameron Island, c. 1917.

Winnie and Donald, Parklands, 1925.

Parklands or the McCulloughs' estate. Others show the men with their slicked-back hair, parted at the side, lounging on Parklands's dock in unflattering black wool swimsuits with white belts. They relaxed on picnics, played croquet, and climbed on the old Great War cannon D.A. had installed on the Parklands property. In the evenings they played music on the crank-handled Victrola, singing and dancing along with it. Or they played auction bridge, a simple forerunner of today's elaborate bidding system. This Great Gatsby existence (with limited liquor for the women) must have been costly. Yet even these expenses did not achieve the desired result.

Winnie's failure to marry at an appropriate time could not have been caused by her appearance. She was among the more beautiful — if not the most beautiful — of the young women offered up for marriage. It was true that she did not have the lean figure fashionable at the time. Whether she suppressed her ample breasts under cloth bands, as some did, I don't know. Yet photos show that she had inherited Dollie's striking beauty. Her dark brows above merry blue eyes were set off by ash blond hair. She had none of Dollie's habitual melancholy, though: always smiling, Winnie loved being with friends, just like her father. She was a good-humoured, strong-willed young woman, secure in her place in the universe. Her small hands and feet and well-turned ankles were strong points in someone who loved dancing as she did.

Why, then, did she not marry in the mid-'20s like so many of her friends and suitors? It was *not* because all the young men in her generation were killed off during the war, no matter which war she meant. There are many possibilities that come to my mind now. Did Dollie cling to her for companionship and stability? My mother said that Winnie shared her fearful mother's bed when D.A. was off hunting or fishing, as he continued to do. On one of these trips in 1913, he had gone with bank president Edmund Walker to fish for salmon in Trinity

D.A.'s personal piper, Alasdair MacPherson, leading Sir Edmund Walker, President of the Canadian Bank of Commerce (left), and D.A., Manager (right), on a salmon fishing trip to Trinity Bay, Newfoundland, 1921. Within four years, Walker and D.A. would both be dead.

Bay, Newfoundland. D.A. wore his kilt on this occasion and took along piper MacPherson to pipe them up and down the shore for their daily walks. I gave my grown son Hugo, by then a piper himself in the 48th Highlanders, a photo of one of these occasions, along with the green-grey tweed vest and jacket with leather buttons his great-grandfather was wearing in the photo, which had somehow fallen my way. Dollie's nervous disorder — whatever it was — seems to have become worse as time passed. It may have been difficult for Winnie, knowing that Dollie's mother had abandoned her at age fifteen, to "abandon" her as well.

Perhaps my mother was right. Perhaps Winnie was "too difficult" to marry anybody. She was accustomed to giving orders, not to taking them. Her beaux may have sensed that she was someone who would not comply with the expectations of a married woman. One of those expectations would have been bearing children. After witnessing, at age ten, Dollie's terrors and pain at Donald's birth, Winnie might herself have dreaded the thought of childbirth enough to forego marriage altogether.

Perhaps her emotional life centred on women more than men. This seems unlikely. Though she was enthralled with clothes, pretty eighteenth-century paintings, and the company of her "great friends," she spoke and wrote of her attractions to various men. Inhabiting a woman-centred world was expected of all the heavily chaperoned debutantes. There could be other reasons that Winnie did not marry when she might have, but, as my father used to say, "You can speculate all night until dawn and be no further ahead."

It was not that Winnie lacked proposals. Cyril Backhouse was probably one. Among her odds and ends of papers is an undated letter from John Pritchard, who mentions that this is his second marriage proposal to her. By today's standards of casual tweets and texts, the carefully handwritten letter to "Miss Cameron" is endearingly formal:

Your departure made me realize how much I am in love with you. I have to risk your displeasure by writing to you once more. From the start of our acquaintance, I have wanted to ask if you would consider marrying me. But perhaps because you never gave me any encouragement, I lacked the courage to ask what I felt might be a very unwelcome question. My admiration & respect for you date back many years. You will always have that. Will you marry me? I would be devoted to you & take all the care, & in good faith. In all sincerity I say that you would not regret it.

Always sincerely yours,

John Pritchard.

John Elton Pritchard was the son of John Pritchard, an Oshawa MP for Wellington North. He was a student at the University of Toronto when Winnie made her debut. The same age as Winnie, he earned his Bachelor of Arts in 1924, and graduated from Osgoode Hall Law School three years later. After success in his private law practice in Toronto, he became an Ontario County Court judge. After Winnie refused him he married Grace Helen Kyle, with whom he had two children.

There were no doubt other proposals for Winnie's hand. A few letters in her scrapbook give tantalizing evidence of her familiarity with some of her other beaux. One letter from Hugh Kindersley, dated July 1920 and written on Pacific Ocean stationery — possibly when he was returning to England after finishing his education at U of T — seems like a note of simple friendship: "With affectionate regards to my tennis partner at 'Benvenuto' in memory of two very pleasant evenings." Benvenuto was Sir Alexander Mackenzie's baronial home on Avenue Road, south of St. Clair Avenue West. Mackenzie, knighted in 1919 for bringing Brazil into the Great War, was president of Brazilian Traction at the time. The Benvenuto Toronto, on the site today, is an upscale condo complex with an expensive restaurant, Scaramouche, downstairs. Another letter is an apology from George Hendrie, dated January 1922, for forgetting to give his brother Bill his mail. Among Bill's letters was an invitation to dinner from Winnie, which Bill received too late to attend. More promising is a note from George Beardmore suggesting some degree of courtship. On "Chudleigh, Toronto" stationery in January 1924, he wrote, "My dear Miss Cameron, I am pleased to have that sweet and beautiful photograph of you. I shall always treasure it. With many thanks & best wishes for you & yours. My sincerest."

Much later, I would come to wonder about two of Winnie's rings, both of which I inherited. One was a spectacular diamond ring in the shape of a flower, half a dozen large diamonds circling a large central diamond. It was stolen and never recovered in a burglary at my home in Deer Park, Toronto in the late 1980s. The other was a small simple gold band. It fit only my little finger, but on Winnie's tiny hands it would have fit her ring finger. When and how she came by these two rings I don't know. Yet I wondered if they might symbolize Winnie's marriage to herself.

Even in the early '20s there were slight gusts that presaged the winds of change for spinsters or old maids. A 26 December 1923 article in the *Toronto Daily Star* was titled "Unmarried Girl May Now Hold her Head High." The author, Julia Nott, argued that parents must allow their daughters to choose a career, just like their sons. If a woman is not prepared by her family for a career, "she starts out handicapped when entering into competition with boys (all of whom have been brought up with the idea of a job in mind) or with girls endowed with more intelligent and far-seeing parents." Otherwise, she might be "a drag on the family" or "an object of pity." Coming from a family that had allowed her to evade education at BSS, and that emphasized instead the utmost importance of making a good match, Winnie was in a vulnerable position when marriage passed her by.

19

YOUNG
DONALD

Donald Cameron quietly passed through childhood in a female household. His sister Winnie's debut into society was the focus of the Camerons' family life from the time he was nine years old. Talk of dresses, hats, shoes, and hair dominated every meal. Invitations rained through the door. Preparations for parties at 162 Isabella Street engaged everyone, except Donald. Happy to be overlooked, he retreated to the garage where he had been allowed to raise his pigeons. It was one of the few things from childhood that he recalled with pleasure. He would grow up hating Toronto.

During the flurry of fashion and socializing that his sister's debut triggered, he silently rebelled. Debuts were silly, he concluded. What was the point of marrying into Toronto society with its false manners and skewed values? When he was about six, he had been dressed up in Highland gear and made to dance for Mary Pickford, the Toronto-born Hollywood star who often visited her hometown. He was — and would remain — an exceptionally graceful dancer, but being on display did not appeal to him. He was a shy boy, who liked reading history and disliked parties. Much later, Winnie's friend Mildred Holden told me of a birthday party at which young Donald hid behind a door throughout the festivities. He was happiest alone, stroking his pigeons, admiring their motley colours, seeing them lay their eggs and raise their fledglings. Certainly he rejected the role of Lord of the Manor that his father played. In later life he liked to irritate my mother by stating, "I'm just a plain dirt farmer." This always drew disapproval. "Oh, *Donald*!" she'd exclaim in exasperation.

When Donald was an adolescent, D.A. decided it was time to make a man of him. D.A. had been disappointed to see him recoil when one day, with rifle in tow, they'd sat under a pine tree filled with crows at Parklands. When D.A. shot straight up the crows fell — thud, thud, thud — around them. His son was horrified. It was time to send him to a boys' school.

D.A. no doubt chose Appleby School for his son because the president of his bank, Sir Edmund Walker, had founded the place in 1911 with former UCC prep school headmaster John Guest. It was my mother who told the story of my father's first trip to Appleby by horse and carriage in the fall of 1923. The school on Lake Ontario, west of Oakville, was about thirty miles away. On the journey, twelve-year-old Donald, in a turmoil of anxiety about leaving home, threw up. D.A. whipped him by the side of the road.

The Appleby School Donald entered that fall had about sixty-five students, almost all boarders. He was one of the seventeen new students that year paying $750 for the "sound" education that prepared them for the Ontario matriculation examinations, the passport for entrance into Canadian universities. He would study the basics: English, French, mathematics, and science. In addition he would take classics (literature), Latin grammar, history, moderns (British literature), music, and physical training (Swedish drills). All students joined the Cadet Corps. These subjects were taught in eight classes a day from 9:15 to 3:00, with an hour for lunch at the dining hall.

It took the sensitive adolescent in Form III (Grade 5) some time to adjust to his new surroundings, but he eventually took wholeheartedly to a male-centred world as different as he could imagine from life at 162 Isabella Street. There Winnie ruled, and Dollie and Kate obeyed. It was the first time he had been surrounded by men and boys. Gone were the governesses, the long ringlets he'd had until age five, the lacy white dresses he'd worn as a toddler, his fragile mother, and — most of all — his autocratic sister. Life at Appleby was refreshing. No more chitchat about beaux, clothes, and parties. Now it was the rough play and crude jokes of his peers. Now there were meals at a dining hall with friends instead of tense, formal meals with family in the dining room. It was all wonderful except for bath night. He had come to hate the baths his governesses gave him. Now, as he told me, he could rebel by running the bath behind a locked door when it was his turn without getting into the tub.

20

AN UNTIMELY DEATH

With the suddenness of a clap of thunder, Winnie and Donald's father fell down on Yonge Street, dead of a heart attack. On New Year's Eve 1924 he had been at the bank during the day as usual. On New Year's Day he had been making his calls, according to the Scottish custom of "first footers," which included a visit to Lieutenant-Governor Henry Cockshutt at Government House. According to this old-country custom, the first person to cross your threshold on New Year's Day determined your fortune for the coming year. If the "first footer" had black or fair hair, you would have good luck. If his hair were red, your fortunes would fall. D.A. was in good spirits, hoping his greying dark hair would bring good fortune here and there. He was looking forward to representing Ontario at a conference in Quebec at the end of the month, to which he had been invited by the Honourable Narcisse Pélardeau, lieutenant-governor of that province. He had another reason to be in good spirits. The previous October he had been promoted to the position of assistant manager at the bank, a position he was to assume the next day.

Yet the next day, 2 January 1925, as he was walking to the bank for his first day as assistant manager, he collapsed, dead. He was with his old friend Walter Gow of Blake, Anglin and Cassels, Toronto's leading corporate lawyers, chatting as they walked. The two men hadn't proceeded far after turning onto Yonge Street from Isabella when he dropped. Gow ran to a nearby store for help, but it was fruitless. D.A. never regained consciousness.

D.A. Cameron, photo taken for his promotion to Assistant Manager of the bank, October 1924. His promotion would not take effect until the New Year.

D.A.'s death was a shock to Toronto's business community. A man who was being praised for his promotion that very day was ironically mourned in obituary after obituary. "He was one of the finest specimens of a rugged Canadian Scot I have ever met," said R.A. Stapells, president of the Board of Trade to the *Toronto Star*, "and a man that nothing could stop after once starting for some objective. He applied excellent judgment and filled every position in the [Canadian Bank of Commerce] with impressive responsibility. He was a staunch Britisher, a man of infinite resources and always a true gentleman." A colleague from the bank wrote that D.A. "showed the same respect and courtesy to a switchboard operator as he did to any of the officials." *The Globe and Mail* noted, as did many, that he was "the first banker to be elected to the Toronto Board of Trade" (he was made president in 1922). His many posts as president or treasurer of organizations were duly noted. So were the various charities he served. The loss of Major Cameron, Adjutant since 1914 to the 48th Highlanders, was sincerely mourned. His steady progress from lieutenant (1913) to captain (1919) to major (1921) is traced. The *Toronto Star* obituary went so far as to say, "even the Empire will be affected by his death."

Caduceus, the Canadian Bank of Commerce staff magazine, printed a long tribute with a photo of D.A. on the front page of that January's issue. After expressing "great shock" at "the terribly sudden death" of D.A., the article summarizes his service to the bank, his work as a "pioneer" in Greenwood, Seattle, and Dawson, and notes his rapid promotion from rank to rank.

Caduceus notes his leisure activities of tennis, rowing, fishing, and shooting in the Parry Sound district, where he owned Cameron Island from 1898 on. His exploits with Captain F.C. Selous are highlighted. Indeed, he is called "The Selous of the Yukon" after outdoing Selous himself with trophy heads that now "adorn the Head Office" in Toronto.

His wide fame as an active Toronto citizen and his Scottishness are praised in *Caduceus*. His service as vice president, then president of the St. Andrew's Society from 1915 and 1920, and his life membership in the Caledonian Society — both Scottish organizations — is offered as proof. Lists appeared of the many clubs of which he had been a member.

With hindsight, he had been one of those many Scots who had stepped into the timely gap between traditional politics and the dynamism of the market in North America. A traditional Conservative — a breed on the wane even then — he was an important business, financial, and social force in Toronto. Had he lived, he would probably have filled even more important positions and contributed greater service. He probably would have become president of the Canadian Bank of Commerce. Undoubtedly, he would also have become an even wealthier man than he already was.

D.A.'s death followed closely on the deaths of several of Canada's wealthiest men, as an era began to wind down. Archie Mackenzie, father of Sir William, died during Winnie's debut year; famed lawyer

Zebulon A. Lash of Blakes died in 1920; in 1921, Sam Hughes died; Senator Fred Nicholls, who had built Parklands, and Lord Mount Stephen, one of the last Canadian Pacific Railway tycoons, died that same year. In 1923, Sir Alexander Mackenzie died. D.A. had been one of his pallbearers. All these men represented a way of life that was already being replaced by one more democratic, more American.

Had D.A. lived longer, he might have insisted that Winnie marry, steering her towards a rich young man he liked. Young Donald would have continued at Appleby School, and after his graduation D.A. would have advised him as to which university program he should take. D.A. would also have seen to it that Donald became one of the beaux at the parties that followed the debuts of the young women his age. After his university graduation, D.A. would have used his contacts to situate his son in a lucrative position in Toronto's business or banking community. In all likelihood, my father would not have been my father at all. He might have married a Toronto debutante around the mid-1930s and settled into a job arranged by his father. D.A. would also have continued to "make a man" of his son,

Winnie, Donald (right), Hans Selwye (left), and a friend at Parklands, c. 1924, the year before D.A. died.

taking him along on his hunting and fishing excursions. As for Dollie, she would have continued under the illusion that her husband was protecting her from her many fears.

When Donald Alexander Cameron died he was only sixty-one. His daughter Winifred was twenty-three; his son Donald was thirteen.

21

A MILITARY FUNERAL,
1925

Major D.A. Cameron's funeral was a grand affair befitting his grand obituaries. The gun carriage drawn by four horses and a military escort of 48th Highlanders arrived at 162 Isabella Street at three p.m. on Sunday, 11 January. Pipe Major Fraser played the funeral procession of the coffin from the house to the gun carriage. The coffin was placed on the gun carriage and draped with the Union Jack, on top of which Cameron's 48th Highlanders feather bonnet was placed, according to custom. The Regimental Pipe Band played the "Pibroch of Donald Dhu" (a traditional dirge based on Sir Walter Scott's poem). The escort commanded by Lieutenant Colonel I.N.R. Sinclair consisted of three officers and 100 NCOs and men. This escort was followed by a procession of pipe, brass, and bugle bands, the gun carriage and pallbearers, and finally Cameron's horse, the personal mourners, and the soldiers of the regiment.

This impressive cortege, pictured in the Toronto papers, proceeded on foot about two and a half miles through the snow along Isabella

Street to Jarvis Street, south on Jarvis to King Street, and west on King to St. Andrew's Presbyterian Church. (Both St. Andrew's and Rosedale Presbyterian Churches had voted against union with the Methodists six months earlier.) At the church, the pipe band played "The Flowers of the Forest." The song narrates the death of a Highland man who leaves a woman behind and is mourned by all of nature, when flowers fail to appear in the spring. My son Hugo, a piper in the 48th Highlanders himself, played the same tune at my father's funeral decades later in 1996. The choice had been his grandfather's request, probably to echo his own father's funeral. Major Crawford Brown, Regimental Chaplain, and the Reverend J.B. Paulin conducted the service for D.A., which was followed by "The Last Post" and "The Piper's Lament." The coffin was then transported to Port Elgin, the town where D.A. was born. There it would be placed in one of the drawers in the Cameron mausoleum.

Surely this funeral procession and the services at St. Andrew's and Port Elgin made a great impression on Winnie and young Donald, but I don't recall either of them talking about it. Why weren't we raised to know and value this family history?

22

A WATERSHED

The death of Donald Alexander Cameron was a watershed for the family. Gone were the expectations of increasing wealth and the Camerons' extravagant British lifestyle. The fine Toronto house and the Parklands acres with the Big House, gatehouse, tennis courts, stables, lighthouse, and docks, where D.A. had created his Scottish baronial retreat — these might have to lapse. Young Donald was only thirteen, far too young to have any say in the decisions that would have to be made. He would return to a life he now enjoyed at Appleby to complete his second year. Certainly Dollie was uninterested or unable to carry on the Camerons' lifestyle on her own, though she signed the appropriate documents in her small, back-slanting hand. Perhaps D.A.'s death was another abandonment she could not cope with. With her husband gone permanently, she grieved not only for him but also for herself. She seldom left the house afterwards.

Before long, Winnie, Dollie, Kate, and the chauffeur left 162 Isabella Street and rented 128 Huntley Street, a three-storey brick house with a

128 Huntley Street, Rosedale, where Dollie and Winnie moved with Kate and the chauffeur after D.A. died. The street became part of Mount Pleasant Road in 1952.

green-fenced garden and garage opposite the Rosedale Presbyterian Church.

D.A.'s most recent will was dated 1910 and had been prepared by the law firm of Blake, Lash, Anglin and Cassels — two of whose partners were fathers of Winnie's beaux. As the will predated young Donald's birth by a year, it was speculative regarding children other than Winnie. The executrix was Dollie (along with the National Trust Co., Ltd.) who was to receive the income (interest) from the trust fund set up with the National Trust. She was to use and apply this income for her own maintenance and for the education and maintenance of Winnie — and any other children — until she or they reached the age of thirty. Dollie was also free to use all furniture and property until her death. Should she decide to sell anything, the proceeds were to go into the trust fund. Under these provisions, Dollie was to receive and administer income from the trust fund until her child(ren) turned thirty. D.A. had made a special provision for Winnie: when she reached that age she was to receive $10,000 of her own. By the time she received this money in 1933, it would have been worth about $170,000 in 2013 dollars; at the time the will was made in 1910, it would have been worth $250,000. Simply put, as far as D.A. knew in 1910, he was leaving his daughter today's equivalent of a quarter of a million dollars.

Dollie and Winnie decided that Parklands would have to go. The property was D.A.'s dream world, not theirs. It was possibly a final visit to Parklands that prompted the 8 July 1926 announcement in the social pages of *The Globe and Mail* that "Mrs. Donald Cameron and Miss Winifred Cameron have left for their summer place at Lake Simcoe." It was Dollie, as D.A.'s executrix, who signed the documents that transferred the property to the National Trust, who managed the property until it was sold that September to Maude Louise Holden, wife of John Bell Holden. The Holdens already owned half of Parklands, having purchased it from Nicholls, Northey, and O'Brian in 1921. They now owned the whole estate, much as it had been when Senator Nicholls built it. Later, my mother used to say that it was stupid of Dollie and Winnie to sell the entire property. "They could have reserved a small waterfront portion for the family's use," she maintained by way of complaining in the heat and humidity of Barrie's summers.

Possibly it was her husband's death that nudged Dollie — already phobic and nerve-wracked — towards dementia. I remember her after about 1947, when I was four, only as an impossibly ancient woman at Huntley Street swathed in sweaters who sat all day in the upstairs living room with its fireplace and collection of sinister, grinning Toby jugs, rubbing her eyebrows until they disappeared. The chauffeur still drove the Auburn, and Kate still kept house, cooked, and did laundry in the Gothic row of steaming vats in the basement. Winnie had no household responsibilities apart from helping Dollie pay the bills, and enough money to make forays to dressmakers, or Creeds and Simpson's, to buy clothes.

At the very point when Winnie might finally have married, she became the mainstay of the household. She helped Dollie with the lawyers who probated the will, the bank officers who allocated her pension, the question of what must be done about Parklands. Probably on advice from some of the wealthy families of her friends or banking colleagues of her father's or — most likely — officials at the National Trust, she made these decisions. This, I think, was the final obstacle to her marriage. Surely D.A. would have pressured her to marry in 1925 or soon after. As a last resort, he might well have forced her to choose a husband. Certainly he would have continued to supervise and limit the household expenses. The upheaval after his untimely death interrupted the smooth unfolding of social events Winnie was accustomed to. Knowing — probably for the first time — that in a scant six years she would receive $10,000, any economic necessity to marry evaporated. With her mother in shock, she had another reason to stay home. She was needed as a companion and support for Dollie much more than ever.

If "before" had been a Great Gatsby fantasy tempered by Anglophilia, "after" was a heavy fall into unpleasant realities that Winnie could not avoid. As compensation, she would now hold the purse strings. Though her mother would sign the important papers, Dollie would do very much what Winnie told her to do. Without a father or a husband, and with what would have looked like endless money, Winnie entered a period in which she had no one to account to but herself.

In her imagination, Winnie replaced her father with the whole 48th Highlanders Regiment to which he had belonged. After his death, she began referring to herself, only partly in jest, as "The Daughter of the Regiment." It is doubtful she had any idea of the 1840 comic

Winnie and Donald in the Auburn at Parklands, the summer before D.A. died.

opera by that name by Gaetano Donizetti. She never went to the opera, considering it "caterwauling." If she had known the work, she might have married a member of the 48th just as Marie, the heroine of *The Daughter of the Regiment*, marries a soldier from the regiment that adopted her as an orphan.

23

RETURN TO
APPLEBY SCHOOL

It seems that Appleby provided a steadying environment for Donald after his father's death. Because it happened while he was on Christmas vacation, D.A.'s death did not disrupt his education. Donald returned to Appleby for the second term of his second year, Form IVb (Grade 7), without a hitch. Oddly, there was something in the circumstances that induced Donald to excel. Perhaps he had simply "taken to" Appleby by this time. Perhaps he was determined not to follow the path his older sister had followed: her disdain for education; her social frivolity; her dislike of any physical activity apart from dancing and her daily walk; even, perhaps, her unquestioning regard for all things British and a fixed social hierarchy. Perhaps he felt freed from his father's "sporting gentleman" view of masculinity and his pressure to make a hunting and shooting man of his son. Now he could define masculinity for himself.

He even blossomed physically. Fourteen-year-old Donald joined the Second Rugby team that spring. In the team photo he is tall, but no taller than the two other boys standing in the back row. He looks relaxed, smiling despite a rugby accident during the season in which he lost his two front teeth. He also threw himself into his academic work. The following year, he was now to choose between Greek and science for an additional course. He chose Greek. It was a pleasure he occasionally referred to later. "I studied Greek," he used to say, without giving any idea of where or when. "It was fun." That year, in Form IVb (Grade 7), he was captain and goalie on the Third Hockey team. His best friend was Tony Griffin, a grandson of Sir William Mackenzie.

Tony Griffin, whom I met and interviewed in 2011 just after he turned 100, remembered Donald vividly. "He was four square," he recalled. "He was always true to his duty as prefect. Once, when I had played a prank — rewiring a doorbell so it would not stop ringing — he had to punish me. He didn't let me off. He told me, 'I hate to do this, Tony, but it is my responsibility, and I must give you the usual ten lashes.' He was respected and liked by most of the boys at Appleby. That didn't mean we never got up to anything. He had a witty sense of humour."

It was the following year that Donald grew — and grew. A photo of the prefects (boys chosen to have limited authority over their peers in each form) in the fall of 1927 shows him a head taller than the other five boys. By the spring of 1928, in a photo of the First Cricket team, he has grown even more, to his full height of six-foot-four-and-a-half. During those last two years at Appleby School Donald came into his own. The final two forms, V and VI (Grades 9–10 and 11–13), prepared students for Ontario provincial matriculation exams in two English, two science, and three mathematics courses. The boys continued to study scripture and trained with Cadets. His unusual height helped him excel in sports, and he continued as a respected prefect. Donald passed matriculation in the spring of 1928, winning prizes in mathematics and Greek. The following year took him even higher. He passed Honours Matriculation, earning honours in ten papers.

Donald (top, 3rd from left) on First Cricket Team, Appleby School, 1928–29.

At Appleby School's graduation day, 23 May 1929, Donald took more awards than any other student. In one Toronto newspaper photo, he is shown holding four different trophies. He was Head Prefect (Head Boy). He was senior athletic champion, and had won the high jump (5'2"), the half-mile race (2 min. 18 secs.), and had tied for the 120–yard hurdle race (19 min. 4.5 secs). He secured the highest athletic honour of the school: the Victor Ludorum (Winner at Sports) Trophy. He also graduated as Head Cadet. His academic awards included the Mr. Colley's Prize for Greek and the Mr. W.R. Campbell's Prize for French.

The prizes that spring were presented by Governor General Lord Willingdon and Lady Willingdon. Lord Willingdon was dressed in a double-breasted dark coat and bowler hat. Lady Willingdon wore a pastel coat and a matching cloche hat with a wide brim that almost hid her face. They sat in the front row of wicker chairs set up on the lawn for the audience. In what *The Globe and Mail* called that "brightly-clad throng" sat Dollie and Winnie, who also attended the reception for the viceregal party after an athletic demonstration outside. In the Toronto newspaper photos Donald is a lean, well-groomed young man, his thick dark hair coming to a widow's peak like his sister's. He looks more serious than the other winners.

He would not have been serious because of the speech given by Lord Willingdon. In this speech, after eliciting cheers by announcing a school holiday, His Excellency told the boys that they were the stepping stones of the British Empire, and must become upright Christian gentlemen. He pointed out the value of sport in building character and spirit for the game of life. "Cultivate the spirit of public life," he proclaimed. He said that those who were to guide the Empire in future had a heavy responsibility, particularly in Canada, which was the Empire's greatest asset. "This country want[s] people with steady heads and stout hearts to maintain the traditions," he advised. It was pure Kipling.

Prize Giving Day, 23 May 1929, with the Governor General, His Excellency Lord Willingdon and his wife, Lady Willingdon (right), and the Head of Appleby School, John S.B. Guest. Donald holds his trophies for Head Prefect and Victor Ludorum (Outstanding Athlete).

What Donald thought of this speech we can't know. He never spoke of his stellar performance at Appleby. Judging from the way he led his life, I might guess that, unlike Winnie, he was somewhat skeptical of the "traditions" of the Empire. Yet not entirely. He would give public service in later life, notably in his many years on the Barrie Police Commission. He joined the 48th Highlanders after his graduation, suggesting that his allegiance to Scotland and the military were the main "British traditions" he embraced. These were the aspects of manliness he accepted from his father. He enjoyed sports, but did not continue playing them. He would remain an independent thinker, choosing his values rather than following advice like Lord Willingdon's. He would have thought the grand reception somewhat pretentious. Winnie, of course, adored the gathering around the Willingdons. She no doubt claimed their acquaintance, since she had presented Lady Willingdon with a bouquet of roses at the ninetieth-anniversary St. Andrew's Ball in Toronto in 1926, a mere three years earlier.

24

THE UNIVERSITY
OF TORONTO

The Great Depression struck with the Wall Street crash of October 1929, a month after my father enrolled at the University of Toronto. Toronto was hit hard. By 1931, seventeen percent of Torontonians were jobless. By 1933, the worst year of the Depression and the year Donald graduated, that figure had almost doubled to thirty percent. Two years later, in 1935, twenty-five percent of the city's population was still on relief. Construction almost ceased, and manufacturing was cut back, declining to an all-time low in 1933–34. That year relief funds hit $10 million, and the number of strikes was greater than in any other year.

Yet in some areas, the Depression had little effect. The working class was devastated, and construction and manufacturing was decimated. Yet because saving — even among the middle class — had replaced investment in industry, Toronto's financial institutions, and the men who ran them, were financially stable. In addition, affluent businessmen refused to pay higher taxes and continued to buy new homes in subdivisions recently annexed to the city, such as York, Forest Hill, Leaside, and Etobicoke. The combining of Toronto stock exchanges in 1934 and the tight auditing of the Ontario Securities Board helped prevent bankruptcies. Ironically, in Toronto the Good it was thanks to liquor and beer sales that Toronto's stock markets took precedence over Montreal's. As the postwar modernization of the 1920s grew, white-collar jobs grew too. Although civil servants, teachers, and professors were paid less, their dollars were worth more because prices had dropped. Radios, cars, refrigerators, and other appliances were manufactured and sold on a grand scale.

The Cameron family was among those who were not affected by the Depression. After D.A.'s death, his money — and the proceeds of $34,000 from the sale of Parklands to Maude Holden — had been invested in the National Trust, one of the saving companies that had replaced stock investments for the wealthy. In addition, Dollie received a pension from the Canadian Bank of Commerce, one of the benefits fought for by D.A. in 1910. (Perhaps it was this discussion of pensions that prompted him to make his will the same year.) Winnie had not been the least bit interested in having an education, but Donald was. Financial provision for any education he chose had been made in his father's will. In fact, the Camerons might have been somewhat worse off had D.A. lived. Although he would have continued to earn a high salary, he would probably have continued to invest. With the collapse of the stock market in 1929, he might have lost money.

Donald enrolled in the degree program for Commerce and Finance at the University of Toronto in the fall of 1929, only a month before the crash. He had returned to live at home with Dollie, Winnie, Winnie's Persian cat Timothy, and Kate, but "home" now meant 128 Huntley Street, not 162 Isabella with its unpleasant memories. His classes at Bloor Street and Avenue Road were walking distance from Huntley. He could also call on the chauffeur, who lived nearby.

D.A. would have approved of Donald's course of study. Although Donald differed in many ways from his father, he was of one mind with him about a business career. Much later, after a lifetime of reading history for pleasure, he wondered whether he ought to have chosen that subject. In his first year, he studied history along with economics, accounting, actuarial science, and French. Given that he had won prizes at Appleby for mathematics and French, it is not surprising that he got firsts in both subjects. In his other subjects he took seconds, except for history, in which he made only a third. Overall, his standing was a second.

In second year, 1930–31, he continued on with economics, accounting, actuarial science, and French. He had firsts in accounting and actuarial science. In French and economics he took seconds. He almost never spoke of his university experience, but I think he lost interest in economics because Harold Innis, famed already as a political and economic historian, was — as my father said — a dreadfully boring lecturer. "Every other thing he said was 'ah' or 'um,'" my father used to say, shaking his head because he admired Innis's books. "It was all we could do to stay awake." Considering that Innis was only in his mid-thirties when my father studied with him, this is surprising. He ought to have been an inspiring professor, since he had already published *A History of the Canadian Pacific Railway* (1923) and *The Fur Trade in Canada* (1930) — a groundbreaking classic that I taught in Canadian Studies courses during the '90s.

The courses in Commerce and Finance changed during my father's last two years in the program. No doubt these changes were the result of the Depression, by then in its second year. Now my father studied labour problems, money, credit and problems, statistics, and public finance, in addition to accounting. In all these courses he obtained seconds, except for public finance in which he earned a third. In his final year it was economic theory, economic history, economic geography (all of which suggested that Harold Innis had had a hand in altering the curriculum), business conditions, and accounting. His marks dropped here. Only in accounting did he achieve a second. He took thirds in the rest of his courses, except for economic theory in which he did not even achieve that. He graduated from Business and Commerce in June 1933 with a Bachelor of Commerce.

25

THE HEIRESS

When Donald was midway through his first year at the University of Toronto, enduring Harold Innis's lectures, Winnie inherited the money her father had allocated for her thirtieth birthday. By 1931, the $10,000 he had left her in 1910 was worth approximately $120,000. This much-anticipated inheritance must have seemed an enormous sum to a young woman whose expenses, maid service, and chauffeur were covered by her mother's income. It didn't take her long to devise spectacular ways of spending it.

Letters between Winnie and her friend Mary Hendrie, now Mary Cumming in London, England, had been exchanged ever since Mary left Hamilton after her wedding in 1925. Perhaps it was Mary who encouraged Winnie to come for a visit to see the grand royal procession that would celebrate the Silver Jubilee of King George V. (King George himself deplored the "fuss and expense" of the occasion that was suggested by his ministers.) Perhaps she formed the plan on her own. She decided to attend the royal celebration on 6 May 1935.

She crossed the Atlantic on one of the Cunard-White Star ships in first class. The letters to her mother, which Dollie saved as if they were historical documents of the utmost importance, lie faded and worn from much rereading in Winnie's scrapbooks.

Her brother could not have avoided the elaborate preparations for this journey any more than he could have avoided the goings-on when she'd made her debut. Here again were the dressmakers, the chauffeured trips to hairdressers and to shops for shoes, hats, jewellery, and furs. A special trunk was purchased for the trip. Later, when I was seven or eight, Winnie took me to the attic at 128 Huntley Street to show it to me. She approached it as if it were a holy relic. It seemed enormous. Meant to sit upright, it opened to show a rack with small hangers on one side; on the other side were drawers of different sizes to accommodate accessories. I seem to remember the interior being lined with blue satin, but perhaps I embellish. I still have the blue linen shoe bags from that trip, and use them when I travel. Although her brother would have been well aware of the widespread effects of the Depression after his university courses, Winnie would have been blithely ignorant.

Winnie's letters home to Dollie from London are dated 5 May, 6 May, 8 May, and 9 May 1935. They are affectionate and filled with superlatives, all opening with "My dearest Mother." There is something of the child's first time at a fair about them. Written in her strong, rounded, now somewhat careless hand, she seldom writes a complete sentence. Her feelings come in short bursts, separated by sharp dashes. The effect is one of intense breathlessness.

She and her Toronto friend, the redheaded Jean Macpherson, set off for London. Jean had made her debut at the same time as Winnie, though Jean seems to have lacked parents, since one of her receptions was held at Huntley Street. They stayed at a hotel in Knightsbridge that charged six guineas daily for a room and meals. She thought this price ($550 today) "very reasonable." Four friends from her debutante days — in addition to Mary Cumming — were also in London: Nancy

Boyd and her sister Lib, Barbara Northey, and Hugh McCullough.

On Sunday the fifth of May, she and Jean took a train to "Gerrard [sic] Corner" about twenty miles out of London, where they were met by David C. Haig and his wife, Helen (née Muirhead), from Toronto. The Haigs took them for a drive through the English countryside: "Never have I seen such gorgeous flowers, blossoms & places," Winnie wrote. The Haigs then took them to Windsor Castle where they walked about the gardens and park and watched the changing of the Grenadier Guards: "all very marvellous." After lunch, the Haigs drove them around Buckinghamshire — "most lovely country, rivers, hedges & flowers galore" — before dropping them at the Uxbridge underground station to make their way back to Knightsbridge.

Winnie was prepared to find all things English delightful, and she did not hesitate to mention what she disliked, a habit she kept for life. "The town of Windsor is lousy," she complained. As for the underground, "I loath [sic] it," she wrote, "& hope never to do that again, it gave me a headache." She also complained about one of her friends, who would not be seeing the procession. "Nancy [Boyd] is in Scotland for ten days. I suppose she never would bother to mix among the proletariate [sic] to see procession."

The following day was the Silver Jubilee celebration. It was, Winnie reported with joy, "hot & sun shining — grand for seeing the procession." Someone — possibly Mary Cumming — had arranged seats for Winnie and Jean at the Argentine Club (later the Canning Club) right next the Duke of York's (later King George VI) residence. There she sat, sipping "much champagne" with an elegant breakfast served on exquisite china and watching the "fine view" of the parade coming up Constitution Hill, along Piccadilly, and around Hyde Park Corner. "We were lucky to see everything so comfortably," she wrote. Winnie was utterly enthralled.

"Crowds terrific," she wrote to Dollie. "Over 4 million people out to see procession. Had breakfast, then watched various regiments take posts along line to keep crowds back. Most magnificent horses

& fine looking officers & guards. The crowds were splendidly handled — many fainting." The first thing she saw were the two royal princesses, Elizabeth and Margaret Rose, coming out of the Duke of York's house next door and getting into the car to go to Buckingham Palace. They were, she thought, "the sweetest things you ever saw dressed in pale pink bonnets & coats."

The Lord Mayor of London led the procession "complete with mace & trappings." Winnie went on to catalogue the parade. "Next came Ramsay MacDonald [Britain's prime minister] & Isabel, then Premier R.B. Bennett & other premiers [sic] of Australia, New Zealand etc., then lots of Lords & Dukes — all in the most gorgeous uniforms. The Duke and Duchess of York & Princesses preceded by outriders came next, cheering thunderous, the Highland lass from Glamis [Elizabeth, later Queen, and much later the Queen Mother] seems still the favourite & no wonder for she looked a radiant picture in pale blue with gray [sic] fox & bowing & smiling to us all. Princess Elizabeth & Margaret Rose waving and smiling too cute for words. The Duchess [of York, Elizabeth] has tremendous charm which her pictures cannot portray."

Despite a couple of errors — Isabel was not the name of Ramsay MacDonald's wife (it was Margaret Edith) and Bennett was prime minister of Canada, not premier of Ontario — Winnie displays a remarkable grasp of the ins and outs of British royalty. Had this been the subject of study at BSS she might not have dropped out. It is unlikely that she knew that Ramsay MacDonald was the illegitimate son of a ploughman.

Not missing anything, Winnie goes on. "After this came the Captains Guard of the Horse Cavalry escorting the Prince of Wales, the Duke of Gloucester & the Queen of Norway." She describes Edward Prince of Wales (later Edward VIII, with whom she had danced at the York Club in Toronto in 1924) as "fussing as usual with gloves, swords etc." The Kents came in another carriage, "she glorious in dusty pink." Princess Mary (third child and only daughter of

George V and Queen Mary), Lord Harewood (her husband, the sixth Earl of Harewood), and their sons dressed in kilt followed, "she in pale pink & fox, but the most awkward & stiff person I have seen."

The King and Queen's escorts "was [sic] most wonderful of all" consisting of Queen's Own Lancers, horse cavalry, gunners, and many others, with "Her Majesty [Queen Mary], very magnificent in silver satin, gray fox & diamonds, just like her photos." Then came more carriages with the Duke of Connaught, Earl of Athlone (later governor general of Canada) "& all the Indian potentates. They simply glittered with jewels." Winnie raved about the parade: "This was altogether the most wonderful sight in my lifetime & one never to be forgotten."

After the procession ended, Winnie "listened to the service at St. Paul's, had lunch & came home very tired as ever." Yet she was not too tired to write home to Dollie about her plans for the evening. "Tonight we go to dine & dance at Maidenhead 20 miles out at an English Castle called Great Fosters." Great Fosters, which still exists as a four-star hotel in Surrey today, is an elaborate Elizabethan country house set in fifty acres of gorgeous gardens. At that time, long before Heathrow Airport was built seven miles away, it would have been a bucolic heaven.

Before closing her letter, Winnie seems to have a touch of homesickness. She hasn't heard from Dollie or Donald yet. "Certainly will be glad to hear news from home. It seems years since I left you all." Yet she soon resumes her commanding air. "Call up & tell Mrs. Northey news as B[arbara] of course has not written a line home." As always, her closing is effusively fond: "Hope you are giving pussy [her Persian, Timothy] lots of milk & water. If I could just get some rest but everything comes at once ... Lots & lots of love & hope you are both well & happy — From Winifred"

By 9 May she had received a letter from Dollie. Again Winnie complains of having so little time she can scarcely find a minute to wash or go to the bathroom. Yet she is having a wonderful time.

She found London "superior to Toronto and the countryside better than Park Lands [sic]." She has lost several pounds from all the activity and complains that her clothes "hang like sacks & consequently fit abominably." Nonetheless she has not lost her zest. "London is a most marvellous city & each day I see more of it, Toronto seems to compare only with Bird's Eye Centre ... Yesterday we lunched with Lib at the Berkeley [a five-star luxury hotel in Knightsbridge]. Never tasted such food in my life, how I shall ever settle down to fare at 128 Huntley again I don't know. After lunch, Lib drove us in her car with chauffeur to call at Canada House. I of course am keenly interested in seeing all the people & know who many of them are which amuses everyone greatly."

Her friend Mary Cummings held a "most elegant dinner" for forty in honour of the Silver Jubilee. "The table was covered with Jubilee decorations," Winnie wrote Dollie, "red white & blue flowers, crackers & gorgeous silver, menus on table, etc. Delicious food, wines, & lovely ladies all covered with diamonds." Her dinner partner, Craig, was the son of the mayor of Ulster.

This was a second chance for Winnie to enter the marriage market. Yet she seems not to have been interested in any of the marriageable men introduced to her. She was more interested in getting the who's who straight and observing what the women were wearing. She found the men "difficult to talk to ... The Tommy Erskines, Margaret Hay & husband & several titled people were there — all so far ahead of anything in our native city. Mary is *au fait* with all the nobs in London — away ahead of Lib." Mary, who was on the Silver Jubilee Committee, "had the best tables [for her guests] in the room, almost beside the Kents (Duke and Duchess)."

She was pleased with the expensive clothes she had brought from Toronto, and with good reason. She was now at the height of her beauty. "I wore all my trappings. My new dress looked lovely — glistening in pearls and diamonds all on the satin. Much to my surprise Joyce Greenly [wife of Colonel Greenly], George Drew & Marion Hay [née Beck, wife of "Stratty" Hay] with a male friend at the party. All Mary's party wore ermine, diamonds & very high brow. Grosvenor House is a *grand* place & the Ballroom & decorations very lovely. There was a Cabaret, a raffle of diamond clips, draw done by Marie Tempest aged 70 & looks 40. Music excellent but awful crowd. One girl sitting at our table wore the most lovely tiara, necklace & bracelets. Lady Dufferin & Ava [Guiness] wore her tiara & many others. The Philip Kindersleys [the Honourable Philip Leyland Kindersley, son of the 1st Baron Kindersley, and brother of Winnie's friend Hugh] are being divorced. One man told me last night that only the middle classes lived with their wives over here.

"The Duke & Duchess of Kent [George, younger brother of Edward VIII and George VI, and his wife, Princess Marina of Greece and Denmark] arrived at 11:30, had a dance & supper. They walked the whole length of the Ballroom, she smiling & bowing to everyone, quite shy & the most adorable creature, wore gold lamé & her diamonds. Quite obviously in the family way. I watched her all through supper & she is quite human, smiles, chats & seems to enjoy herself." It was as if thirty-four-year-old Winnie were still a debutante at even more lavish parties than she had known in Toronto fifteen years before.

The next day, Winnie went at Jean's initiative to the House of Commons, where "Sir Robert Horne [Conservative MP, a Scot and a womanizing bachelor] & Sir Arthur Shirley Benn [another Conservative MP and 1st Baron Glenravel] had given Jean seats in the front row of the Ladies' Gallery." There they heard Ramsay MacDonald, who had led the Commonwealth prime ministers in the Silver Jubilee procession, Stanley Baldwin, who the following month would replace MacDonald as prime minister, Sir Neville Chamberlain, later to become prime minister and best known for ceding the Sudetenland to Nazi Germany in the Munich Pact of 1938, and Lady Astor, the first woman to sit as a Member of Parliament. These politicians and their views in 1935 were crucial in setting the stage for the Second

World War. Though Winnie reported that the debate was "very interesting," I doubt that she understood anything. She and Jean had not climbed into bed until 3:30 a.m. the night before, and the speeches centred on the League of Nations and the possibility of increasing armaments against the possibility of a second world war would have bored her. As for Lady Astor, who supported women's suffrage as a role for a radically different concept of woman's place in the world, she could not have fathomed it. She was more interested in the "magnificent buildings" of the House of Commons than in anything that went on inside them.

Such a visit would not have been complete for Winnie and Jean without at least a glimpse of Scotland. On Monday the twelfth, they took the night train to Edinburgh. There Colonel Greenly had arranged a car for them. "He has given us a *Rolls Royce*," she wrote enthusiastically, "& *chauffeur* at our disposal, *free of charge* to motor through Scotland for one week — pretty nice!!!" The night they arrived they went to the theatre with the Haigs, then went on the following day to a reception at Mrs. Ferguson's. They spent the weekend with Lib in the country. They dropped in at Achnacarry Castle, but could only see the outside and grounds. It seems they visited Lady Leith, since Winnie had sent her a note before they left London. They had a box for Olympia and the Derby, and Jean had arranged for them to see a polo match at Ranlegh, near Oxford.

After reporting that Hugh McCullough — one of her earlier beaux — will stay two weeks longer in London, she closes, "Very best love to you three dears — from *Winifred*." As a final P.S., she adds, "The shops are simply gorgeous — I long to buy *everything*."

A BREAKDOWN

It is impossible to know what caused Donald's nervous collapse. At twenty-two he seemed like a young man on the threshold of a lucrative and outstanding career. He had excelled above his peers at Appleby School. He had completed a degree in Commerce and Finance at the University of Toronto. He had received a third on graduating, but his grades in accounting — the career he was most likely to follow — had always been firsts and seconds. Thanks to Harold Innis, the very professor he could not tolerate, he was among the first generation of university students to be trained in the latest social, political, and financial aspects of commerce and business ushered in by the Great Depression.

He seemed to enjoy his time away from his studies, too. Sometime during his university years he learned the Charleston. He occasionally danced it with me when I was a young woman visiting for Christmas, rolling his trousers up over his knees with a big smile. He spoke of open cars and drinking, and he sang Roaring Twenties songs such as "Bye, Bye, Blackbird" and "Five Foot Two, Eyes of Blue."

A couple of decades ago, I found a scrap of paper that records a canoe trip — or part of one — in his back-slanting, round hand-writing, which was smaller than Winnie's. It is dated June 1930. It traces a trip including portages of between twelve and fifteen miles a day through the Kawartha Lakes. Leaving from "G's," they camped on Mud Turtle Lake, went on to Coboconk and Norland, then to Minden and on to Mount Lake. It interests me that, in accountant-like fashion, my father kept detailed track of times and distances. Even more interesting, he records the things he lost: a knife on the first lap of the trip, a razor guard on the last lap. At the end of his record of the second lap, he declares with obvious satisfaction, "Lose nothing." Who went on this trip with him? Who or what was "G"? I have no idea. It might have been Appleby friends or university classmates. He never said.

The only way I could get my father to talk to me at any length when I grew up was to treat him to lunch in Barrie. He used to order things like liver, which my mother never cooked. Perhaps it was this canoe trip he meant when he told me at one of those lunches about a prank he and his friends played. They had stopped at someone's vacant cottage for a skinny dip. On the dock, one of them had found a camera loaded with film. They took turns taking pictures of each other grouped in the nude, then put the camera back. How my father laughed as he recalled their glee in imagining the owners' bafflement and embarrassment upon developing the film!

Yet something caused Donald to retreat to his room at Huntley Street and refuse to come out. It was an avoidance reminiscent of his hiding from his governesses and his hiding at parties. Was it a delayed reaction to his father's death? Was it the expectations of him he knew others now held? Was it the sudden falling-away of the structured life of school and university? There, decisions were made for him, schedules were fixed, expectations were clear. Did he fear marriage, especially if it involved a woman from Toronto "society," a woman like Winnie? Was it the prospect of living without a foreseeable end in the female household of his mother, his sister, and Kate?

By this time, Winnie's authority in that household had been fully established. My mother often said, "Dollie was a lovely, gentle soul, but she was no match for Winnie." With the added clout of her large inheritance and the habitual relationship between her and her ever more timid mother, Winnie at thirty-two would have been a powerful force. Social patterns with her Toronto friends were now well established. Her values — with which her brother largely disagreed — were taken for granted at Huntley Street. Her unbridled spending and autocratic treatment of Kate and the chauffeur — even of her mother — would have been blatant. Where and when was he to escape? In that limbo between the end of education and establishment in a job, he faltered.

My father never spoke of this. My mother told us about it, but since she had not met my father when this happened her report is suspect. She said that Dr. Brock Chisholm, outstanding psychiatrist and later the first director-general of the World Health Organization, was called to the house to talk him out of the room and into treatments with him. How long these continued I don't know. But somehow, through these treatments, Donald made the transition to the world of work. He took a job as an accountant in the investments branch at the reputable Confederation Life Insurance Co., Ltd.

"FOR ONCE I FELT
LIKE A DUCHESS"

So successful was Winnie's visit to England and Scotland for the Silver Jubilee that she could not resist a second. The occasion was even grander: the coronation of George VI, whose house she had sat next to for the Silver Jubilee and whose table was near hers at Mary Cumming's dinner party for that occasion. This all happened quite suddenly and unexpectedly, four months after the abdication of Edward VIII for the woman he loved, Wallis Simpson. The date meant for Edward's formal coronation remained unchanged. His younger brother simply replaced him on the twelfth of May 1937. Suitable young unmarried women from Britain and the colonies of the British Empire would be presented to the Duke and Duchess of York, instead of to Edward VIII, a week before the coronation.

Among these young ladies from the colonies was Winifred Cameron. I suppose it was the fact that she was still unmarried that qualified her for presentation at court. Certainly at thirty-six she was hardly young. Yet she had contacts enough in Canada and the UK to help her arrange it. Again she was off to London, with her large elaborate trunk filled with even more expensive clothes and accessories. She boarded another grand Cunard-White Star liner. Most likely it was the Queen Mary, which still sailed from New York and crossed the Atlantic to Southampton in luxury, ignorant of the world's economic collapse, ignorant even that the company providing such luxurious travel was itself in financial difficulty.

Her letters to Dollie were as effusive and affectionate as ever, maybe more so. They are still full of spelling errors, dashes, and incomplete sentences that at times make them almost incomprehensible. She reports visiting Mary Cumming, who may have had something to do with Winnie's presentation, for lunch on Wednesday the fifth of May. "I ... saw the children [Mary's daughters, aged nine and six] & had a good talk with Mary as we were alone." Her idea of "a good talk" was an exchange of information about status, material goods, and social plans. "She & Ronny have bought a yacht & they will go there every week-end somewhere near Portsmouth. She intends taking Bill [Mary's brother and Winnie's former dancing partner in Toronto] there nearly every week-end & seems to have arranged several week-end parties. Bill is to be here for 2 months — hardly enough. They are going to see the naval review at Spithead in one of the Sea Lords [sic] yachts just behind the Royal Yacht Victoria & Albert." At this lunch, Mary offered to lend Winnie "the most gorgeous turquoise feather fan I have ever seen to wear to court. Five times as big as mine with ivory handle & costing $150.00 [about $2,300 in 2013]." Winnie, ecstatic, accepted.

Winnie was presented at Buckingham Palace on the sixth of May. Her Friday 7 May 1937 letter to her mother the next day is the essence of Winnie. "My dearest Mother," she writes. "Well, the great day is over & I have been presented."

The "great day" began at 3:30 p.m., when all the young women to be presented gathered to dress. Winnie reported that "Unks [Marion Hays's Uncle James Hay, who lived in London] and Mary D. came to see us dress." Alice Waters, another of the young women from Toronto being presented, bothered Winnie: "[she] is a terrible fusser & was very nervous." The official escorts arrived at six o'clock for a small meal. "We had sandwitches [sic] & fruit salad & some rye & this was all the food until breakfast next day." Then they were off to Buckingham Palace. "We had a grand car & 2 splendid chauffeurs & for once I felt like a duchess. The crowds were all around us while we drove over to the palace — we were let in the gates at 7:30 sharpe [sic] & then the cars had to wait in the inner court until 8:30. Everything was on the dot as to time. It all seems now like a dream of fairyland — & I would like to go every night."

Winnie tells her mother that it would take pages to write about the "marvellous" inside of the palace. She will tell her more when she returns to Toronto. Meanwhile, she offers a "brief" description. "We sat in rows of gold chairs in a throne room of gold & crystal with the walls of mirrors which reflected a most wonderful sight. The jewellery, uniforms & gorgeous dresses were by far the most magnificent sight of my life & one quite worth coming over to see. At sharpe [sic] 9:30 the Royal party came in & I was thrilled to the core."

The moment draws near for Winnie's presentation. "I was not in the least nervous & when my turn came there were 6 men to take my card & fix my train & [make] a large space to make curtsy. The King is very like Edward the same ruddy complexion. He nodded & smiled slightly while I swept to the floor & brought the fan around in front, then on to the Queen. She was simply perfect in a silver dress that glittered like a mirror & her wonderful diamond tiara. She is far prettier than any picture ever portrays — her smile & complexion are radiant & I shall never forget the smile she gave me as I came up & smiled to her."

Since Winnie was seated in the front row with the Beefeaters as the royal procession left the room, she was able to see almost everyone. "I could not stare at them all. The Duchess of Buccleuch [who was to hold Queen Elizabeth's canopy at the coronation] was in silver with diamonds & emeralds. I lunched at Premiers next to her on Wednesday. She is a real beauty & last night looked simply radiant. The jewels on Lady Londonderry [renowned society hostess and wife of a Conservative MP] nearly blinded me — the Indian princes are very attractive headed by the Aga Khan who wore a black fez. Marian [Marian "Crawfie" Crawford, governess to the royal princesses Elizabeth and Margaret] was too lovely in pale pink lamé — the Princess [sic] Royal looked very nice. As the Royal procession left the Throne room & the King, Duke of Kent were so close I almost touched them. We bowed again as the King & Queen passed us hand & hand & she is a dream."

Although Winnie complained that their meal of sandwiches, fruit salad, and rye at 3:30 would be the only food they had until breakfast the next day, there was a supper after the presentation. "We had supper & drank the King's champagne while the Masseys introduced us to a great many celebrities including L[ord] & Lady Chamberlain." Neville Chamberlain was then prime minister of England. Vincent Massey, who had been on the board of the Canadian Bank of Commerce from 1922–25, and his wife, Alice, were living in London then because Massey had been appointed Canadian High Commissioner to the U.K. in 1935. Now that Winnie had more time to "stare," she concluded, "My dress looked as well as any but my jewels could not really rival the Royal Parties [sic]." She reported to Dollie that "Mrs. Massey said she was very proud of us & from the dias [sic] several people had remarked on what charming girls & this was the Canadian girls."

Then they were seated for supper. Probably all Winnie could hear was that intoxicating fanfare, the voice of happiness itself. Was it possible that she would see this night end, watch it become the past? This night was so beautiful, so perfect. Surely it could not be forgotten.

After the supper was over the "girls" had their pictures taken by Dorothy Wilding in Old Bond Street. It was two a.m. when she got into bed. "To-day," she writes the next day, "we have to sign the book at Buckingham Palace."

There is a sense of letdown in the days after the presentation. Almost enviously, she writes, "[this] week-end I shall be alone. Shirley [Haldenby] is going to the country with the Masseys. [Massey, a patron of the arts, would have known Shirley's husband, the famed architect Eric Haldenby, with whom Winnie had danced long ago.] Next week I shall write each day & hope I won't get lonely. I may move over to Shirleys [sic] after the 14th but they go for 5 days to Paris." Instead, she focuses on the plans she does have. "We think we'll go to the naval review at Spithead [which Mary had mentioned at lunch] in one of the CPR boats — cost $20.00 & Mary may take us to the Caledonian Ball — on May 28th that is the Highland Ball. Neil has asked me to lunch next Thursday with Marg Griffin [the granddaughter of Sir Alexander Mackenzie]."

With this, Winnie closes, after complaining that she has had only one letter from Dollie. "How is my darling pussy and Don — Tons of love & kisses, from *Winifred*."

Winnie was thirty-six when she was presented at court. She was a real beauty. The portrait photograph of her taken the night she was presented could be that of a movie star of the era. She looked somewhat like Gertrude Lawrence, the actress and friend of Noël Coward who had starred with him in *Private Lives* a few years before. She also slightly resembled Greta Garbo, whose film *Camille* appeared that same year. Winnie is wearing a long, sleeveless, sequined silver dress with a V-back. Draped over her shoulder sweeps a luxurious white fox stole. Her ash blond hair is bobbed and Marcelled into fashionable waves. Her pronounced widow's peak shapes her lovely face into a heart. She wears powder on her nose and lipstick only, but her thick, dark eyebrows — an Ireland family feature — make her look unusually striking. 6 May 1937 was the high point of her life, the "wedding" she never had.

28

CONFEDERATION
LIFE

In 1933, the same year that Donald finished his degree in Commerce and Finance, a young woman from Saskatchewan arrived in Toronto to train as a secretary. It was one of three choices — typical of that time — offered by her mother: nurse, teacher, or secretary. Bertah Roy was lucky to have any choice at all. It was the worst year of the Depression. Her father, Robert, had died a slow, ugly death of cancer in 1926. She was nine then, the youngest, and his favourite. She remembers his intervening on her behalf with her mother after she dropped a tray of fine china. She also remembers his foul-smelling room the last year of his life. Loving him as she did, she was torn between going into and avoiding that room. Afterwards, she could not abide the scent of spring orange blossoms, which had been the flowers at his funeral.

Robert Roy was a Scottish immigrant from Tillicoultry, Clackmannanshire. He had been an accountant, but industrialization had taken its toll on his wool-weaving community. He aspired to a civilized and reverent Presbyterian family life in Canada. He read to his wife and three children from the Bible and his favourite poet, Robert Browning. Photos show him a well-groomed, slightly self-satisfied man in well-tailored clothes. He and his wife, Henrietta, known as "Hinny," had sailed from Glasgow for Canada in 1910. Two of his brothers had emigrated with them but settled elsewhere. The day before they'd left, the three brothers had visited their family in Tillicoultry for a last climb among the moody Ochil Hills.

After their father's death, the three Roy children scattered to allow their mother time to recover from her grief. Elsie was sent to the University of Toronto to study medicine; Gregor went to live with another family, probably relatives; and little, dark-haired Bertah was sent alone to relatives in Kamsack. There, abandoned and stricken, she studied music, playing the piano. "It was the one thing everyone approved of," she told me, "working and working for that degree." By age fifteen she had her Associate diploma from the London College of Music. She would have obtained one of the highest levels, the licentiate, two years later if the three families in Kamsack with daughters ready to try that exam had been able to afford to bring out an examiner from England.

After Robert died, with Elsie at university in Toronto, and before there was a social safety net in Canada, Henrietta's money had soon run out. To support herself and her three children, Henrietta taught at a nearby Indian reservation. My mother used to tell me about a hemophiliac boy she had saved on the reservation. She was twelve, he was hurt and bleeding, and she was the only one around. She got him into a truck and drove him to the hospital. Yet others of her stories betrayed a racist outlook, no doubt handed her by her mother: Indians were shifty, drunk, and incurably lazy.

Gregor had enrolled in teacher's college around 1931. By 1933, as the Depression deepened, there was not enough money to send Bertah to university. This was to be a lifelong wound to her. She had matriculated at sixteen with an average of ninety-three percent, the best in her class. She had achieved — overachieved — in music as well

as in school. To attend Shaw College in Toronto was a sharp come-
down. There she learned shorthand, typing, and other secretarial
skills, her face a national flood disaster. She had joined her sister and
her friends, Joan Sterling and Evadne, in an old Toronto mansion on
Beverley Street, opposite the Art Gallery of Toronto. To come home
from Shaw to no piano and a sister attending the university she herself wanted to attend was humiliating. At night she wandered
Toronto, stalking happiness. "I felt like the Little Match Girl," she
used to say, "looking into all those lighted windows. Families having
dinner, talking, laughing, playing games." She escaped into the glamorous world of the "talkies," took up smoking in imitation of Bette
Davis, and window-shopped the fashions of the time. She had a feisty
nature that in the long run proved irrepressible.

Shaw College prided itself on finding positions for all its graduates. Bertah landed her first job at age seventeen with Confederation
Life. There, in the handsome seven-storey redbrick Romanesque
Revival building still at 14 Richmond Street East, she became secretary for a group of Confederation Life accountants. One of them was
twenty-four-year-old Donald Cameron.

From the little that was said about this situation, my mother —
along with the other Confederation Life employees — was agog
over the daily arrival and departure of the tall, handsome Donald
in his chauffeur-driven car. I think she cheered up generally after
finding herself in a good job with a paycheque. She loved clothes,
and the fashions of the mid-'30s with their tailored wide shoulders
or puffed sleeves and shaped skirts suited her petite, slim figure well.
So did the hats, decorated with feathers or cloth bows, worn jauntily
aslant the face and surrounded by curls. This was an era of ensembles,
gloves, pearls, and heeled shoes. Though she was only five foot two
(the same height as the high jump record Donald had established
at Appleby School), she would have been a pert, efficient presence at
Confederation Life. Whether she had access to a sewing machine I
don't know, but I remember watching her sewing her own clothes

— even suits and coats — as well as ours throughout my childhood. She had come from a family that included milliners, and was as expert and precise a seamstress as she was a secretary. To a Saskatchewan girl from a family diminished by the death of her father, Toronto probably seemed glamorous and fun — especially now that she, unlike so many, had a job. Now she could window-shop along Yonge Street just around the corner, or take the streetcar up to the Bloor shops.

I don't know how much of Shaw College's philosophy Bertah absorbed. The college's founder, William Shaw, had advertised the institution's motto in 1892: "Be up with the times and always progressive." Shaw College was one of the first of such places to teach modern professions, which meant education in practical arts to meet the needs of industry. He touted what he called "new-world ideas." Though Bertah was exceptionally deft at typing and shorthand, her crushed dreams of university probably blotted out any message the college hoped to instill.

Coming from this institution into the world of Confederation Life represented a clash of values. The Confederation Life Insurance Co. was a conservative capitalist organization founded in 1871. It was a major Canadian insurance and financial services provider with operations in the U.K., the U.S., Bermuda, and Cuba. It was a business somewhat like Brazilian Traction, or the Canadian Bank of Commerce for that matter: Canadian-owned, but with many international offices. Had Confederation Life been "progressive," as Shaw College claimed to be, it might have allowed women to pursue careers. As it was, women like my mother were little more than flunkies in a system in which male owners and male accountants made money partly from the low-paid labour of the company's staff. Shaw College was indeed "meeting the needs of industry," but not the needs of its graduates.

Donald, however, was not quite typical of his class or of Confederation Life, despite the chauffeured car. Private school, university education, social connections, family wealth — none of this had turned him into a man like his father. He had his own ideas, and they had been formed by his temperament, his courses at U of T that took the Depression into account, his resistance to his father's outdoors- and club-based lifestyle, and — perhaps most of all — his observation of his sister Winnie's wantonly spendthrift ways. He had kept the Scottish military association of the 48th Highlanders and a strong sense of duty from his background, but not much else. Donald's ideas about life were actually closer to Bertah's than might at first appear. Both had been raised as avid Scots and imbued with the culture of Britain (though she more than he), both were accustomed to the world of accountants, both were skeptical of organized religion, both were drawn to music (he by then played the bagpipes), and both were deeply convinced of the importance of education.

Nothing was reported to me about Bertah's first introduction to Dollie and Winnie at 128 Huntley Street. It could have been any time between 1935 and 1938. It isn't hard to imagine Winnie's dismay at her brother's growing interest in Bertah Roy. She probably said, "I've never heard of such a thing!" — one of her favourite sayings, and a frequently used one, since she knew so little. "*What*? A girl from *Saskatchewan*? Where *is* Saskatchewan? A *secretary*? No family of any worth? Why wouldn't you want a nice Toronto debutante from a good family?" She probably proceeded to name a few. Mother was even at a disadvantage vis-à-vis the Camerons in matters Scottish. She believed (wrongly) that she was descended from Rob Roy MacGregor — possibly the most reviled and criminal of the clan chiefs. So great were his offences that he was not only imprisoned and stripped of all his land, but his name was made illegal. Mother's maiden name was Roy, the name used after MacGregor became taboo. (For some reason, my parents saw fit to give me the middle name of MacGregor. I like to think they were forecasting trouble.) Overall, the MacGregors were Lowlanders, and therefore inferior to Highlanders like the Camerons.

For her own part Bertah, who was intelligent, accomplished, and who knew how much her accountant father had valued literature, music, and education, disliked Winnie. She thought her a deplorably ignorant bully. Her later observations about Huntley Street were not flattering. "Dollie was such a meek soul," she used to say. "She was timid and fearful. Once I noticed that her toenails had grown far too long, and I trimmed them for her. What she said was, 'That hurt more than men have hurt me.' She did not have a happy life." Mother could see that Dollie was dominated by Winnie, whose behaviour — in her opinion — was abominable. "One day Winnie came home with a very expensive hat she had bought. She didn't really like it, so she began trimming it. She clipped off one feather after another, then finally threw it down the front stairs yelling at Kate to come and throw it out." Winnie did not heed the advice of contemporary advisors in etiquette that, in the title of a 1924 *Toronto Daily Star* article, "Rudeness to Servants is a Lack of Breeding."

Possibly the only thing Winnie and Bertah had in common was an interest in fashion. Yet even here they differed. Winnie draped herself in the tweeds and cardigans and the silks and satins she associated with Britain and the Royals, clothes that spoke of wealth and tradition. Bertah, whose tastes were being formed by the movies she loved, liked the stylish, shoulder-padded tops and fitted skirts of the modern American world. Partly this was due to their physical shapes. Winnie, who seemed taller than her five feet and five inches, became more and more stout as time passed, her bosom dominating her shape, projecting like the continental shelf. She thought my mother needed to eat more, and said so. Bertah, seventeen years her junior, was slim and shapely, like the movie stars she admired. I remember her mentioning Katharine Hepburn, Greta Garbo, Olivia de Havilland, Deanna Durbin, and Norma Shearer. She disliked Mae West and Jean Harlow because they were vulgar, and she positively loathed Shirley Temple. Her idols were Errol Flynn and Bette Davis. Her Presbyterian background ensured she wore nothing daring, but she was attractive and vivacious. She found Winnie's weight repulsive. Unlike Winnie she wore her dark hair in longish curls that would become a stylish, sleek pageboy by the 1940s. Later she would be compared often to Vivien Leigh in *Gone with the Wind*. Winnie continued to wear Marcell waves, oblivious to contemporary change, absolutely certain that her clothes were the best because they were the most expensive. Winnie's grand, slow-moving presence dwarfed Bertah's five-foot-two-inch liveliness; she expected to dominate this hayseed girl half her age. Yet Bertah had a strong personality too, and her acute fashion sense made her stand out.

29

COLLISIONS

By the time the Second World War exploded in 1939, Donald and Bertah were together. As a member of the 48th Highlanders for a decade, Donald enlisted in the Canadian Armed Forces. Mother said he was turned down for overseas duty because of his anxiety. This was to be a sore point, as I discovered a few years after the war ended. I was about age six, out in the old Studebaker with my parents. I piped up, as I often and annoyingly did, to blurt out, "I know why Daddy didn't go to war. He was scared." This caused instant and long-lasting silence on the subject.

Instead, and greatly to his credit I now see, he was stationed at Canadian Forces Base Borden on a glacial moraine twenty miles west of Barrie, Ontario, where he became an outstanding instructor to soldiers headed overseas. He always said he enjoyed Camp Borden. There he returned to the same kind of structured life with men that he had come to enjoy at Appleby School. At first he was company commander, teaching both shooting and orientation (map reading and practical forays into unknown territory using maps and a compass). I can't imagine his shooting anyone, not even an animal, yet he eventually became a major and the chief instructor with A-11 Canadian Machine Gun Training Centre. Much later, when my sister and I were in our early teens, he taught us to shoot a BB gun. There was never any thought that the gun would be used for anything but the stationary target he set up at the end of our dead-end street. As for orientation, I suppose it suited him to pretend being in enemy territory rather than actually being in it, for he was still subject to an anxiety much like Dollie's. I know he enjoyed reading maps. I have one of the books he used: *Manual of Map Reading, Photo Reading, and Field Sketching*, published by the British War Office in 1929, then reprinted in 1939. Donald has stamped *D.S.F. CAMERON* on the cover and on the first page. The content is extremely complex and difficult. The textbook has many fold-out maps, lists of terms like "defile," "re-entrant," and "magnetic meridian," and symbols indicating almost anything a soldier on the ground might expect to encounter, such as "dangerous bogs," "wind-pumps," and "battle sites." Instruments used in field sketching such as the "alidade," "the aneroid barometer," and "the trough compass" are illustrated. The reading and sketching of ordnance maps of differing scales readied soldiers to deal with the realities of night marches, when they would need to negotiate the way to or away from battles and know where to find refuge. The preface rightly pointed out that these were "necessary items of military education and aim[ed] at enabling the student to visualize, appreciate, and make good use of, the tactical features of the ground." I trust that my father's instruction saved the lives of at least some, possibly many, of the soldiers he taught.

From Camp Borden Donald wrote letters to his mother and to Bertah. His marriage proposal also arrived by letter. That must have been about a year or so into the war, because Donald and Bertah were married on 21 December 1941 at Rosedale Presbyterian Church, just across from 128 Huntley Street. Bertah's mother, Henrietta, attended

Donald's military
wedding to Bertah
Roy, Rosedale
Presbyterian
Church, 21
December 1941

the wedding. Though she visited occasionally, and I was taught to call
her by the Indian word for grandmother, Noko, I never really knew
her, as she died when I was three. Photos — and a brief 30 mm. film
of the wedding party outside — depict a military wedding. By that
time my father was a major in the regiment. In the photo I have he is
wearing the kilt, Glengarry, and sporran of the 48th Highlanders, and
he and Bertah walk beneath the crossed swords of his fellow Highlanders. His most prominent feature is his bony knees and those
long, long legs. Mother always said he was sedated for the wedding,
and his drooping eyes suggest that that could be true. Bertah is in her
glory. Her simple satin dress is the backdrop for a waterfall bouquet of

white roses. Her feet in white open-toed pumps peek out from below. Around her shoulders is a lush white fox cape. Yet it is the headdress that stands out. It is shaped like a Dutch girl's hat in two transparent peaks of net. A mid-length tiered veil stands out from behind this headdress. The effect is doll-like: coy, elfin, and virginal. Her brides-maids were her sister Elsie and her friend Joan Sterling, who had roomed with her on Beverley Street and later became my godmother. In the film, there is a quick shot of Dan Chisholm, Elsie's husband, turning his back on the camera and flipping up his kilt. Dan was a brother of Brock Chisholm, the psychiatrist who had helped Donald with his anxieties. Dan had courted Bertah for a time, before deciding to marry her older sister instead. It took years for us to discover this connection, and its basis for the series of "Uncle Dan" songs that my father created to make fun of his wife's first boyfriend, the man who was now his brother-in-law. It's the closest he came to jealousy, though Uncle Dan was a quiet, unobtrusive fellow, and I think my father was fond of him. One of these songs — some sung to the tune of "Barney Google," a 1920s foxtrot made popular by Spike Jones — went like this:

> *Uncle Danny, with his goo-goo-googly eyes,*
> *Uncle Danny, took a trip to par-a-dise.*
> *And the paradise he headed for, was the local liquor store,*
> *Uncle Danny, with his googly-woogly eyes.*

> *Uncle Danny, with his goo-goo-googly eyes,*
> *Uncle Danny, Elsie cuts him down to size.*
> *Every time he says a word, Elsie says, "Don't be absurd!"*
> *Uncle Danny, with his googly-woogly eyes.*

Another, sung to a different tune, went like this:

> *Uncle Dan, Uncle Dan,*
> *Was a very, very, very nasty man.*

Every year he took the prize, for taking wings off flies,
Uncle Dan, Uncle Dan, old Uncle Dan.

Uncle Dan, Uncle Dan,
You will usually find him sitting on the can.
He spends many hours in there, keeping out of Elsie's hair,
Uncle Dan, Uncle Dan, old Uncle Dan.

My father never sang these songs in front of Dan and Elsie, or their children. Yet he made sure that we — and my children a generation later — knew these undeniably hostile songs by heart. He often turned this same humour on himself. He always said, for instance, that his initials D.S.F. stood for "Damned Stupid Fool."

At first Donald and Bertah rented a house on Whitehall Road in Rosedale, not far from Huntley Street. Donald, of course, could only be there on his fortnightly weekend leaves from Camp Borden. Bertah probably left — or was forced to leave — her job at Confederation Life. Married women, especially during the war, were thought to be unpatriotic in taking jobs needed by men with families. Mother told me that she and Joan became acquainted with a young German professor from the U of T who lived nearby. He used to bring his German friends over to visit and dance. Mother used to laugh about this, insisting she had no idea that she and Joan might be encouraging national enemies.

Donald, meanwhile, was now company commander and instructor at Camp Borden. As the dangers of smoking gradually penetrated social consciousness, he would tell me about exercise marches he used to go on from Borden to Newmarket or other villages nearby. "We had no idea that smoking was a health hazard," he would say, laughing. "We used to march for an hour, then take a ten-minute break. Every soldier would immediately light up and smoke furiously for the entire break." I remember him rolling cigarettes from blue tins of Player's Navy Cut tobacco. He'd set up the little cigarette-rolling machine like a small press on the dining room table and make half a dozen cigarettes at a time.

30

A WAR
BABY

Under what circumstances Bertah moved from Whitehall Road to Huntley Street I don't know. It could have been because she fell pregnant with me in the spring of 1942. Perhaps it was decided she ought not to be alone. Donald would be at Borden until 1945, helping with the process of demobilization. Certainly Kate's practical care-taking would have been welcomed by my mother, who didn't enjoy cooking. Even so, cohabiting with Dollie and Winnie could not have seemed much improvement on solitude.

My father was at Camp Borden when I was born. Much later, he told me that I was conceived on one of his leaves, when he had a very high temperature. I'm still not sure what his point was. It is not difficult to imagine the hysteria at Huntley Street on the night of 9 January 1943, when my mother went into labour during one of the worst blizzards to be unleashed on Toronto. Winnie told me this story over and over. What a frightful blizzard it had been! How she was terrified my mother would be stuck somewhere in the snow on the way to the Toronto General Hospital! Dollie was wringing her hands, stricken. Even my plucky mother was frightened.

I was duly born early on 10 January 1943, as the blizzard raged on. Both my mother and Winnie often recalled that night. Winnie always spoke of it as some kind of miracle: that my mother made it to the hospital, that I was the loveliest baby in the nursery, the excitement when my mother brought me home to Huntley Street. No doubt this account owed more to Winnie's imagination than to reality. My mother's account could not have been more different, and it was probably closer to the truth. "I had ulcers during my pregnancy because you kicked me so much," she used to say. "You were born with a huge strawberry birthmark over half of your face (I still have one on my left calf). I spent two endless weeks in the hospital crying. When I got out I was as weak as a kitten. You were so ugly. My stomach was all wrinkled and flabby like an old potato." For years, I believed that I had *caused* the blizzard, that I had assaulted my mother before I was even born, that I was ugly, and that I had ruined my mother's figure.

Among the many sentimental cards of congratulations kept by my mother is one accompanying a bouquet of yellow mums, signed in Winnie's broad writing: "With fond love from 'Hubby' who is not here as usual to write card, per. W." Her own card features a patch of white cloth meant to be a diaper held by a puzzled father labelled "D." The card goes through several warnings about the difficulties of dealing with a baby, and is signed, "Oh, Boy!" There is a card featuring a little girl in an elaborate bonnet watching blue birds, signed "With love & song, Mother Dollie."

Both my parents had been the youngest children in their families. Neither of them had ever held a baby. Nor had Winnie or Kate, and Dollie wasn't much use since nannies and governesses had dealt with Winnie and Donald. They couldn't cope. "We had to call in a VON nurse to give you your first bath," my mother told me. Mother had chosen a pediatrician who tended to Toronto's elite. Dr. Neil Silverthorne followed Dr. Benjamin Spock's principles — now discounted — of child rearing: fresh air, rigid schedules of feedings every four hours, various measures against "spoiling" the baby. "I had to put you as far away as possible so I couldn't hear you screaming between feedings," mother told me. "Finally I took you to Dr. Silverthorne in desperation. He made out a prescription for sedatives. I gave them to you for eighteen months."

I know only what I was told later, of course. Though neither the Camerons nor Henrietta went to church, I was christened on 26 September 1943 at Huntley Street in a long lacy robe and cap. All of my own children were christened in that same outfit, which I still have.

Winnie used to savour recollections of taking me out for walks around Rosedale in my pram. "You were the cutest baby," she used to say, glowing with pride. "I'd ask you about all the animals — 'What does the birdie say? What does the doggie say? What does the cow say?' — and you knew *all* the answers."

"Sure, she took you for walks," mother responded when I asked about this, "but she did *nothing* else. I'd get you all ready in gorgeous clothes and blankets that Kate had washed and ironed. I'd take the pram down the front steps. Then Winnie would appear. She'd bring you back, ring the doorbell, and expect me to take you in and carry the pram up the stairs." Mother insisted that I was a difficult baby in many ways. Not only did I scream between feedings, I threw up when I *was* fed. "You had a love-hate relationship with eggs," she always told me. "I never knew whether you would want more than one or throw up at the first spoonful." Among the jumble of papers my mother saved is a prescription for the antacid Amphogel to be taken after every meal.

Life went on so at Huntley Street for eighteen months after I was born: my father returning only on his leaves from Camp Borden, my mother gritting her teeth, Winnie indulging me, Kate doing all the chores, and Dollie becoming more anxious. "Dollie had no finesse dealing with babies," my mother used to say. "She'd poke you a few times in the chest and say a few words, such as 'How is Miss Mouse?' You'd burst into tears. You were scared of her."

31

28 DUNDONALD STREET, BARRIE

By the summer of 1944, Mother was pregnant again. She and Donald rented a cottage at Shanty Bay, "by the lake" and next door to a cottage rented by her sister Elsie, who by then had a son, Robbie, a year older than me. This cottage provided cool air and company for my pregnant mother, who spent much of her time sitting outside in a lawn chair with skeins of wool draped around her neck, knitting for the new baby. The only story she told me about that summer was of my hanging a garter snake around her neck and saying "Pretty wool!" Her reaction resulted in my fear of snakes.

That fall of 1944, my parents left Huntley Street for good. They rented the upstairs of 28 Dundonald Street in Barrie, which was then a small town of roughly 11,000 about sixty miles north of Toronto. It formed a horseshoe around the end of Kempenfelt Bay on the western end of Lake Simcoe. Our Victorian brick house stood on the brow of a long steep hill that was later excellent for controlled tobogganing. Across the street was a little wood, where I used to gather violets for my mother in the spring while I waited for her to wake up. Her brother Gregor — also at Camp Borden — lived downstairs with his wife Muriel ("Mike") and son Robert, who was also a year older than me. There was much fighting between Gregor and Mike. They had loud arguments that spilled out onto the front lawn. Gregor disciplined Robert, and he also disciplined me.

Two incidents when I was about three show that I desperately wanted to return to Aunt Winnie. I was snatched at the last minute from a train at the railway station downtown while my mother was shopping. I said that I was going to see Aunt Winnie. On the other occasion, Gregor found me naked at the bus stop on the busy street at the bottom of the hill. "He spanked you all the way up that hill," mother told me, in a tone that implied I deserved it. My nakedness was common. I used to take my clothes off once I got outside, returning to explain to my mother, "I put my tummy in a puddle." On one occasion, my mother watched in humiliation as a city crew dug up the street and removed a set of my clothes that were blocking the sewer.

These misdemeanours, I later saw, were the predictable result of a lack of supervision. To say that my mother was a night person hardly conveys the reality. She did her housework after we were put to bed. I can still remember the drone of the vacuum cleaner and the lurching rattle of the old wringer-washing machine as I turned over in bed, with our cat Amber stretched out beside me. After the housework she read, mostly novels, Victorian and otherwise. She liked Henry James, Jane Austen, D.H. Lawrence, Evelyn Waugh, Dostoevsky, Tolstoy, and mysteries by Agatha Christie and Dorothy L. Sayers. The rules were that we were *not* to wake her up, and we were *not* to knock on her closed bedroom door in the morning, and, when she did get up, we were *not* to speak to her until after she had her coffee. The result of this odd regimen — that seemed normal to us — was that my mother did not get up until late morning or early afternoon. Anything my sister and I decided to do on weekend and summer mornings, for better or worse, was done. We made our own bows and arrows and shot them at each other. We flipped our jackknives into the ground beside each other's bare feet, playing a game called "Stretch" (you had to stretch your foot to the place where the knife went in, without falling over). Once, we explored the storm sewers under the town streets in our Wellington boots. In winter we raced in opposite directions from the front door, barefoot in deep snow.

Once the war was over, my father was at home permanently. Yet mother's routine did not change. Since I had only seen him on his leaves until I was four, I had never really gotten to know him. As an every-two-weeks father he was uneasy with me. I'm told that once, when I was about two or three, my mother sent him outside with a sweater to put on me. He returned with the sweater, saying, "She won't let me put it on."

What I remember best and enjoyed most were my father's silly songs. Like Winnie, he enjoyed singing, and he sang well. But, unlike her, he sang tongue-in-cheek, sarcastic, or downright insulting songs. In the morning, she'd burst into, "Oh, what a beautiful morning, oh, what a beautiful day!" When he got up, he sang the army song, "Oh, how I hate to get up in the morning, oh, how I'd love to remain in bed." This was partly a dig at my mother, who in fact was still in bed. As he shaved in the morning, he used to sing other army songs, his Lions' Club songs ("Go, Lions, bite 'em, bite 'em, bite 'em"), and the popular songs of his day, such as "I've Got a Lovely Bunch of Coconuts" or "Bye, Bye, Blackbird." He especially enjoyed anti-Catholic songs:

> *When the Catholic boys come into the town*
> *The stink of their feet would knock a man down.*
> *Teeter-totter holy water, sprinkle the heretics one by one*
> *And if that won't do, we'll cut them in two*
> *And bury them under the orange and blue.*

This was especially mischievous, as he really *was* anti-Catholic. We were not allowed to play with "the kids on Duckworth Street" otherwise known as "dogans" or "mackerel snatchers." (One of them would later play hockey for the Maple Leafs.) Perhaps his most insulting songs, though, were the ones related to his own life. One, called "Filial Lament" from the '20s, went like this:

> *Hooray! Hooray! My father's going to be hung!*
> *Hooray! Hooray! The dirty son-of-a-gun,*
> *For he was very mean to me when I was very young,*
> *And now,* Thank God! *they're hanging Father!*

I have no doubt that this song raised eyebrows among the neighbours. Yet my sister and I were too young to understand, and we sang it with innocent glee.

He also made up his own songs, often about our friends or about us. These, too, were insulting. One was about my sister, who was his favourite, so much so that he teased her by calling her "Fish Face" and by hiding toys in her bed, causing nightly hysterics:

> *Oh Tina, oh Tina,*
> *You really should have seen her,*
> *Her undershirt was full of dirt*
> *And she smelled like a hyena.*

Another was about a neighbouring widow who had married twice — scandalous in Barrie at the time:

> *There's nobody nearer or dearer than Vera*
> *Who lives on the way to the Bay.*
> *She was a McCarthy, and then a Mackenzie,*
> *And now she's a Thompson they say!*

We were encouraged to sing these songs outside to anyone who would listen. He would open his blue eyes wide and profess ignorance if we asked him to sing for our friends.

My father also played the bagpipes. He had bought a set much earlier with a $100 Victory Bond his father had given him. In the summer, when he was in the mood after dinner, he would play the pipes, walking back and forth across the front lawn. Soon he attracted a long line of neighbourhood children marching behind him, as if he were a sort of Scottish Pied Piper. He didn't play in the winter, though. Mother wouldn't allow it. "Bagpipes are an outdoor sport," she would say firmly. She suggested playing them in the garage, but he never did.

128 HUNTLEY STREET, TORONTO

Until my grandmother died when I was ten, we spent Christmas at Huntley Street. I remember these occasions as magical. We used to drive down Highway 11 (Yonge Street) through immense banks of snow. My father insisted we learn the sequence of towns as we passed — Churchill, Bradford, Aurora, Richmond Hill, Thornhill, and then, Toronto. I loved the plain British food Kate cooked: leg of lamb, roast beef or chicken, potatoes of all kinds, lemon pies, cakes, and puddings. She provided three meals a day, on time, at the large mahogany table in the dining room. At last I was offered what Winnie called "a proper breakfast" of bacon and eggs and toast with marmalade. Kate, in her black-and-white uniform, served all the meals there. I still have two of Kate's aprons: short, square, white, and trimmed with lace. To call us to the enormous table she rang a five-tiered brass gong in the front hall. I don't know what eventually happened to that gong and its small wooden baton, but I remember that later it hung in the front hall of our house on Mulcaster Street in Barrie and was used by my mother to call us to dinner. I can still sing the five reverberating tones.

My grandmother would proceed ponderously down the front stairs, gripping the banister, and take her seat at the head of the table. She spoke little, if at all. Her solemn, silent presence frightened me. She had no idea how to speak to children, or perhaps was so far gone into dementia that she was not really there. I remember that my sister always thought the bacon was undercooked. She would take it around the corner into the hall and throw it out the front door, where it would be discovered by the next person to come or go.

One of the great spectacles at Huntley Street was the sight of Aunt Winnie taking a bath. Why we were allowed — perhaps invited — into the bathroom to watch her slidings and bouncings and squeals of glee I don't know. She was like a great walrus or hippo flopping about for the sheer joy of it.

Winnie c. 1939–40 at
128 Huntley Street.

An indelible memory for me is standing in the hall upstairs outside my grandmother's bedroom watching Kate brush her hair for her before bed. Her hair was grey but still thick and extremely long, falling below the seat of the chair in which she sat. Later, when I studied Gothic literature as an English student, this image of my grandmother in profile in a shadowy room came back to me. During the day, Dollie sat in the small upstairs sitting room next to her bedroom. All around the room on a ledge near the ceiling were Toby jugs, flushed and grinning in a way that frightened me. My grandmother sat in front of a fire that was encouraged by a bellows, staring into space and rubbing her eyebrows. I can't recall her ever speaking to me, though she must have.

On Christmas Eve, my sister and I would be tucked into Winnie's double bed. I later learned she spent those nights — and many others — sleeping with her mother. What I remember most about those sleepless nights is the swinging curve of headlights as cars passed below on Huntley Street. That and the photo of Queen Elizabeth, whose eyes eerily seemed to follow me around the room. Whether Winnie's sleeping with her mother began after D.A. died I don't know. Mother told us that Dollie was such a fearful soul that she spent much time gazing out the windows wringing her hands, worrying that there might be a thunderstorm. When a storm actually occurred, she was carried on her mattress into the basement where she would take a sip of brandy — the only times she drank alcohol. Winnie might have been expected to provide comfort.

Winnie always read us "'Twas the Night Before Christmas" with that special gusto of those who have not entirely left childhood behind. Our stockings in front of the unused fireplace in the empty living room were bulging in the morning. Presents were lavish. Mother said that Winnie gave me much nicer presents than she gave my sister, and more of them. I never noticed. I hope my sister didn't either, though she probably did. We spent the day playing with our new toys and games, running up and down the front and back stairs through the door that opened on to the landing. Sometimes we played a game in the perpetually empty downstairs living room, with its scratchy grey-blue horsehair sofa. We called the game Deep Purple, for some reason I've forgotten. Perhaps it was because the sheet music for that song stood on the piano. The game involved running back and forth between the old piano and the long, low footstool in front of the never-used fireplace. We stuck our fingers through the faded blue silk stretched behind the ornately scrolled back of the piano. This made a satisfying "pop!" We picked off the tiny beads that were sewn into an elaborate floral pattern on the footstool. Eventually the five tones of the gong would sound, and we would all sit down to a Dickensian Christmas turkey dinner cooked by Kate: potatoes, gravy, peas, carrots, cranberry sauce, and, for dessert, steamed pudding and Christmas crackers that exploded into magical little toys and bright paper hats. Kate, disdained as a Catholic and whispered to be a Communist, would have attended Midnight Mass the night before.

Yet I especially enjoyed Kate's company when Winnie was out of the house. I used to visit her room in the attic to look at the little treasures she kept in a glass cabinet: a carved white elephant, shells, rosaries, tiny bits of china. I used to watch her do her hair up, twisting the salt-and-pepper sections into rolls like sausages, keeping it in place with the long wire hairpins she kept in a china dish. I used to stay with her in the kitchen, watching her cook. She'd indulge me with chunks of cold lamb ridged with delicious white fat, or give me the spoon to lick after she mixed a dessert. I had begun ballet classes at age four, so I used to entertain her by "dancing" for her in large swirls and dips, while singing songs such as "I Want to Dance with the Dolly with a Hole in Her Stocking." I have no idea where the rest of the household was while I spent these long hours in the kitchen with Kate. Nor can I recall Kate's last name, though I think it was something like Denault. Servants were known only by their first names, and it is one of the frustrations of research that members of Kate's class left no school records, scrapbooks, or news clippings behind.

When I was turning six, we prolonged our Toronto Christmas visit into the New Year so I could be taken to the Royal Alexandra Theatre to see *Brigadoon* for my birthday. Perhaps my sister was thought too young to go, or perhaps it was a special treat for me. I can't recall. We almost didn't go because I had developed a fever. I was not sick, my mother ultimately decided. I was simply over-excited. The musical at the Royal Alex was my first experience of stage performance. From the moment the curtain opened to reveal the "Scotch mist" — actually dry ice — swirling about in the heather, I was enthralled. Winnie kept the memory alive for years afterwards, teaching me the songs and frolicking around, dancing to them with her small hands waving to the beat:

> *The mist of May is in the gloamin',*
> *And all the clouds are holdin' still.*
> *So take my hand and we'll go roamin'*
> *Through the heather on the hill.*

Merry folk prancing about in tartans, the yearnings of courtship, fake Scottish brogues, thatched cottages — this was the Scotland she taught me to love. Much later I made several trips to Scotland, and found it nothing like this fantasy, though I loved it for different reasons.

We were sometimes put out in the fenced garden to play. I hated the damp musty smell there and the sense of being caged by the green picket fence. I was almost afraid of the strange potted jade plants with their fat, round, shiny leaves like dark green Chiclets. In one photo of me in the garden, dressed impeccably in a smocked white dress with puffed sleeves and a large bow in my hair, my face looks like a thunderstorm. It seemed to me that there was nothing to do in that dank patch of grass with no trees. Visiting the place recently, the sight of what is left of that same green fence, faded and rotten now, much of it fallen over, made me shiver.

33

ROYALTY

Aunt Winnie knew everything it was possible to know about the Royal Family. She knew even the names and ranks of the most obscure duchesses and barons. She kept an entire scrapbook dedicated to news clippings about the royals. She especially admired Queen Elizabeth. Elizabeth was Scottish and had lived in Glamis Castle — major points in her favour. She also delighted in clothes and elaborate hats, another point in her favour. She was even, like Winnie, "well-upholstered," as my mother, who took pride in her slim figure, used to say. For Winnie, the comings and goings of the Royal Family — no matter how inconsequential — were matters of intense interest. I don't think she read newspapers, but she must have scanned them for headlines and photos of royalty.

I recall spending hours and hours with Winnie, from about age six to age ten, in the upstairs sitting room at 128 Huntley Street. We would proceed slowly through these articles, while Dollie sat nearby, rubbing her eyebrows. "Look at Princess Alexandra of Kent in this picture," Winnie would say. "Isn't her dress pretty? She's opening a hospital, helping all the sick little girls and boys."

"Look at the Royal Family on the balcony!" she'd exclaim. "There's our Scottish lass (Queen Elizabeth) and Bertie (King George VI), and look at the dear little princesses waving to the crowd!"

"That's Louis, the first Earl of Mountbatten of Burma," she'd explain. It was as if he and the others in her scrapbook were mythological creatures like the gods and goddesses in my favourite book, *D'Aulaires' Book of Greek Myths*. I preferred the Greek myths because the people in them were scamps. By comparison, the Royal Family, as presented by Winnie, were impossibly good. I couldn't imagine them playing the kind of pranks my sister and I did, such as leading our bewildered granny to open the linen cupboard door so that Kate's ironing board would fall out.

A highlight for Winnie had been the births of the royal princesses, Elizabeth and Margaret Rose. She had endless photos of them. Their births had been major events in her life. She would have been twenty-five when Elizabeth, whom she sometimes called by her nickname Lilibet, was born, and twenty-nine when Margaret Rose (Winnie always included her middle name) appeared. By then, Winnie's own friends had married. Some of them were having babies too. Winnie was at exactly the age when she might have been having babies herself, but she was still playing the role of debutante. The year Princess Elizabeth was born, Winnie presented a bouquet of roses to the guest of honour at the St. Andrew's Ball, Viscountess Willingdon, wife of the governor general of Canada, in the Crystal Ballroom of the King Edward Hotel in Toronto. Winnie was written up among the many guests in the paper the next day as "wearing a pretty French frock, the tight bodice of iridescent sequins, with long pearl streamers from the shoulders. The full skirt was done with a design in roses. Silver slippers were worn, also the Cameron tartan, on the shoulder a Cairngorm brooch, and bandeau."

Though I could not realize it at the time, the two royal princesses were her surrogate children. There were photos of them as babies, held by their mother, draped in white lace shawls. Later, there were pictures of them in their little tweed coats and bonnets, standing about the grounds of Balmoral or Windsor Castle or the Royal Lodge. They didn't look to me as if they were having much fun. Winnie was ecstatic about them. "Look at that darling blue coat on little Lilibet! And Princess Margaret Rose! Hers is a rosy colour, just like her name! Isn't she adorable!"

Looking back, I think that Winnie made a rather bizarre connection between the two royal princesses and me and my sister. This was aided by the fact that my name, Elspeth, was the Scottish form of Elizabeth, and that there was roughly the same age difference between my sister and me as there was between them. For her, I think, we represented a sort of rerun of the childhoods of the princesses. I remember being confused about this. One thing was clear, though: royalty was the most important thing in the world, and the more my sister and I resembled these two princesses, the better our lives would be.

Princess Elizabeth and Prince Philip visited Canada in 1951. Surely Winnie must have been in at least one of the crowds that greeted them. Yet I don't remember. What I do remember is Winnie showing me pictures of "our plucky little Princess" as she wore different outfits for the various places she visited in Canada. I remember one in which she is wearing a full skirt, blouse, and neckerchief as she whirls around in a square dance with Prince Philip, probably in Calgary or Edmonton.

At about the same time, Winnie wrote to Lady Hermione, the wife of Donald Cameron of Lochiel. Cameron had just died, and Winnie, in her avid scans of newspapers for news of royalty and others that mattered to her, had read the obituary. She promptly wrote a letter of sympathy on 19 October 1951 to Lady Hermione on behalf of Dollie, "who is unable to do so."

This will be a great loss to the Clan Cameron. You may remember that during your visit to Toronto, Canada, with Lochiel many years ago, my father the late Donald A. Cameron & my mother had the pleasure of entertaining you. I was a child at the time but I do remember Mr. Archie Cameron very well, as he stayed with us several times while on a motor trip through Scotland in 1935. I called at Achnacarry. The factor very kindly allowed me to see the outside of the Castle & the beautiful grounds. This was of tremendous interest to me.

I must tell you too, that I met your eldest son Donald & your daughter Marion, at the Caledonian Ball in London the year of the Coronation. I was there both to see it & to be presented at one of the courts.

Again may I extend deepest sympathy from all my family. We feel we have lost a great chief & one who will always be remembered.

Yours sincerely,
Winifred Cameron

When the Donald Cameron of Lochiel my grandfather had entertained in Toronto in 1913 died, his eldest son, also Donald, became the 26th chieftain of the Clan Cameron. He left his lucrative accounting job in London, donned his kilt, as his father had done, and moved into Achnacarry Castle. His wife, Margaret "Margot" Gathorne-Hardy, was a niece of the third Earl of Cranbrook. Eventually they would have four children. The eldest son, of course, would be named Donald. Once installed in Achnacarry Castle, the affable 26th Cameron of Lochiel welcomed any Cameron who appeared on his doorstep. That eventually included Winnie, and, much later, my sister, and even later, me.

34

VISITS TO WINNIE

Once I was able to insist on seeing Winnie, and she was able to convince my parents that I could go, I visited her in Toronto. The ardour with which I had propelled myself to the train station and the bus stop at the foot of our hill had not waned. I remember taking the bus all the way down Highway 11 on to Yonge Street. Or perhaps that was later, and Winnie drove me to Huntley Street and then back to Barrie. The earliest proof of these visits is a couple of postcards I wrote to my family from Toronto. The earliest of these is dated 1950, when I would have been seven.

I remember my delight at being with Winnie. I was her "Pigeon Pie." She was my "Win Pin" or "Windy" — a reference to her burping. We'd play cards, sit and talk, or go for walks around Rosedale. I recall one occasion when she took me to Britnell's Book Shop and allowed me to choose any book I wanted. I chose *Cinderella*, a lavishly illustrated edition. I also remember my joy at returning to the sonorous dinner gong and Kate's meals, especially her "proper breakfasts."

Winnie with the author as a child at Rosie Point, Shanty Bay, c. 1949.

I also have a vague memory of going with her to visit her "great friend" Alice Heighington. Alice, I now realize, had been Alice Johnson in Winnie's social group in the 1920s. Alice had married Captain Wilfrid Heighington, though I have no recollection of meeting him. Perhaps she was a widow. All I recall is a large, boisterous woman with fly-away dark hair greeting us at the top of a long flight of steps and inviting us in for tea.

In between my visits to Winnie, I received postcards from her. Often they were pictures of the animals from Beatrix Potter stories. Later they were paintings, or portraits of the Royal Family. Only two of these addressed to Miss Elspeth Cameron remain. How they got

saved I don't know. Did my mother put them in with Winnie's
scrapbooks later? Did I save them myself? One, a Margaret Temple
illustration of four teddy bears playing at the beach, called *King of
the Castle*, was sent a few days before my seventh birthday in 1950:

> Read about Princesses. Where is that letter you were writing me?
> Are you going to have a party on your birthday? How did you
> like being back at school? Write soon — Much love to you & T
> — Winnie

The other was sent in mid-January 1952, when I was nine. I would
have just seen her at Christmas — the second-last Christmas we spent
in Toronto. The card is a copy of Degas's famous painting *Les Danseuses*:

> Darling P:
> Am lost without you — sent the book to you yesterday — so be
> sure to write. Has T. found her sleigh yet? How are Ted & Amb?
> Love to all of you.
> Winnie
> XXXXX

"Ted" was Teddy, our black cocker spaniel who was incompletely
housetrained and chased every vehicle that passed as if it threatened
his very life. "Amb" was Amber, my big orange cat, who slept with his
head on my pillow. I often fell out of my bed from edging away from
the heat he generated — not that that stopped me from having him
there with his mighty purring. Like Winnie, I loved animals. I can't
recall when it was, but I joined in her grief when her dear old tabby,
Timothy, was poisoned by a neighbour. It was one of my earliest
insights into the nature of evil.

35

ANOTHER DEATH

Dollie drifted into death in February 1953. The official cause was "hardening of the arteries," which, despite my mother's long explanations, I could not understand. Today we would blame cholesterol, and would possibly insert stents to treat it. Dollie was eighty-five. I was ten. For some reason I don't recall, my mother took only my sister to the interment in Port Elgin. I didn't especially resent this. I was too busy in Grade 5, skipping Double Dutch at recess, and racing about in the fine spring air at Codrington School.

Upon returning from the interment, mother told Gothic tales of the creepy Cameron mausoleum in which various Camerons — including D.A., his parents, three of his sisters, and two of his brothers — lay in closed drawers. Only one drawer was left, she said, and that would be for Winnie. She and my sister complained that Dollie had been put into her drawer wearing a diamond brooch. "Such a waste!" Mother said. I had known my grandmother, yet didn't know her at all. I did not grieve, though I played up my "loss" for sympathy at school. I had no curiosity then about the mausoleum, though I liked saying the word. That would change.

Dollie's death precipitated many unwelcome changes for Winnie. Now she and my father would inherit half of whatever was left in the National Trust fund set up for Dollie by D.A. They would also split the furnishings and decorations at 128 Huntley Street. I recall the visit to the house, during which Winnie and my father — backed by my mother — went from room to room discussing who would have what. All I remember is the thick tension in the air. I wanted desperately to get back home to Barrie.

The whole city of Toronto was changing quickly then. Suburbs were springing up in every direction except south on the lake. Access to the city — especially from Barrie and cottage country to the north and Oshawa to the east — was dramatically increased once Highway 401 was extended from Scarborough to the east in 1947 and Highway 400 completed to the north in 1952. The Toronto Bypass, linking Highway 27 to the 401, soon followed. Mount Pleasant Road, from north Toronto into the downtown at Bloor Street, swallowed up Huntley Street in order to facilitate access to the downtown by 1950, and the Rapid Transit Subway opened in 1954. I vividly recall being taken to Toronto specifically to ride that futuristic contraption that frightened me by going so fast. With all these "improvements" came a vast increase of pace and traffic. The house on Huntley Street, now 128 Mount Pleasant Road, still stands between South Drive and Meredith Crescent, across from the Rosedale Presbyterian Church. It is derelict and forlorn. By 1960 the 401 would speed traffic into, out of, and past the city from one end of the province to the other.

Other changes occurred in a city whose population had now swelled with the inclusion of suburban areas, annexed sections like York, and smaller communities like Weston. Toronto's population had grown from about half a million in 1921 to nearly seven million in 1951. Waves of immigrants surged into the city in the wake of the war. Over a quarter of the city's population in the 1951 census were *not* ethnically British. The social barriers that had protected a British and insular life for families like the Camerons had broken down. Women, many of whom had taken on men's jobs during the war, or like my mother had trained to become secretaries, nurses, or teachers, entered the work force. Women like Winnie had become anachronisms, passed over in the backwaters of a river that was flowing in a different direction. It would never have occurred to Winnie to find a job, apart from her volunteer work answering the phone in the gift shop of the Princess Margaret Hospital. Had she understood the nature of cancer she never would have gone into the place, but she was attracted to the institution's name.

Fashions, too, had changed. After the short-skirted military suits with padded shoulders of wartime had passed, wasp waists and full ballerina skirts with crinolines appeared. This was the glamorous era of Dior and Balmain. These fashions could not have been less flattering to Winnie. Though her "buzzom," as she called it, had been a problem in the straight silhouettes of the '20s, those loose, straight dresses concealed the fact that Winnie didn't really have a waist. The new fashion of tight skirts with cinch belts worn with blouses or sweater sets would draw attention to any waist that had expanded. Her body, beneath the "buzzom," was by then more or less a stout tube. On the other hand, my mother's petite, slight figure was shown to perfection in the '50s, and she set to sewing dresses, suits, and even coats for herself and us, as my sister and I reached adolescence.

Huntley Street had been rented, so it was let go. D.A. believed that owning real estate was a poor investment, and I was later told that he sold off several acres in today's affluent Leaside. It was a given that Winnie would not leave Rosedale. She found a lower duplex at 80 Elm Avenue in a house (now gone) that had once belonged to Robert C.H. Cassels, the father of one of her beaux. It would be the first time in her life that she had to cook, clean, and cope with laundry. She was fifty-two, and she remained indignant for the rest of her life that she was expected to do these chores. She bought herself a grey-blue Chevrolet Bel Air. Oblivious to the dramatic restructuring of Toronto and its province, she did her best to maintain life as she had known it in her twenties. Even on the new highways, she drove at the forty mph speed that was the limit a couple of decades earlier. Mother said she was more likely to cause an accident than anyone speeding.

Winnie had visited us often at Dundonald Street, mainly at Easter and Thanksgiving. She took it for granted that we — her only family — would welcome her on holidays. She would drive up to Barrie, her car laden with gifts for me and my sister. My mother would complain long before she arrived, saying things like, "Donald, do we have to have her *every* holiday?" My father's response to this was to quietly leave the room, or pick up a book. He never, ever raised his voice. Now I see that, much as he disliked Winnie himself, he considered it his duty to have her visit.

Aunt Winnie was as much a morning person as my mother was a night person. She often cited, "Early to bed, early to rise, makes a man healthy, wealthy, and wise," as if it were one of the Ten Commandments. Winnie grew sleepy and began yawning at around nine p.m., then my father at 10:30, just as my mother was really coming to life. Winnie's fatigue came on suddenly. She would move ponderously, without undressing or washing, from the small living room into my parents' bedroom and lie down on my mother's bed. "She never asked. She just disappeared in there," my mother would later tell me indignantly. "Eventually, your father would go off to his bed in there too. I'd look in, and there would be the two of them, sound asleep on our twin beds. I used to sleep on the sofa."

Winnie could not resist commenting on my mother's habits. She never did understand that she should not talk to my mother until after she'd had her coffee. She would accost her as soon as she appeared out of her bedroom to berate her for neglecting us. "Well! This is a fine time to get up, Bertah!" she might say with a merry laugh. Or, she would say things like, "All the girls had for breakfast was a *brownie*! *Standing up*! They should have a proper breakfast!" She would go on to speak proudly of the "proper breakfast" she had given us when we last visited her and how much we'd enjoyed it. Since she would have been lying in wait for my mother since about seven, she had her speeches thoroughly prepared, and they were delivered in a rushed and panicky voice.

I always loved Aunt Winnie's visits. Because of those first eighteen months with her at Huntley Street, I was her favourite. My sister didn't have a chance. "She always arrived with a big present for you — an expensive doll, or toy — and some little thing for your sister," Mother said. Winnie seemed to light up our household: she laughed merrily, gave me hugs, and sat still to talk with me. Mother always zipped around. I rarely saw her sit down. Winnie got up when we got up, and spent hours with us playing card games like Fish, Snap, or Old Maid, roaring with laughter when she drew the Old Maid card. We could always tell when she'd drawn it by the puckish smile on her face. She made being an Old Maid seem like something enviable.

36

"OUR BRAVE LITTLE QUEENIE"

Only three months after my grandmother's death, Princess Elizabeth was crowned Queen Elizabeth II. Winnie was ecstatic. She must have grieved for her mother as Dollie descended into senility, rather than at her death. She showed no signs of mourning. Nor did my father, for that matter.

When Elizabeth was crowned in June 1953, when I was ten, Winnie's excitement around the news coverage overflowed. Her memory of her trips to London for George V's Silver Jubilee and her own presentation to George VI and Queen Elizabeth flooded back. "There's our brave little Queenie. She's wearing the Order of the Garter! Isn't she lovely?" she exclaimed over news photos with me. "Look, they're on the balcony of Buckingham Palace! See them waving?" Winnie was not unusual in viewing the coronation as a major event in Canadian life. Canada was still essentially colonial then. I remember my teacher a short time later in Grade 8 showing us with pride all the red places on the map of the world, and explaining that these were all countries in the British Empire. "The sun never sets on the British Empire," he said. "Britain is the crossroads of the world."

For the great event, our class was shown the procession into Westminster Abbey and the coronation on television. That magical technological device had just appeared in North America the year before, though it would be almost a decade before my parents succumbed. I can recall the awe I felt at actually seeing the whole event at the very time it was happening. Having been prepared by Winnie for years to grasp the significance of the Royal Family, I knew who all the characters were. I recognized the Queen Mother and Princess Margaret easily. I knew that those children standing between them were Prince Charles and Princess Anne. I even knew that the Duke of Gloucester was Elizabeth's uncle. The golden chariot that took the new queen from Westminster Abbey to Buckingham Palace was just like Cinderella's in the expensive book Winnie had bought me. The huge procession with group after group of military men and women — even Mounties on their black horses — was like a fabled spectacle.

Our class was given glossy illustrated booklets about the coronation. I still have mine. It explains the symbolism of the orb, the sceptre, and the various jewels in various crowns, all to impart to us the meaning of this momentous political and religious occasion. Winnie's take on the occasion had nothing to do with religion and little to do with politics. She had a vague sense of the divine right of kings, but could never have defined it, or even named it. To her it was more that kings *were* divine. It was the grandeur of the occasion, the sumptuous clothing all were wearing, the sheer monetary value of all those jewels, all that ermine, all those velvet- and silk-embroidered robes, that enthralled her. Westminster Abbey was a fairytale stage, not a place of worship. She especially liked the "darling little page boys," who perhaps reminded her of my father as a boy. Then there were all the caparisoned horses, the Yeomen of the Guard, the bagpipe regiments, and the soldiers from Australia, New Zealand, and Canada — even "the darkies" as she called them, suppressing her instinct to call them something else, from South Africa, Ceylon, Pakistan, and India — marching to celebrate their place in the British Empire.

Winnie was not unusual in admiring things British, but she *was* unusual in the degree to which she idealized the Queen and Prince Philip. She even knew the names of each of the "darling corgis," especially "Susan," who had been given to Elizabeth on her eighteenth birthday. She especially liked photos of the Royal Family with their pack of corgis waddling about at Balmoral Castle in Scotland. There the Queen wore tartan pleated skirts like the ones Winnie often wore, and unbecoming kerchiefs tied under her chin "against the Scotch mist," as Winnie called it. I saw so many photos of the Royals at Balmoral that I felt as if I had been there.

37

THE ROYAL
WEDDING

I continued to visit Winnie after she moved into 80 Elm Avenue, sometimes with my sister, but mostly on my own. On one of these visits she took me to a movie theatre to see *The Royal Wedding*. This was the marriage of Princess Elizabeth to Prince Philip, Duke of Edinburgh, which had taken place years earlier on 20 November 1947 when Elizabeth was twenty-one and Philip was twenty-six. I was probably ten, and it might have been my first visit to Elm Avenue after Winnie moved in 1953. I wrote a letter home, which my mother later gave to Winnie, who kept it with her muddle of papers. Judging by the content — poorly printed and full of misspelled words — Winnie at least partly dictated it, ensuring I make it clear that Mother did not feed me properly:

Dear Family;

Yesterday we went to Osler Park and had lunch there. At half past three p.m. Winnie took me to the movie. It was called Royal Wedding. There was a lot of dancing in it. Once a man danced on the ceiling. Hope Tina bought Teddy some Pard [dog food] with the quarter Winnie gave her. In Royal Wedding I saw Princess Elizabeth waving to the crowed [sic].

I am eating everything and am finished my pills. I have breakfast at 8 every morning. I have gained two pounds.

Winnie wants too [sic] know if you phoned Miss Wilson. Are Ted and Amber missing me.

> Love and Kisses
> To you all
> P[idge]. |XX|XX|XX|XX|XX|
> B. D. Ti. Te. A. [Bertah Donald Tina Teddy Amber]

I think Winnie experienced the Royal Wedding as if it were her own. She would have been forty-six at the time, and had not given up the pleasure of having admirers, nor would she for a long time to come.

I don't have any idea how long these visits of mine lasted. I don't think my parents would have let me miss school, but there were Easter holidays and long weekends. I can remember still the pleasant musty, perfumey smell of her apartment on Elm Avenue.

38

THE CABIN

Aunt Winnie felt entitled to summers "by the lake." She was determined to maintain the mythical rhythm of seasonal life her father had established: Toronto for the Season, Lake Simcoe for the summer. Parklands was gone, the Cameron half sold to the Holdens a year after Winnie's father died. This, as my mother often pointed out, had been done without retaining even a small section of lakeshore property to be used by the Camerons in future. "But then, Winnie didn't have the sense of a *fly*," she'd add, "and your father was too young, and Dollie would have been too passive."

Soon after Winnie took up the apartment on Elm Avenue, she rented a log cabin in Shanty Bay for July and August so she could be "by the lake." It bore the same relationship to her Rosedale apartment as Marie Antoinette's "Petit Hameau" bore to Versailles. Just as the French queen, bored with the formality of palace life, frolicked around dressed as a shepherdess at her little cottage, Winnie left the Toronto Season for a more relaxed life at what was called "The

Winnie at
The Cabin,
Shanty Bay,
late '50s.

Cabin." Like the Victorians, she covered all the furniture at Elm Avenue with dust sheets before she left. Then she, like Marie Antoinette, dressed the part at her rustic refuge. Winnie wore girlish sundresses, ill-advised Bermuda shorts with halter or strapless tops, and a bathing suit with rubber cap and 1920s rubber slippers against Lake Simcoe's stones. Given her ample figure, and the hourglass fashions of the 1950s, even I could see that these outfits were silly. I remember one of her favourite combinations: turquoise Bermuda shorts and an elasticized, strapless peach top, stretched to the limit over her vast "buzzom." She liked to sit in the sun, painting her nails with Revlon's "Persian Melon," or leafing through *Vogue* or *Harper's Bazaar*. From time to time she used to hold up a picture to show us how much one or the other of us resembled some model. This made us howl with laughter. Our own forays into fashion were yet to come.

The Cabin, perched above a woody cliff over the lake, was approached across a tiny bridge that reminded Winnie of *Brigadoon*, still her favourite musical. It must have been an original pioneer home. It was made of logs that formed the walls inside as well as outside, and the hewn grey-brown logs crisscrossed at the corners. A central fieldstone fireplace heated the space inside. There were five small rooms: a living area, a simple little kitchen with a table beside a window looking over the lake, and two small bedrooms, with a minuscule bathroom wedged in between. It was furnished in a plain, rustic manner. The window frames outside were painted a cheerful red. At the back was a clothesline on which we hung towels and bathing suits when we changed in and out of our suits outside. I don't recall any laundry, but Winnie must have done some, since she took the place for July and August every summer. Perhaps not, since we bathed and washed our hair once a week in the lake. She might have thought that laundry was unnecessary.

The Cabin was part of the Wilson estate. Old, widowed Mr. Wilson and his English second wife lived in the Big House up closer to the road. There was a green sward for lawn bowling and a tennis court near the Big House. Old Mr. Wilson had four daughters, all of whom were roughly the age of my parents. Each of these daughters had a cottage on the estate, all in wooded areas hidden from the others and from The Cabin. Each daughter was married with three children, except the youngest, who had only one son with her second husband, a Scandinavian man. My father used to refer to Mr. Wilson as "Foxy-Four-Eyes." He thought that the crafty old gentleman was supporting some of the summer doings of the Wilson family with the exorbitant rent he charged Winnie for The Cabin. I remember seeing her write out monthly $500 cheques for the place, an enormous sum for the early 1950s, equivalent to approximately $4,500 today.

From the time I was ten until I was sixteen, my sister and I spent most of every summer there with Winnie. I suppose now that it suited my parents to be free of us for the summer. I didn't miss them, and I guess they didn't miss us. Certainly we had a wonderful time. We played games like Kick the Can or Red Rover, and went out in the old green rowboat. We were in and out of the water all day, from the first skinny dip before breakfast to the last one at night before putting on our pyjamas. In between, we mostly wore our bathing suits. I remember days when we never changed out of them. The Wilson kids had a raft anchored about thirty feet from shore, and we dived from it with them. I recall dozing off on that raft, feeling the sun warm my back as I watched the bass and perch curving through the sunlight-streaked water below. On rainy days we played board games wih the Wilson kids in the Bricks, a room at the side of the Big House.

Winnie had her swims regularly at mid-morning and mid-afternoon. In her bathing cap covered with bright rubber flowers, she inched into the water from shore, oohing and ahhing at the cold, and exclaiming "Oh, *Bud*!" as the stones pricked her feet despite her rubber bathing shoes. She had massive thighs, a "buzzom" that overflowed her bathing costumes (as she called them), and tiny feet in her bathing shoes. She shrieked and laughed as she finally immersed herself in the water. She floundered around a bit, swam a few breast strokes up and down near the dock, calling out "Oh, *Bud*!" or "Oh, *Boy*!" every so often, then emerged from the water dripping like a happy walrus.

She always sat on the dock in a reclining chair when we were swimming. She took her responsibilities with us very seriously. She especially enjoyed watching us do duck dives, in or out of bathing suits, our little bottoms thrust out of the water just before we plunged down. To her the bottom was a humourous aspect of the human anatomy — as it was to my father, who used to exclaim "Pants! Ha, ha!" every so often. She laughed heartily even to hear the word "bottom," and simply roared when we did duck dives.

The food was simple, but there was always lots of it. Winnie believed that our thin frames indicated that we were being starved at home. She took it as her mission to fatten us up. We'd sit at the tiny kitchen table, looking out of the window to the lake. Instead of grace she would say, "Pin back your hair, MacDuff, and dig in." Usually for dinner she would put a roast in the oven, which would provide many meals of cold lamb, chicken, or beef to follow. Lunch was simple sandwiches. She always stewed her strawberries because they were "too acid." We were provided with lots of cookies, store-bought cakes — especially pound cake — and the ever-present British Taverners fruit drops. We disdained the sliced tongue she relished. Otherwise, we were perfectly satisfied with the "good plain food," though my sister was fussier than I was. If she asked Winnie what was for lunch or dinner, Winnie would laugh and say, "Boiled mouse!" After a while, my sister realized that it was only a joke.

When we got the inevitable scrapes and cuts, she administered bright red Mercurochrome from a bottle with a glass dropper, and applied bandaids. When mosquito bites were unbearably itchy, she made a solution of water and baking soda and dabbed it on them. These remedies were long outdated — especially Mercurochome, which would be taken off the market due to its mercury content in 1998 — but they worked.

Now that I've raised children of my own, I am deeply ashamed that we took advantage of what we knew was her concern for our safety. As we got older and more devious, we used to "hide" on the roof of The Cabin, climbing up the logs that crossed at each corner. Eventually Winnie would miss us, emerge from The Cabin, stand right below us, and call us at ever-increasing volume. Eventually our giggles could no longer be stifled. We knew she would be relieved, not angry.

Later on, and more deviously, we would hide under the raft, in the air space between the old oil drums that held it up, until she missed us, called everywhere, and finally came down to the dock to see if we were there. Once she became frantic, we would emerge, laughing. After these teasing games, she would threaten to call our parents. Since that would mean driving into the village to use the phone at the store, we knew these threats were hollow.

When we were bored, we visited up and down the road to the village. Our favourites were the Kortrights and the Rossers. Dr. Francis "Frank" Kortright — who in 1979 would establish the Kortright Centre for Conservation in Kleinberg, north of Toronto — had a large speedboat. He enjoyed taking us for rides in his boat, letting us steer. He used to cut the motor far out in the lake and give us cigarettes to smoke — a major adventure. The Rossers — Lee and his wife, Bobby — had moved to Barrie in the late '50s when Mr. Rosser became head of Mansfield Rubber, beside Highway 400 at the south end of Barrie. The Rossers were American and proud of it, which meant that my parents had an uneasy relationship with them. (I now realize that this was partly because Mansfield Rubber was one of the branch plants quickly lining Highway 400 that were undermining Canadian manufacturing.) Mother used to imitate their broad Midwestern accents — "Y'all," "cute," and "darling" were staples of their vocabulary. The house they designed along Shanty Bay Road bore no resemblance to the British structures beside them. Possibly inspired by Frank Lloyd Wright, their house was a one-storey structure with many windows and much wood, and a central stone fireplace that opened on two sides and heated all the rooms off it. The Rossers, who had no children, travelled widely, especially to Hawaii. They used to bring me a menu from each of the exotic restaurants they went to. I pored over these as if they were poetry. Their house featured many Hawaiian paintings of partly naked women and other mementos that Mother would make fun of. When we visited the Rossers, we were always greeted with American friendliness and compliments about our cute swimsuits or darling ponytails. We soon learned not to stop in after lunch because Bobby was "down at the lake." Much later, I figured she was probably tanning nude.

The village store was a special place for us. Once we understood that Winnie had credit there, we used to walk up to the store — a good two miles or so — and stock up on potato chips, chocolate bars, and Cokes, which we would consume on the way back. "Charge it to Miss Winifred Cameron," we would say. When Winnie eventually realized from her bills what was happening she told us to stop it, but, without any consequences, we continued to make our trips to the store.

Occasionally, our parents came out to The Cabin for a swim. Winnie would tell them of our various misdemeanours. Mother would tell us to stop whatever they were, but we soon discovered that there were no consequences with her either. These summers, with other children to play with, swimming at any time, an endless supply of treats, and an aunt who was never really angry with us, were a child's dream. If Winnie were alive today, I would thank her over and over for giving us such summers, so much better than the camps most of our friends went to.

When I was twelve, I was sent to one such camp on an island in Parry Sound called Wahcahmie. I was miserably homesick, so homesick the director sent for my mother. She and my sister drove all the way there in our landlord's Rolls-Royce. Their visit helped me turn a corner. Soon I was known as "The Garbage Can," as I finished what the other girls left on their plates. That year I grew a foot taller, reaching my full height of five-foot-eight at age thirteen. I joyfully learned to water ski and to play the ukulele. Yet I missed all my family, especially Winnie. In my first letter home, on tiny child's stationery that pictured golliwogs and donkeys, I asked my sister how the cats were, and told her she would love the director's "little spaniel Goldie, [who] jumps in after you when you go in swimming." To my father I wrote, "Still haven't recovered from the [goodbye] kiss you gave me." I wrote to Winnie, "I am feeling fine. I will write later as I haven't much space. I didn't get to sleep till 2:00 a.m. ... as our cabin was an uproar last night. Love, Pidgie." In another letter home, I reported that I "got Winpin's letter. Thank her very much for me. It is so nice to get mail." The following year, I was back at The Cabin.

39

"SEE THE BROAD HIGHWAY IN YOUR CHEVROLET"

Winnie loved cars, and loved driving them. She had been taught in the old family Auburn at Parklands by the family's chauffeur. As with almost everything, Winnie locked into place the things she learned in her youth and did not change them. Her driving remained the same in the 1960s as it had been in the 1920s. Her maximum speed was still around forty miles an hour. This had served well enough in those days. It was sufficient for the roads back and forth between Toronto and Lake Simcoe. Highway 27, then a one-lane highway that curved through farms with their livestock, crops, barns, and silos, or Highway 11, the extension of Yonge Street, which poked its way though Thornhill, Richmond Hill, Aurora, Bradford, and Churchill to Barrie, were two-lane roads. Once Highway 400 between Barrie and Toronto and the 401, the many-laned bypass across the north of Toronto, were completed in the early 1950s, the speed limit soared from a leisurely pace to sixty miles an hour. Winnie did not feel safe driving faster than forty, so she didn't. My mother used to say, "No one expects *anyone* to drive that slowly." Certainly Mother didn't. I was present on several occasions when she talked her way out of speeding tickets by asking the officer if he knew her husband, D.S.F. Cameron, who was on the Barrie Police Commission.

When we were at The Cabin, going for a drive was one of Winnie's favourite pastimes. Usually that meant she was headed to one of the antique stores in towns such as Craigleith near Shanty Bay, and that we would stop for ice cream cones somewhere along the way. As she drove, Winnie would sing. She would already have sung "Oh, What a Beautiful Morning" from *Oklahoma*. Her repertoire was almost completely hits from Broadway musicals: "Some Enchanted Evening," "Shall We Dance," "I Could Have Danced All Night," and, of course, most of the songs from *Brigadoon*. She was also fond of belting out Scottish songs like "My Bonnie Lies Over the Ocean," "Roamin' in the Gloamin'," or "You Take the High Road." She sang in tune and had a strong voice. She swayed to the music as if she were dancing. I can see now that she was reliving the dances of her youth: those foxtrots and waltzes had been upstaged by musicals, and the Scottish ballads were sometimes used as dance music too. At the same time, she conveyed an ideal world where life was carefree and filled with fun and costume, a world where romance did not involve sex or childbirth or the necessity of compromising.

Her cars were always Chevrolets. Why, I don't know. Perhaps she was influenced somehow by the McLaughlin family in Oshawa, who first manufactured the popular McLaughlin car, and later changed the company name to General Motors. Probably someone told her that these were good cars, and like so much else, she stuck to her early convictions. The car I remember best was her pastel blue Chevrolet Bel Air. That was the car she first had at The Cabin. I have good reason to remember this because I learned to drive in it. I was so eager to drive, in those days before automatic gears, that I began "practising" in Winnie's car at age thirteen. It was parked in the large open field of long grass on the other side of the little bridge that led to The Cabin.

I used to take the keys and jerkily back the car up a few feet, then stop, change into first gear, and drive it back into place. Sometimes Winnie was unaware of my "practising." Other times, she heard the car and came running across the bridge shouting in a high-pitched, hysterical voice, "Pidgie, get out of the car!" — despite the fact that, by then, I was usually already out of the car.

At both The Cabin and Elm Street, Winnie listened to CFRB Radio. I recall her "arguments" with the cantankerous Gordon Sinclair, who — among other things — opposed the singing of "God Save the Queen" in Canada. "Oh, *Bud*!" she'd exclaim. "That's *bilge-water*!" Perhaps because Sinclair was Scottish and had served on reserve in the 48th Highlanders during the Great War, she'd forgive him and ready herself for the next bout the following day. The station featured a recurring jingle advertising Chevrolet cars, and Winnie loved singing it as she puttered along in her Bel Air:

> *See the broad highway*
> *In your Chev-ro-let*
> *The Rockies way out west*
> *Are calling you.*

> *See the broad highway*
> *In your Chev-ro-let*
> *Where fields of waving wheat*
> *Pass in review.*

"The broad highway" would have resonated for her, since one of the few books she read was Jeffrey Farnol's *The Broad Highway* (1910). It was a romantic historical novel of adventure on the road, based on his childhood in England — the kind of book my mother called "claptrap."

Winnie replaced the old Bel Air with another Chevy: a splendid turquoise-and-white two-tone Impala. It was an iconic luxury car.

It had more trim and more chrome than the Bel Air, and a sleeker body. Like the Bel Air it was a two-door that looked like a convertible without actually being one. My father just rolled his eyes. We all knew why. How could she afford it? She must be "dipping into her capital."

Between songs, Winnie was given to affectionate nonsense directed at her two "chicken pies." "Fuddy-buddy was a bum, I know, yes sir-*ee*!" That's as close as I can come to transcribing one of her favourites. No one could have doubted the love with which these illogical outbursts were voiced. She often called me "Pigeon Pie" or "Peachy" — variations on Pidge. After she saw *South Pacific*, she called me and my sister "honey bun," from the line "A hundred and one pounds of fun, that's my little honey bun." One of the songs she made up for the two of us was:

> Barrie on the bum, Barrie on the bum,
> Me-oh-my I love my Pidg-eon.
> Barrie on the B, Barrie on the B,
> Me-oh-my I love my Tee-Tee.

She radiated good humour and a delight in life. Looking back, I would say she was the merriest person I ever knew.

She was an ideal person to deal with adolescent — or pre-adolescent — girls. Her inner age was much the same. Like us, she loved sweets, and there were always plenty around: Taverners fruit drops and Laura Secord chocolates. She played her popular music all day on the radio. In those days before rock and roll transformed music and life itself, she was happy to listen to songs of adolescent yearning, such as Perry Como's 1953 hit "No Other Love Have I," or "Old Cape Cod" by Patti Page, or Rosemary Clooney's "Mangos," both 1957 favourites. She would play cards with us for hours, even though we'd moved on from Fish and Old Maid to Canasta. She allowed us to experiment with her makeup, which consisted of Elizabeth Arden face powder applied with a soft peach puff with a peach satin bow, a couple of lipsticks in peach or pink colours, and blue eyeshadow that she almost never wore. I hate to think of the sight I must have been emerging from her dark bedroom into the strong summer sunlight. The other kids laughed, but I didn't care. She never really got angry with us. She never punished us for anything. I learned to discipline myself a bit from the sheer affection I had for her.

Occasionally Winnie had friends visiting at The Cabin. I recall the red-haired Jean Macpherson arriving for weekends. Like all of Aunt Winnie's "great friends" that I met, Jean spoke with an affected English accent that seemed snobbish to me. Winnie herself never mastered this accent for some reason, though she always said "Spadeena" instead of "Spa-dine-a." (I understand now that Spadeena was used for the upper, elitist section of the street, whereas Spadina was used for the lower, working class part.) Beside these friends she seemed like a jolly country bumpkin. It was obvious Jean didn't like children, so we kept clear. I did not realize that she was someone Winnie had known at the height of her glory as a young woman in England until I read Winnie's letters of her visit to the House of Commons with Jean in London in 1935.

I don't know how Winnie knew Anne White from Ottawa. But Anne was a lovely blond who looked and acted like a movie star — June Allyson comes to mind. Anne was there with a handsome, slick, dark-haired man called Bill, and we were forbidden to go down to the dock when they were there "sunning themselves," which was most of the time. I have a vague recollection that Anne was divorced, or that this man was courting her, or both.

A much more dramatic friend was Jimmy Dacosta. She provided the occasion for much giggling. She had long, curly hair that she dyed henna — that color of red that is almost purple. She had very long pointed fingernails that were painted bright purple, and she spoke with an accent — Italian, I now guess — in a loud voice as she gestured wildly. I have some recollection that she was involved in politics in Toronto.

Winnie also encouraged us to bring our friends to The Cabin. She was generous and friendly with them, and our friends always liked her. I remember one friend I took there named Louise Mellion, who had come to Canada from England. Because she had an English accent, Winnie liked her especially. (Louise has since become an antique dealer on Fifth Avenue in New York City.)

One year my sister and I discovered a small photo pamphlet in Winnie's desk drawer. We were probably snooping for anything that would tell us her age. Each photo showed a naked woman doing something outside: sitting on a beach, walking through the woods, swinging high on a swing. This last photo reminded me even then of the Fragonard painting *The Swing*, a print of which Winnie had in her apartment on Elm Avenue. In both, the erotic possibilities of watching a woman ride high on a swing were exploited to the full. In the photo, the pubic area was visible but blurred, as it was in all the other photos. We showed this prize to the Wilson children. When I met one of them again for lunch years later, he remembered this first glimpse of pornography as being hilarious.

Every year, Winnie had a cocktail party outside on the lawn of The Cabin. To this she invited all the "Wilson clan," as she called them. She also invited some of the cottagers along the road to the Village. Her favourites were the Rossers, whose outgoing American charm she appreciated. My sister and I had the job of passing plates of hors d'oeuvres. It was a job we relished because it gave us the chance to sneak food to the Wilson children, who lurked around or under the bridge, and to overhear all sorts of comments and gossip that we would later exchange over giggles.

Later on, we no longer wanted to go to The Cabin in the summer. I preferred to hang out with friends seeing Friday night movies, or dance with boyfriends at the Pavillion ("the Pav") in Orillia or the Lucky Star at Oro Beach, where one night motorcycle rumblers had a knife fight on the dance floor.

40

AUNTNESS, AUNTISM,
AUNTDOM

Auntness, or Auntism or Auntdom, was Winnie's vocation, her calling in life. She identified with the role of aunt more than with any other — even more than with debutante. It was a good way to have children without the catastrophe of giving birth. It gave her a sense of her genes living on into the next generation. It gave her a connection to her only close family member, her brother, who disliked her. After she lost the companionship of her mother, she became even more ardent as an aunt.

Winnie's own Aunt Pussy might have been a model for her. She had grown close to Jean Forsyth in Dawson City, where Aunt Pussy had lived with the Camerons the year Winnie turned six. She always spoke fondly of her aunt, and I got the impression that she loved her dearly. Visits to her aunt in Vancouver after they all left Dawson were events of great fun and excitement, according to Winnie. She was excessively fond of the portrait of Aunt Pussy that hung at Huntley Street, a sentimental work in a gilt frame that would have

Portrait of Pussy as a child, Chatham, Ontario, c. 1856–57.

been done in Port Elgin in 1856 or 1857, when Jean was five or six. The sweet-faced child is wearing a white lace dress arranged to expose her shoulders. Her fair hair falls in thick ringlets not quite touching those shoulders. She raises a garland of flowers. This painting was later moved to my parents' living room on Mulcaster Street, and now hangs over my fireplace.

Photos of Aunt Pussy as a woman suggest that this sweet-faced girl with ringlets was not being flattered by the artist. Jean Forsyth was a beautiful woman. An article in a series called "Canadian Women in the Public Eye" for the *Edmonton Journal*, dated 22 September 1923, observed: "Anyone who has ever met Miss Forsyth is unlikely to forget her ... She [is] always effectively dressed, witty and fair to look upon, with cornflower blue eyes and fair hair ... Her verve, gaiety and esprit ... and her rare gifts as a comedian [make] her much sought after."

Aunt Pussy remained a spinster all her life. She appears to have enjoyed this independence. Though her family was wealthy enough to commission a portrait and could have supported her, Jean Forsyth had a career. She sang soprano in Winnipeg's Holy Trinity Church and gave vocal lessons. Once she settled in Edmonton, her creative flair expressed itself in the way she lived. Housing was scarce in the postwar boom, so she rented a large new store with double windows. She converted this business space into a studio and lived there. She covered the walls with dark green chintz embellished with huge roses. Rugs, cushions, and potted plants transformed the bays of the curtained windows into Victorian alcoves. In addition to teaching singing, she wrote a regular social column for the *Edmonton Journal*. Yet her career did not inspire Winnie to emulate her. In many ways, Winnie remained stubbornly Edwardian — my mother would have said Victorian — whereas Jean Forsyth was a striking example of the "new woman": financially independent, in favour of the vote for women, friends with other career women like Judge Emily Murphy. Despite her unconventional nature, though, Jean was also deeply engaged with feminine fashion.

Aunt Pussy was clearly a strong-willed woman who loved life. Her "niece" Winnie was much the same. My mother used to have a photo of four-year-old Winnie beautifully dressed, her thick hair tied in a large bow, prominently displayed in a mahogany frame in our upstairs TV room. "Did you ever see such a sullen determined little face?" she used to say.

What really raised widespread awareness of the importance of aunts was the appearance of the Broadway play *Auntie Mame* in 1957, with Rosalind Russell as the freewheeling Mame. The play was based on a 1955 novel by Patrick Dennis. In 1958 the play was transferred to the silver screen, with Rosalind Russell reprising her starring role. It was the top money-maker of the year, earning a net profit of $8,800,000. It won two Golden Globes, and earned eight Oscar nominations. By 1958, everyone knew about *Auntie Mame*, and Winnie basked in the reflected glory.

Winnie identified with the flamboyant, madcap Auntie Mame, who is suddenly saddled with an adolescent nephew, Patrick, when her brother dies. Mame attempts to rescue young Patrick from his stuffy, conventional outlook. Aunt Winnie did not resemble Rosalind Russell's Auntie Mame in most ways. She was not witty; nor did she drink excessively; nor was she unconventional, except for the fact that, having been groomed to marry, she had not. Winnie was eccentric, not unconventional. What Aunt Winnie did have in common with Auntie Mame — apart from using a long cigarette holder, which she revived from her days as a debutante in Toronto — was that she enjoyed her independence, was gregarious, and focused much of her time on the way she dressed. Both were filled with *joie de vivre*. As Auntie Mame says, "I may be odd, but I'm loving."

Auntie Mame was a deliberate comic. Her lines were widely quoted. When she sees Patrick launching toy airplanes, she exclaims, "Oh, you know I really am fascinated by aviation. I didn't know they did it all with rubber bands." When Patrick opens a curtain to unleash sunlight on a hung-over Mame, she says, "Child, how can you see with all that light?" One of Mame's expressions, "bust a gut," entered Winnie's vocabulary. "Don't you girls bust a gut now!" she would say when we were giggling at her.

Though Aunt Winnie had an appetite for humour like Auntie Mame's, she was comical inadvertently. She was given to statements that were jumbled versions of well-known sayings. "Murder is its own reward," she would say seriously. Or, "A bird is worth two in the bush," or "Where there's fire there's smoke," or, "He who laughs first, laughs last." My sister and I used to collapse into giggles at these, sometimes falling off our chairs and rolling on the floor holding our stomachs. One of Aunt Winnie's favourites was, "You can't lead a horse to water with a ten-foot pole." In fact, as we later figured out, many of her "sayings" related to horses. "Time to put on the feed-bag," she'd say when dinner was ready. Bedtime was announced by "Time to hit the hay!" She would tell the two of us to "stop horsing around." Clothes were "trappings." When she had groceries to buy, she'd say, "I'll just trot over to the store and haul back some things" (this even though she drove to the grocery store). As we grew older and became better educated than Winnie had ever been, it came to the point where almost anything she said with seriousness was cause for a fit of giggles. Luckily, like Auntie Mame, she took it all in good humour and laughed at herself, even when she had no idea what we were laughing at. I can't remember her ever being hurt or upset when we laughed at her. She so enjoyed our company, and so enjoyed being our "Auntie Mame," that not much could have offended her.

41

MORE VISITS
TO WINNIE

In 1957, I spent my fifteenth birthday with Winnie at the opening of an art show at the Art Gallery of Ontario. She lent me her beautiful jewelled and gold-braid turquoise top for the occasion. It was pinned down each side with safety pins so it would fit me. She did not frequent art galleries, but this show featured paintings from the eighteenth century — Winnie's favourites. Most of the paintings were of royalty or aristocrats dressed in powdered wigs and gorgeous materials in her favourite colours: pastels, especially blues, and peachy pinks. I loved it.

I would continue to visit Winnie by bus through my teens. Highway 400 was built at about the same time as my grandmother died, linking Barrie to Toronto much more quickly. I would board the bus at Barrie and tell the driver I wanted to get out at Crescent Road in Rosedale. It was not an official stop, but in those days drivers used to accommodate passengers.

I would eagerly watch as we approached Crescent Road, which

entered Yonge Street only from the east. There was a bench in Ramsden Park, right where the bus stopped, and Aunt Winnie would be sitting there waiting there for me. Probably she had been waiting for a long time, since she was early for everything. She would welcome me with smiles and hugs and all sorts of expressions of her happiness at seeing her "Pigeon Pie."

Her lower duplex at 80 Elm Avenue, across from a little park called Craigleith Gardens, was an oasis of happiness to me. The upper duplex was rented by a bachelor named Eric Aldwinkle. Winnie had no idea that he was famous, so I didn't either, until much later. If anyone had tried to explain his career to her, she wouldn't have understood. When she moved there in 1953, he was a graphic designer for Imperial Oil, the University of Toronto, Ryerson College, and the Stratford Festival. In 1955, he visited the Soviet Union as part of a cultural exchange that included Group of Seven painter Frederick Varley, and Aldwinkle wrote up the trip for *Maclean's* magazine. He also designed the Great Seal of Canada for the Canadian Mint. He was a gifted eccentric: on top of being a graphic designer he was an accomplished chef, a raconteur, an astrologer, a composer of music, a playwright, and a social critic. I don't think I ever met him. Winnie didn't like him. He was famous for mentoring young artists. All Winnie ever talked about were the frequent visits of young men and boys to his place where they made "a helluva racket horsing around" upstairs. "What are they *doing* up there," she used to complain, "at all hours of the day and night?" Had his visitors been female, she would have understood at once.

Winnie's favourite colours were turquoise and peach, and she used them to decorate her apartment. Her favorite artist was the French painter Fragonard, not that she knew his name. She did know and admired his painting *The Swing*, which reminded me of the naked women booklet we'd found at The Cabin. There was a framed print in her apartment. The painting is ornate and erotic. A young woman rides a swing pushed high by a man behind. She wears a jaunty straw hat and a peach dress of luxurious material. She kicks one of her white-stockinged legs high, smiling down at another man in blue silk, lace jabot, and white powdered wig, who reclines in the lush foliage in such a way as to have an excellent view up the girl's dress. This painting was done in 1767 as one of many to grace the courts of Louis XV, only a couple of years before the Austrian princess Marie Antoinette arrived at Versailles to marry the Dauphin. Aunt Winnie could be said to favour the eighteenth century, and the French court at Versailles in particular. With no concept of history, she often said that she wished she could have lived at Versailles. Mother used to tell her in reply, "It's fine to wish yourself back into Versailles, but how do you know you wouldn't be a servant?"

Winnie decorated her small apartment with the same grandeur as Huntley Street. The first thing you saw as you entered the tiny front hall was a romantic watercolour of Bonnie Prince Charlie in Highland regalia and a powdered wig. All the rooms fanned off this central hall that contained an ornate table with a telephone and a stool. There was also a brass umbrella stand by the door and a small china cabinet full of antique china and various knick-knacks, such as Doulton figurines. A mahogany table that could have seated ten or twelve filled the dining room on the right. Chairs were jammed smack into the table, and a large sideboard filled with English bone china cut off access from one side. It looked as if the dining room at Huntley Street had shrunk its walls to a quarter their size around the grand furniture. No one could have gotten into those chairs to sit at the mahogany table. There wasn't space to pull them out. The room was never used because Winnie never entertained. She was a frequent guest at the homes of her "great friends," but, as she explained, she did not cook and had no staff. "It's too hard to be Lady Jane and Mary Jane at the same time," she used to say. She ate all her meals in the living room.

Her living room was also crammed with elegant and valuable furniture — much of it needing repair — and every surface displayed

antiques she had inherited or continued to collect: a few of the grinning Toby jugs from Huntley Street, cranberry glass vases, moustache
cups (that must have reminded her of her father and her beaux),
Dresden figurines, and Staffordshire dogs. On the walls were crystal
teardrop lustres that gave off the dim light she preferred. She had
two sofas: one in the bay window, the other against the opposite
wall facing her small black-and-white television. There were large,
shaky coffee tables in front of each sofa. Like my father, she had no
thought of repairing broken furniture. There was a small bathroom
with the little geometric black-and-white tiles that were typical of
Toronto in the 1920s.

Her bedroom was stuffed with more antiques: Dollie's mahogany
four-poster double bed; a dressing table with silver brush, comb, and
mirror; a heavy, silver-lidded lead crystal inkpot, inscribed with her
mother's initials (and which I still have); a Victorian hair receiver;
and perfume bottles with rubber bulbs for spraying. These items and
the entire room were chaotically doubled by the gilt-scrolled mirror
above the dressing table. At the foot of the bed was a low recliner like
a one-sided sofa. This left a mere foot between it and the dressing
table stool. There was a small window on one side of the room in
front of a small closet, which was always open and overflowing with
clothes; on the other side stood a huge mahogany bureau (now owned
by my son, Hugo), which left about a foot and a half between it
and the bed. Over net curtains on the window were turquoise silk
drapes embossed with gold *fleur de lys*. On the bed was a matching
bedspread.

The apartment would have been overstuffed with only half of
these objects in it. To enter it was to feel stifled and claustrophobic
immediately. My mother used to say acerbically, "Winnie won't
throw anything out. She identifies with her belongings. And there are
mirrors everywhere you turn in that place." When we relayed this,
Winnie used to say, "I don't like to throw anything out because I
want you girls to have it someday."

Winnie was extremely tidy. Someone had convinced her that beds must be made, clothes put away, and dishes washed at once. Nothing, however, was clean. Without Kate to dust, wash floors, and launder, and having been waited on for fifty-two years, she was at a loss. She sent her laundry out, leaving a large bag on the doorstep and receiving last week's perfectly pressed items in return. Occasionally she had a Scottish maid named Mary (pronounced "Mee-rry") in to clean. Mary dressed in a black-and-white maid's uniform like Kate's. She seemed a poor cowed creature, constantly clasping her hands, bowing, and saying in a thick accent, rolling her r's, "Yes, Miss Winifrrred" or "No, Miss Winifrrred." I don't think she cleaned well or often. My sister once wrote a note that said, "This note was left here on [such-and-such a date]. No one has cleaned this since then." She stuffed it into one of the knick-knacks. I don't recall how long it took Winnie or Mary to find this note. I believe it was months, possibly years. Mother, who was a brisk and thorough cleaner of everything and whose frenzy of spring cleaning was an annual ordeal, was disgusted by Winnie's inattention to dirt. "Ugh!" she'd say grimacing, "her dishcloth! The *dust* everywhere! There's nothing worse than all that grimy peach stuff! I can't go near the place." She didn't. I don't remember my mother ever visiting Winnie there, though she must have. Winnie's indifference to dirt never bothered me as much as my mother's manic housekeeping, though I enjoyed the clean home where I grew up.

The only things I ever saw Winnie wash — and this was rarely — were her girdle and waist-length bra. These imposing items could be seen hanging over the shower rail from time to time. They resembled Amazonian armour, and Winnie had to struggle in and out of them in the narrow space between her bed and the bureau to exclamations of "Oh, *Bud*!" or "Oh, *Boy*!" To keep these two garments from separating, she pinned them together at what should have been her waist with a large safety pin.

My parents held out against television until the year before I left for university in 1961. I was only allowed to walk over to my friend's place to watch *I Love Lucy* once a week. At Winnie's, though, I could watch television for hours. I remember especially the cartoons. My favorite was the *Road Runner*. I would lie on the lumpy antique sofa watching pretty much anything that came on the few stations in those days. It was such a welcome relief from my strenuous routine at home. I took school very seriously under the watchful eye of my father, who signed all my report cards. I was also heavily involved in sports. My mother had enrolled us in just about every kind of lesson: art, music, riding, dancing, swimming, and skating. When I got to Winnie's I did nothing. The only physical activity we did was going for a daily walk — something Winnie believed was good for one's health.

While I lay about watching television, Winnie would sit on her chintz sofa by the window — often doing needlepoint, which she must have learned at BSS, or plucking hairs from her chin — and ask me questions: Who were my friends? What did their fathers do? Did my mother give me enough to eat? Where did I get that sweater? Why did I wear jeans? This was not annoying at all because she paused for a long time between questions, thinking up the next one, and she didn't really require answers. In the evenings, she would join me for her favourite programs: *The Perry Como Show*, *Liberace*, and *The Lawrence Welk Show*. Since the debonair Lawrence Welk and Perry Como, with their slicked-back hair parted on the side, resembled the beaux she had danced with in the '20s, I assume this was the kind of man she was attracted to. Liberace's melodrama made her laugh. She loved popular music, and I now realize she was probably reliving those many dances at Jenkins' Art Galleries and elsewhere when she came out. Often she'd get up and dance about the limited space in the room, holding both her small hands up and waving them in time to the music. For a big woman, she was light on her feet. She especially liked the bubbles that surged up at the beginning of every *Lawrence Welk* episode as the announcer welcomed "Lawrence Welk and his champagne music." I thought those men were too wimpy and oily, but she raved about them. She disapproved of Dean Martin's inebriation. (Much later I read that it was all a gag and that he had apple juice in his glass.) Even Winnie thought Liberace was a bit over the top, though she loved the candelabra on his piano, his (often eighteenth-century) costumes, and the flourish with which he played.

When I visited Winnie I slept with her in her double bed. This was heaven. She went to bed when I did, around nine o'clock. She used to rub my back and tell me stories, mostly about the Royal Family. Sometimes she told me naughty jokes. Since her sense of humour had been arrested at approximately the same age I was then, these were hilarious to me. "Have you read *The Open Kimono* by One Hung Low?" she would ask, and then break into peals of laughter. "Have you read *The Sodden Mattress* by I.P. Knightley?" She might also recite a bit of doggerel verse:

> *Where e'er you be*
> *Let your wind blow free,*
> *For to hold it in*
> *Was the death of me!*

Most of her humour was bathroom humour; her own nickname for herself was "Windy," because of her frequent burping. I was able to recycle her jokes with great success to my friends once I got home.

Eventually, she would cuddle me into her arms and we'd both fall asleep. I never felt more loved. Later my mother told me, "I knew all about those *orgies* with Winnie, you know." I was speechless. As a mother myself by then, I couldn't comprehend how any parent would allow such behaviour if they believed this was true. My mother was probably exaggerating, but since she and my father slept in twin beds with the door open and hardly ever touched each other or us, she and I might have differed on what constitutes an orgy. Winnie never did anything that crossed the boundary between affection and abuse.

She was simply expressing her love. Later, when I was having therapy for any number of things, the therapist asked me to identify a really safe place so I could visualize it. What came to mind at once was Aunt Winnie's bed.

In the morning, Winnie woke before I did and got up to make us breakfast. Since I seldom got breakfast — and never a "proper breakfast" — at home, and since Mother slept until around noon, this was a treat beyond treats. I could hear the radio in the kitchen giving what Winnie called "the noos," and I could smell bacon cooking. Winnie might be singing "Oh, What a Beautiful Morning," depending on the weather. In she would come with her old, dented turquoise tin tray with roses on it, carrying a plate of bacon, eggs, and toast, and a glass of orange juice. No one, in any luxury hotel, having room service in the Royal Suite, could have enjoyed it more than I enjoyed those breakfasts in bed.

Bacon and eggs was pretty much Winnie's *tour de force* as a cook. I watched her try to make Jell-O without success. Our meals were plain. Since the dining room was clogged with furniture, we ate off the shaky coffee tables in the living room. For lunch she heated up a can of Campbell's soup. She knew my favourite was Scotch Broth. Bread and butter with sliced ham or tongue (one of her favourites) went with this. Then store-bought cookies for dessert, mostly Peak Freans. For dinner she usually baked or boiled a potato, heated up a tin of green peas (always *petit pois*), and fried up some minced steak. Occasionally she would put a roast in the oven: a leg of lamb, a sirloin tip, or a chicken without stuffing. Dessert was usually something from the bakery: chocolate éclairs or — her favorite — Charlotte Russe, lady fingers and custard topped with whipped cream. She made Maxwell House instant coffee for herself for breakfast, and always had Shierriff's Good Morning marmalade on her toast. She often rhapsodized about Kate's meals while she ate. Sometimes, she ate her meals out of a teacup so she'd have fewer dishes to wash. I now think it might also have been comforting to her, as she was probably fed from a teacup when she was small.

Winnie did her phone calls right after breakfast. Since she got up about 6:30 or seven, this meant that she phoned her friends before eight. I often heard her saying to them with a laugh, "Oh, I thought you'd be out of bed by now." But she would call the same friends at the same time and say the same thing the next day. Her most important calls had to wait until nine when the shops opened. She would pass the time by smoking, or rather by puffing on a Matinee filter cigarette in her Auntie Mame cigarette holder. Eventually she would leave, reach Dom and Tony's, the fruit and vegetable grocers at 379 Bloor Street near Sherbourne (an easy walk away), right at nine. Her voice would be sharp with annoyance, but once she got going with her list of things to be delivered she would calm down. She also called Brown Brothers, the butcher at 1–3 St. Lawrence Market, to order ground steak or a roast and bacon, also to be delivered.

After that, while I watched television, she would leaf through *Vogue* or *Harper's Bazaar*. Sometimes she would work on her needlepoint. Every so often, she would hold up a page for me to see, saying, "Look at *this*, Pidgie. I wouldn't wear that to a *dog* fight!" She herself could not have worn anything pictured in those magazines, as she was many sizes larger than the models that wore them.

Quite often Winnie took me shopping. She had a sort of route she followed among her favourite stores. These were all on or near Bloor Street at Bay Street. She loved expensive clothes. They had been the focus of the whirl of social events after she came out, and she never changed. The store she prized above all others was Creeds, which no longer exists. After all, she had modelled clothes there in 1924 with other debutantes to raise money for the Junior League. Originally Creeds was known for its furs, but by the time I was visiting Winnie it was *the* high fashion store in Toronto. Winnie was well-known there, and the staff almost cow-towed when she sailed in. "Good morning, Miss Cameron," was discreetly murmured here and there. I remember being awed at the almost religious atmosphere of the place: the scent of perfumes, the impeccably dressed clerks, the slim, slim models who walked slowly about, turning and striking poses in strange outfits with hats and gloves. One salesgirl in particular dealt with Winnie. Her name was Lexi, and she had bleached blond hair pulled back in a chignon and wore more makeup than I'd ever seen on anyone, except the Paris whores in mother's book about Toulouse-Lautrec.

Dealing with Winnie meant selecting clothes that would flatter her stout figure. I was included in the dressing room as Winnie heaved herself into various skirts and dresses and blouses and jackets, all the while exclaiming, "Oh, *Bud*!" or "Oh, *Boy*!" She could never do up the zippers. Lexi would come in and discreetly put pins in to mark where things needed to be let out. "We can just alter this here a little, Miss Cameron. This is a very becoming little frock. The colour suits you; it brings out your blue eyes." The staff always made a fuss over me too. I had no idea it was a sales pitch. Later, when I had developed a bust, Winnie occasionally bought things here for me too. I hate to think of what they cost. In my case, the pins were needed to mark where things needed to be taken in. I was thrilled.

After Creeds, we went to Birks (at the time Birks-Ryrie) on the southeast corner of Bloor and Bay. There, too, the staff all knew Winnie. I didn't like Birks. It smelled old, like silver polish, and the clerks behind their glass counters looked remote and cold. (This has not changed.) Winnie liked to browse. She'd ask the price of items that interested her, mainly necklaces. The only things I remember her buying were bits of costume jewellery that seemed incredibly expensive to me, trinkets like little animal brooches studded with rhinestones or necklaces with fake pearls. She termed such items "darling" or "pretty." Sometimes she bought something whimsical for me. Much later, I recall asking her for a pair of real pearl earrings. She hesitated a little, but when she saw how much I wanted them she bought them for me. They cost forty dollars. I still wear them.

From Birks we would proceed to Ada Mackenzie's, a block above Bloor. Ada Mackenzie's was not grand like Creeds. The little shop was owned by Ada herself, an international golf champion who had opened the shop in 1930 to provide quality sportswear for women. Here Winnie, who was far from sporty, would look over the latest imports from Scotland and England, picking out sweaters, blouses, and scarves. Liberty to Winnie did not mean freedom; it meant the gorgeous patterned silk scarves imported from Liberty's in London.

After Ada Mackenzie's we were off to my favourite place, the Albert Britnell Book Shop on Yonge Street just above Bloor. I now realize that it was a replica of the small family-run book shops in England. It was narrow but deep, with shelf after shelf and table after table of books. I could have spent hours there, touching the vast array of children's books, opening them, feeling the paper and smelling that indescribably exciting aroma of paper and print. Winnie usually bought me a book. It would take me a long time to make a choice. I recall getting the book of Greek myths there that I still have today. *Robinson Crusoe* was another I remember, and Scottish books about a character called Curdy. I no longer have it, but every now and then I look at the illustrations in George MacDonald's *The Princes and Curdie* when I'm at the library. I still find them exquisite, lush, and romantic.

The only difficulty of shopping on Bloor Street was parking. Winnie had learned to drive from the chauffeur at Parklands, so she had never learned to parallel park, or to back up for that matter, since Parklands consisted of a series of loops that intersected. She would circle the block over and over until a space appeared at one end of the block or the other. Then she could pull directly into the spot. As she circled, she'd say things like, "That fool is taking my place," or "Last week it wasn't this bad," or, when she found a place, "Jiminy cricket! There we go!" This circling and circling was part of the anticipation of shopping, for me as well as for her.

On other days, Aunt Winnie took me to Simpson's downtown on King Street. We would survey the clothing, shoe, and jewellery sections, as well as what she called "notions." This included things like gloves, purses, scarves, and umbrellas. Sometimes we went to the underwear department, where she would purchase her gigantic waist-length bras or a girdle that looked like an elastic shield. Winnie liked frilly, floor-length nylon nighties, so we often looked to see if they had any peach or turquoise ones in Winnie's size. I had no interest in these. I liked flannel pyjamas, and still do. Winnie would always stop in at the Elizabeth Arden Hair Salon, which was on one of Simpson's upper floors. There she would have her hair "styled." What this meant was that someone would comb it and push its permed waves into place at a cost of fifty cents. I was never there when she got a permanent, or the rinses that were supposed to transform her white hair into blond. The result was actually streaks of orange.

The highlight of our shopping trips to Simpson's was lunch at the Arcadian Court. This restaurant had been built to suggest the dining room of a luxury liner like the ones on which Winnie had crossed back and forth over the Atlantic. She would always begin her order of what she called "good plain food" with "I'll just have ..." She delighted in the fact that my sister and I were always assumed to be her daughters. My sister, with her blond hair and blue eyes, actually resembled Winnie a great deal. I had my mother's hazel eyes and my father's long face, but people thought I was her daughter anyway. I was allowed to order anything I wanted. Since I was — and still am — experimental about food, I'd try something exotic like duck casserole. She might have a fruit salad plate, or sliced chicken breast with peas and potatoes. We always had dessert: delicious pastries or cakes stuffed with cream brought round on a trolley.

On very special occasions, she would take me to Winston's for lunch. Winston's, at 1120 King Street, was *the* place to lunch in Toronto then. It was very expensive, and Toronto's society matrons and businessmen could usually be found there. Often, one of Winnie's old friends from her debutante days would pass by. Winnie would light up, and the two would chat and laugh. I was introduced, but soon became an observer.

On Sundays, Winnie sometimes took me to Lichee Gardens just south of Dundas Street in Chinatown. How she overcame her racism to do this I have no idea. I wish she were still here so I could ask her.

Probably the place was fashionable in her set in the early '20s. Maybe it was the only restaurant open on Sundays in Toronto the Good. I can think of no other reason why she would have gone to a place where most of the staff and customers were Chinese. What she found there to eat that qualified as "good plain food" I don't know.

Since my parents never took us to restaurants — except very occasionally after dinner in the summer to Lakeview Dairy for a chocolate marshmallow sundae — these lunches out with Winnie were wondrous.

42

MEN

By 1956 I was interested in men. This new interest took the form of vague longings, a despairing interest in fashions that did not suit me, and an instant connection to the vibrations of the new music. I vividly remember the first time I heard Elvis Presley sing "Heartbreak Hotel." I was with my Grade 8 girlfriend, who was having menstrual cramps. I couldn't tell whether she was writhing in agony because of the cramps or because of Elvis. But I doubled over too in spasms of excitement. We couldn't decipher the words, but we *knew* Elvis was far, far above any other singer. When his first movie *Love Me Tender* came out later that year I campaigned for a visit to Winnie. Movies then opened in Toronto on release, but didn't reach the three Barrie theatres for three or four months. I couldn't wait. So I got myself to Winnie's and persuaded her to take me.

She was full of questions as the film began and Elvis appeared as a poor Civil War-era Southern farmer plowing a field. "Is *that* Elvis? What is he supposed to be doing? What Civil War?" Once he started into his first song, Winnie got up, covered her ears, and left. I knew she'd wait in the car for me, so I feasted rapturously on the rest of the movie. When I got to the car, she laughed and said, "He sounds like an *alley cat*!" From that day on, whenever she heard rock and roll music, which was more and more often, she always said, "Who's *that alley cat*?"

Perhaps it was this awakening, this uneasy tingling which I had no idea was sexual, that tuned my antennae to the men in Winnie's life. It seemed more than extraordinary that Winnie would insist on my sister and I dressing nicely for a visit to Frank Hayes. He was her financial advisor at the National Trust with an intimidating office somewhere downtown. She trotted us out to shake hands with Frank, who paid us little attention. He and Winnie, however, paid each other a great deal of attention. They were discussing the boring subject of money. I did not understand. What I did understand was that Winnie was unusually merry, laughing and straightening her dress and gloves.

Sometimes, she would take me and my sister on a drive to the beach where she would treat us to ice cream cones. Then she would drive to Frank's home nearby and park opposite his house. While we attended to the ice cream cones, she gazed steadily at the house. I sensed that this was too odd and too intense, that this — not the ice cream — had been the purpose of the outing.

I remember visits from Alex Aziz at The Cabin. He was her last obvious beau. I think he was younger than her. I recall a photo of my baby sister on his lap at Mulcaster Street, so he must have visited there with Winnie, too. I remember especially a pair of Wrangler jeans he gave me when I was about twelve. He was somehow connected to an importing business in Toronto that handled that brand. They became my favourite pair of jeans.

At The Cabin, my sister and I stayed put in the twin beds. Winnie gave Alex her double bed. She slept on the sofa. Alex was good-natured and seemed to enjoy being with us children. In the mornings, we headed as always to Winnie's bed and crawled in. Alex told us firmly to get out.

During the day, Winnie and Alex sat outside in the sun. They would go down to the dock for regular morning and afternoon swims, Winnie, as usual, in her flowered bathing cap and white rubber bathing shoes. By this time, Winnie had large blotches of white skin on her chest, neck, arms, and face amidst her deep tan — a disease called vitiligo, I later learned. (It was the disease Michael Jackson much later claimed had lightened his skin.) This disfigurement — which elicited comments of disgust from my mother — did not stop Winnie from wearing her sundresses and bathing suits.

In the evenings we all played cards — usually Canasta. If it was clear and warm, Winnie set up the card table outside overlooking the lake. She had her radio playing near the window so we could hear the latest popular songs. I remember especially the Four Aces' "Love

R.M.S. MAURETANIA
West Indies Cruise. 1955.

Winnie on the *RMS Mauretania*, cruising the West Indies, 1955.

is a Many-Splendored Thing." Such slow, sultry songs with their coded allusions to sex had already been replaced by the raw sexual onslaught of rock and roll, but they remained Winnie's favourites. As she went in and out for drinks — always one gin-and-ginger ale for herself, ginger ale for us, and who knows what for Alex — she would dance around a bit and sing along, waving her small hands to the music.

Alex was swarthy and handsome, the culmination of Winnie's attraction to "darkies," as she called them. She had thought the "Indian potentates" wearing their "glittering jewels" in the 1935 parade in London handsome and exciting. The Indian princes, headed by the Aga Khan in his black fez, at her presentation at Buckingham Palace in 1937 also seemed "very attractive" to her. She had enjoyed a shipboard romance with "the Maharaja," as she called him, sometime in her fifties. Perhaps Indians and Middle Eastern men were all right, whereas blacks were not. Or maybe the colour barrier in her mind dissolved if the man in question was rich. Who knows? No one looked for consistency in Winnie. This *Arabian Nights* view of what we today call visible minorities was romantic and naïve. I suppose it aroused the thrill of the taboo for her.

43
∽

ANOTHER VISIT
FROM SCOTLAND, 1957

The new 26th chief of the Clan Cameron visited Canada in the summer of 1957. It was one of his occasional visitations to the colonies, where he was welcomed by thousands of loyal Camerons. This Donald Cameron of Lochiel was a jovial, round-faced, balding fellow who enjoyed meeting people. I have no idea whether Winnie had kept in touch with him since her letter of sympathy to his mother, Hermione, on the death of his father in 1951. Perhaps she had already made one of her pilgrimages to Achnacarry by that time, returning — as always — to complain, "It was not only damp, it was *dank*!"

There would have been much prodding of my father by his sister about how he planned to entertain Lochiel, since their father had entertained his father in 1913. My father succumbed, and there are photos of my parents with Lochiel and his wife, Lady Margaret, in the garden at Mulcaster Street. Winnie had her plans, too. I would have been fourteen at the time, but I remember nothing. Perhaps that was the summer I spent a month with the Caouette family in

Quebec on a Visite Interprovinciale in one of my many unsuccessful attempts to become fluently bilingual. I certainly heard about Lochiel, however. I can't recall what my parents did, but Winnie entertained him at the exclusive and expensive York Club in Toronto, where her father had entertained his father. There was much discussion after the visit about how it was she could have possibly paid for the costly reception. Mother said she had no idea how Winnie could pull this off, since by then she was running low on her inheritance money and could not have afforded the York Club's membership fees or the cost of entertaining a crowd. Probably she was able to persuade one or more of her "great friends" to help sponsor the occasion. I recall my father using the phrase "dipping into her capital." It was a phrase that also came up whenever Winnie took one of her cruises in the West Indies during the winter. The winters she didn't "go south," as she called it, she complained bitterly that "all her friends" had "gone south." She must have forgotten entirely her early preference for the climate of Dawson City over that of Toronto, or perhaps D.A. had misrepresented her when he told Stefansson all those years ago that she liked the cold. She complained loudly about the snow, began wearing her old opossum coat and mink hat inside on winter visits to Mulcaster Street, and kept the temperature in her Elm Street apartment at a tropical pitch.

After the Lochiels' visit, she made at least one more pilgrimage to Achnacarry Castle, which, she reported, was horribly drafty and cold. No doubt she made this view known to her host and hostess. Yet she returned more than once, the draw of Scottish romanticism and social status trumping discomfort.

I did not really grasp what the Lochiels and Achnacarry Castle were all about until much later, when my younger sister also visited the Castle on Loch Arkaig at Spean Bridge, Inverness-shire — no doubt on Winnie's strong encouragement. I believe she went sometime in the early '60s (probably the summer of 1964 or 1965), when I was a student either in Vancouver at UBC or in Fredericton at UNB. She would have then been in her late teens, a year older than Lochiel's eldest son, Donald, who later became the 27th chief of the Clan Cameron after his father died at age ninety-three in 2004.

My sister was a much more astute observer than Winnie had been. She came back with tales of the goings-on at Achnacarry that explained to me Winnie's enduring reverence for the place. I believe my sister was taken salmon fishing in the Arkaig River which tumbled through Lochiel's land close to the castle — a major occupation there. I'm not sure whether she stalked deer on the 100,000 acres that Lochiel owned (once 130,000 acres and the largest landholding in Britain of any commoner), but that, too, was one of the main pleasures of the Lochiels. She saw several mementos in the castle, including the two waistcoats worn by Bonnie Prince Charlie. At dinner, she said, they spoke often of '45. At first she had no idea what they were talking about. It was not *nineteen*-forty-five, when the Second World War ended and she was born, she eventually realized. It was *seventeen*-forty-five, when the Camerons comprised the largest number of soldiers — some of whom were mere cottars on the Cameron estate — at the Battle of Culloden early the next year. Lochiel and his family spoke of it passionately, as if the tragedy had occurred yesterday. Although Cameron of Lochiel had served in the Second World War with the Lovat Scouts, the wound to the clans left by the defeat of Bonnie Prince Charlie (whom the Camerons had guarded the night before Culloden), and the Highland Clearances which followed, in which the Camerons lost more land than any other clan, were indelible. All these details were lost on Winnie.

THAT CHAIR

To understand the dynamics in my family, you have to know about *that* chair. We had moved from the upper floor of the Dundonald Street house to our own house at 135 Mulcaster Street in the spring of 1955 when I was twelve. My father used his inheritance from his mother to purchase the two-storey Victorian building on an acre and a half of land for $13,500. It sat at the end of a dead-end street. Mother joked that we were now the Dead-End Kids. Father joked that we now lived on Mouse-catcher Street, probably a sly dig at Captain William Mulcaster of the British Royal Navy, who had fought in the War of 1812 and after whom the street was named. Instead of sharing a garden with our landlords at Dundonald Street (named after Scotland's greatest eighteenth-century naval admiral), who had replaced Uncle Gregor and his family, we had our own treed acre of garden to play in. My sister and I immediately set up a baseball diamond of sorts with the neighbourhood kids and destroyed the grass.

One of Mother's proverbs was "New house, new baby," and, sure enough, a year after we moved in to Mulcaster Street — where my parents briefly shared a double bed with a candlewick bedspread — my mother gave birth to another girl. She said she was going to call her Jezebel, after her favourite Bette Davis movie, if it was a girl. Yet when her third daughter was born she relented. The new baby got the same type of intensely Scottish name as we did: Alexandra Fiona Forsyth. Winnie — age fifty-five by then — took almost no interest in this child. She still focused on me and my sister.

Renovations swiftly followed the move. The renovated kitchen soon had a long, pale green Arborite counter along the length of the large picture windows that now gave onto the garden. There were two end chairs, but family meals there were likely to involve people sitting in a row, often reading newspapers. The room was big enough to have accommodated a table in the middle of the room, but that would have involved eye contact and communication. Mother preferred to look out at the birdfeeders and attempt to reorganize nature. She didn't like squirrels or pigeons. When these appeared, she'd leap up and bang on the window to scare them off. She had binoculars at hand to watch the other birds: lovely cardinals, chickadees, juncos, and sparrows. She was iffy about blue jays. They were beautiful, but sometimes they bullied the smaller birds. Later these binoculars were used to observe and report on the goings-on at the properties beyond the garden.

In a corner of the room, there was a large, pale green Naugahyde easy chair with a big matching footstool. It was the only chair in the kitchen, other than those along the counter. My father generally sat there for the lunch he made himself of peanut butter sandwiches, reading *The Globe and Mail* that mother had just finished at her breakfast around noon. He enjoyed this as a break from his job as general administrator of the Royal Victoria Hospital — a position at which he excelled for 35 years. Our only family meal was dinner, a meal my mother sometimes avoided, saying, "Now that I've cooked it, I don't feel like eating it." When Winnie visited, she upset this intricate routine by installing herself in the green chair. It served her as a sort of sentry post from which she could engage members of the family in conversation as they passed by or snacked in the kitchen. My mother referred to it as *that* chair, rolling her eyes. *That* chair afforded her many variations on the theme "All the Camerons do is *sit!*" She was right, and Cameron photos bear this out. Dollie, especially, appears not to have done much except sit on the Parklands veranda in the summer and in her upstairs sitting room at Huntley Street in the winter. Although mother had picked out *that* chair, she never sat in it at all.

For that matter, my mother hardly ever sat at all. She ate her lunch of cheese and crackers standing up; she darted about cleaning things or gardening; she zipped about town in her little green-and-white Nash Metropolitan convertible, shopping. I don't think I ever saw her just *sit*.

Winnie hated to see my mother doing things instead of sitting. When she saw her up on a ladder changing storm windows while my father, fearing heights, held the ladder below, or digging up a flower bed, or any other of her frenetic activities, Winnie would say in a strident voice, "Why don't you hire a man to do that and pay him a dollar?" Worst was the year my father dug a wall around what would become the flagstone patio outside the kitchen. He explained to us that it had to go lower than the frost line. Wearing his ragged old Appleby toque and the old grey flannel trousers with the broken zipper that were held together with a safety pin, he was in full view of the kitchen window on weekends for weeks. Mother said it was like watching someone in the salt mines of Russia. He actually looked worse than any hired man. Winnie couldn't stand to see this, and said so. "Donald, why don't you hire a man and pay him a dollar?" His reply was "I'm just a plain dirt farmer" — a line he used often. With perfect timing, my mother's invariable exclamation would follow: "Oh, *Donald*! Stop that!" Once, much later, I asked him what career he would most have liked. His answer was so quick that I knew he must have harboured this fantasy for years. "A butler," he said. And in some sense he was. Later, when asked why she didn't get a dishwasher, my mother used to say, "I already have one — your father."

As for my father, he continued to sing and make up silly songs. He composed at least two political songs: "Gerda Munsinger, That East German Swinger" and "I Wonder Who's Kissinger Now":

> *I wonder who's Kissinger now?*
> *I wonder who's telling them how?*
> *The wogs and the frogs, and the kikes and the spics*
> *Are all getting wise to those Kissinger tricks.*
> *I wonder how Kissinger felt*
> *When he learned how much Watergate smelt?*
> *He's been in a fix since they ostracized Nix*
> *I wonder who's Kissinger now?*

His *tour de force* was a song about himself called "Dirty Daddy":

> *Just how dirty can you be*
> *Just ask little Pidge and Tee*
> *To tell you all about their dirty Daddy.*
> *Grubby socks and dirty hair*
> *He'll never change his underwear*
> *That* dirty, dirty *Daddy of ours.*
> *Mum has to hit him with a club*
> *Before she gets him in the tub*
> *Oh, that Daddy.*
> *He sat beside a pig one day*
> *And the piggy got up and walked away*
> *That* dirty, dirty *Daddy of ours.*

Much later, when we were both grown women, we were expected to sing this song at my parents' annual New Year's Eve *ceilidh*. By then, we knew the song was true to a point. He hated baths, and my mother always had to remind him to take one.

These songs were actually gestures of affection. My father once told me that a servant who was whipped by his master riding by was likely to say, "He noticed me." I suppose this idea lay at the basis of his humour, as well as his tricks of speech and the puzzles he posed to us. We tussled for years over whether that pound of lead was heavier than the pound of feathers. He would send us to our mother for some "elbow grease." It was so bad, we began asking our mother "Is that true, Mum?" about everything he said. He'd state, "Today's Army Day" on March 4th, and point out, "It's a great day for the race." "What race?" we asked. "The human race." His only physical gesture of affection was to pat us rather hard on the head as he passed by, saying, "I love to pat little heads." He made up no songs about Winnie. Now I see that that was a crushing insult. He wouldn't pay her the compliment.

On very rare occasions he could drop the sarcasm. One such occasion was one of the Robert Burns celebrations my parents went to every year. "Gentlemen," he said, "Robert Burns, during his career some two centuries ago, said as part of his many verses:

> *She has my heart, she has my hand*
> *By sacred truth and honour's band!*
> *Till mortal stroke shall lay me low,*
> *I'm thine, my Highland Lassie, O."*

He continued, "Tonight I would like you to join me in these sentiments and to drink a toast to our Bonny Ladies, O." It was the closest he got to expressing affection publicly for my mother. They did not share a bed; they never held hands or hugged; the word "dear" or "Bertah dear" was his only endearment. He was as undemonstrative as his sister was effusive.

Father rarely spoke to Winnie. One of her visits could go by entirely without his saying a word to her. When one of my husbands asked him what Winnie thought about something or other, he replied, "I don't know, I haven't spoken to her since 1920." It was an exaggeration, but not much of one. If Winnie began addressing questions to my father, or tried to engage him in chit-chat, he left the room and sat in his chair in the living room, reading a book. If she followed him there, he took his book upstairs and lay down on his bed to continue reading. This infuriated my mother, who was left to field the stream of questions and orders from Winnie sitting in *that* chair. "When are you sending the girls to a private school? Why don't your friends play bridge? Why does Donald keep the house so cold? Let the cat out, he's meowing at the door." Or, conversely, "Let the cat in, he's been out for two hours now." This my father would do, muttering under his breath, "Damned cat!" My mother liked to recall the few times when Winnie and Donald did engage in conversation. She especially savoured the day when Winnie was going on about how we girls should go to private schools and come out as debutantes in Toronto. I now understand why Winnie was so fervent about this. The high point of her life had been the social flurry that for years followed her debut in 1919. To my sister and me, her insistence on Toronto private schools was laughable. We knew that any Barrie girls who went to such schools were being punished for being unmanageable at home or at school or both. As for "coming out" — then an innocent expression — it was one of those sayings of Winnie's that caused us to erupt into giggles. "Coming out of *what*?" we used to cry between bouts of hysteria. "A *cocoon*?" Winnie was especially persistent with my father on this subject. "How will they ever meet marriageable men in a *dump* like Barrie?" she urged, as determined as a dog digging under a fence. Eventually my father said quietly, "I want my children to sit next to the garbage man's son in school." Winnie was outraged. I don't remember what it was that Winnie had said to provoke him, but on one occasion he was as close to anger as I ever saw him. "Winifred," he said, "it's people like you who caused the French Revolution." To this Winnie replied, "But Donald, I've never *been* to France."

MERRY CHRISTMAS

Even in the new house, Christmases continued to be an exercise in evasion. Winnie always came to Mulcaster Street for the holiday. She had habits at that season that irritated my mother and father more than usual. Mother would have spent much time and creativity in decorating our Victorian house. The tree changed from year to year: sometimes it was traditional red and green; one year it was white and silver; another time everything — even the angel hair and tinsel — was blue. Winnie had many observations on the tree. The only one she liked was traditional. Mother's lovely experiments drew comments such as: "Bertah, why on earth did you do the tree *blue*? I never heard of such a thing!" She might say of a white-and-silver tree, "Bertah, that tree could do with a little colour. Shouldn't you put on a few red and green balls?" Like a child, Winnie used to try to peek at the gifts we and her "great friends" had given her. When she thought no one was around, she'd try to unwrap and re-wrap her gifts. Since her wrapping was clumsy (unlike my mother's, who was noted for making perfect packages without using Scotch tape), this was no secret.

She sat in *that* chair wrapped in her ratty opossum coat, her mink hat pulled onto her head, complaining at intervals about the cold. By then, my sister and I agreed with her. We regularly used hot water bottles. I recall getting up in the night, my teeth chattering, to wrap a blanket around me before getting back into bed. It was three against one. We turned the thermostat up; my father turned it down. Winnie kept a close eye on my mother's cooking, in case she used spices or that "peasant food," garlic. Mother used to say she slipped these in, since she enjoyed strong flavours, and Winnie ate it all anyway without noticing. For dinner, Winnie often told my mother, "Just boil me an egg," as if preparing two different meals were easy. This nursery food she would eat out of a teacup at the kitchen counter before the rest of us ate.

On Christmas Eve, my family — which later included various husbands and boyfriends — sang Christmas carols at the baby

grand piano, with Mother accompanying us. These were occasions on which my father allowed himself more than two drinks. Once we were older, we drank too. The carols became more spirited as the evening wore on. Winnie did not drink

Winnie shutting out the sound of the annual family carol sing on Christmas Eve, Barrie, Ontario. Bertah played the piano, her granddaughter, Beatrix, played the violin, c. 1978.

or sing carols. She sat in her furs in my father's chair in the living room with her hands over her ears, saying things like, "Oh, *Bud*!" or "You sound like *alley cats*!" Eventually, she would go upstairs to bed, leaving the rest of us to caterwaul.

Christmas morning was always dicey. Mother wanted to keep to her routine, sleeping in until eleven or so. When we were small, she had relied on overflowing stockings to keep us busy until then. We knew our "big presents" were not to be opened until she got up and had her coffee. Winnie and my father got up at seven or eight. What my father did after his toast and coffee I can't recall. Perhaps he shovelled snow. Winnie established herself in *that* chair, her eyes fixed on the entrance to the kitchen from the back stairs, where my mother would eventually appear in one of her Bette Davis nighties and matching negligees.

Winnie would work herself up into a frenzy of anxiety in case she missed the annual speech from "our dear little Queenie." My parents were late getting television, predicting — correctly — that it would undermine everyone's reading. When they succumbed in the early '60s, almost a decade after TV was available, they set up a tiny TV room — actually an alcove at the top of the front stairs with room for only a single small sofa. The sofa blocked the doors to a tiny balcony over the front porch. Since no one ever went out on the balcony — or used the front door for that matter — this made no difference. Right next the TV room was the door to my parents' bedroom, a turquoise sanctuary with a 1940s dressing table and twin beds. Usually the door stood open, so watching TV was out of the question until mother got up and had her coffee. Since the Queen gave her Christmas address to the Empire at ten o'clock a.m., tension filled the house after about nine. If my mother was up, Winnie was upstairs in the TV room watching Queen Elizabeth, whose speeches back then always began, "My husband and I ..." Sometimes Winnie would persuade me to watch this stiff ten-minute monologue, whether or not Mother was up. If she wasn't, she soon was. As the Queen read her slow, over-rehearsed speech about those less fortunate (read: poor beyond her imagination) or the blessings we enjoyed at this season (read: the Anglican church was a fine institution and the birth of Jesus an inspiring event), Winnie would point out her tiara, her hairdo, the red, white-bordered sash that represented the Order of the Garter, and so on.

My father never watched the Queen's speech, and Winnie never gave up pressuring him to do so. In her mind, it was one of the highlights, if not *the* highlight, of the season. To my father, it was a lot of damned nonsense.

After mother had her coffee, we went to the living room to open our "big presents," having read the comics, eaten the candy canes, and played with the toys from our stockings. Since it was either noon or close to it by then, my parents (and in later years my sister and I)

numbed the stress with glasses of sherry. Winnie made it clear she did not approve of this. She heaved herself up from *that* chair in the kitchen after needling my mother

Winnie opening a Christmas present from one of her Toronto friends, Barrie, late '70s.

about her lateness and telling her how marvellous "our dear little Queenie's" speech was. In the living room, she established herself in my father's chair. He never protested.

Since Winnie had a good idea by then of the nature of all her presents, she feigned surprise as she opened each one. She liked to wait until the rest of us had opened our presents before opening hers. "Oh," she'd say, "this is a bar of Yardley's soap from Barbara. You'd think she could do better than *that*!" Or, as she held up a package of cocktail napkins with roses on them, "Mildred gave me *these*! She knows I never have cocktail parties — or teas for that matter!" Or, on opening a large box of Laura Secord chocolates from my parents, she would say, "Do any of these have *nuts* in them?" in a voice that implied nuts were more or less poison. Later, she would drive my mother wild by "testing" each chocolate — including those in the even larger box of chocolates given to my father by someone at the hospital — to see whether there were nuts inside. Within hours, the Christmas chocolates looked as if a small rodent had nibbled a corner from each one. Meanwhile, my father was in an agony of guilt as he opened gifts from his colleagues at the RVH (now the Royal Victoria Regional Health Centre). Since the RVH grew dramatically like other Ontario hospitals in the 1960s, these gifts were sometimes from contractors or the heads of companies who had been hired by the board (of which he was chairman) to build and equip additions. He felt especially guilty about the bottles of his favourite Scotch or rye that were often given to him. As he quickly put them down out of sight, he would say things like, "So-and-so shouldn't have given me this. He must know it smacks of a bribe." He hated Christmas, and always had. His favourite Christmas story was Stephen Leacock's "Hoodoo McFiggin's Christmas," about a boy who is given practical gifts he dislikes and nothing that he has asked for.

As for us, we were given all sorts of wonderful things. As always, Winnie gave me more and better presents than she gave my sister — something that irked my mother and, no doubt, my sister too. Mother was a generous person, and for her Christmas was the one time of the year to spoil us. One year during the war she sold some of her jewellery to buy us presents. She took as much delight in watching us open our gifts as Father felt apprehension at what the New Year's bills might be.

Christmas dinner was festive, despite Winnie. Mother would be frazzled after preparing the feast, a captive to Winnie's comments and questions from *that* chair, where she would sit until it was time to go upstairs and dress for dinner. That's when Mother would touch up the meal, adding lots of black pepper and a jigger of Scotch to the gravy.

We all dressed for Christmas dinner, in striking contrast to most of the meals we took sitting along the kitchen counter like an audience at a play that didn't exist. Mother considered Christmas dinner the challenge of the year. She cleaned the house. She polished the silver — not just the silverware, but also the silver coffee pot and tea set on their silver tray, which were never used. She decorated the table with a red felt tablecloth, neatly hemmed with grosgrain ribbon that she had sewn. She placed shiny Christmas crackers at each place. Finally, she arranged a stunning centrepiece of something like red carnations and pine sprigs in the silver punch bowl which had been given to D.A. when he left for Greenwood in 1898. Immaculate white linen napkins were folded beside each place. Crystal champagne glasses and her best Coalport china were at the ready. When the time came, she rang the five-tone gong that had announced the meals at Huntley Street.

We could not tell what special dress Winnie had put on for dinner. No doubt it was an expanded Creeds model, lavish and expensive. It could not be seen because over it she had put on her increasingly shaggy opossum coat. Though father seemed not to notice, my mother could not help saying things like, "Winifred, it's *Christmas*, for heaven's sake. Take off that *damned* coat and hat just this once." Winnie would launch into a speech about how terribly cold it was in the house. "I'll catch cold if I take them off." Fortunately, Winnie had by then taken her one pre-dinner drink, and the rest of us had had at least two on top of the sherry we'd been sipping all afternoon.

Father may have seen himself as "a plain dirt farmer," but he knew the niceties of the dinner table. Winnie, as the eldest guest, sat on his right, in my accustomed place. He sharpened the carving knife dramatically and carved the turkey in precise, thin slices. Though he well knew our preferences, he would ask each of us what we would like. He duly placed the meat on one of the china plates in front of him, asked about stuffing, served that too, then passed each plate in turn to my mother at the other end of the table to serve the vegetables. As the guest Winnie was served first, my father addressing her as "Winifred." She took only white meat, and declined stuffing, no doubt because she didn't know what my mother had put in it. She always took potatoes and gravy, but when offered the vegetables she might say things like, "I don't like turnips!" or, "Brussels sprouts give me indigestion!" or, "Just a few carrots," or, "Bertah, why didn't you have peas?"

As soon as Winnie was passed her plate, she "dug in." We had been taught to wait until everyone was served, and we did. Sometimes my mother just had to say something in a tense voice. "Winnie, can't you wait until the rest of us are served?" To this, Winnie always said the same thing: "But Bertah, my food would be cold by then!" Year after year, my father ignored the whole thing, proceeding with the slow and proper ritual he always followed. Winnie ate steadily, not looking up or talking or putting down her cutlery for a moment. By the time all of us were served, and my father (or one of our boyfriends or husbands) had circled the table to pour the champagne, she had finished her meal. She would then ineffectively suppress a burp or two, each time saying with a laugh, "Pardon me, same trouble!" For the rest of the meal, she would pepper us with comments and questions, such as "Too bad Kate isn't here to make the dinner," or, "Where did you get that Tom Turkey, Bertah?" Though she was offered plum pudding with brandied hard sauce, she always declined. Who knew what my mother had put in them? The high point of this holiday meal for Winnie was snapping open the Christmas crackers. Like a child, she was mildly scared by the bang but loved the supremely breakable little toys and the fortunes or jokes inside. After dinner, to my mother's displeasure, she picked succulent bits of turkey off the platter in the kitchen and gave them to whatever cats and dogs were resident at the time.

46

MY MOVE TO
TORONTO, 1961

When I left home at eighteen to study English Language and Literature at Victoria College, I saw Winnie more often than ever. My parents tried to induce me to go to the elitist, Anglican Trinity College, but I rebelled and chose the United Church College instead. My first-year residence at Victoria College was close enough to walk to 80 Elm Avenue.

It says much about my naïveté and general ignorance on the subject of Canadian literature that, unbeknownst to me, E.J. Pratt, Jay Macpherson, and Northrop Frye were teaching English there, and Margaret Atwood and Dennis Lee were fourth-year students. I took my studies seriously, enjoyed the social life of the college, studied ballet with the Russian Boris Volkoff, who carried a cane and did not hesitate to use it on our legs, and played basketball for the U of T women's team. Yet I found time to visit Winnie often.

I thought of her crammed, dusty apartment as an oasis, just as I had when I'd visited from Barrie. I could always count on the usual simple meals and a chance to lie about watching TV. If I stayed over, the routine was the same as it had always been: cuddles and jokes in bed, then breakfast brought to me on the dented turquoise tray in the morning. I couldn't read or study there because I would inevitably hear "If you don't stop reading, you'll ruin your looks." We used to take walks together around Rosedale or have picnics in Craigleith Gardens. Sometimes we'd go shopping, as in the old days. Creeds, Birks, Ada Mackenzie's, Britnell's, and sometimes Simpson's. She still circled the block at Bloor and Bay for as long as it took to find a parking place she could drive directly into. She continued to give me gifts: a pair of shoes, a blouse, or costume jewellery. It never occurred to me that she couldn't afford these presents. She still occasionally "went south" on cruises in the winter, and she still drove her big Chev Impala everywhere.

She also still fretted about the noises "at all hours of the day and night" from Eric Aldwinkle's apartment above hers. "Why," she continued to ask, "do those young boys keep going up there?" At the time, I had no more idea than she did why this would be so. She still phoned her friends so early she woke them up. I would hear her merry laugh and remarks like, "You should be up at this hour!" or, "I've already had my breakfast!"

My father had put me on a limited budget at university, so I used to get Winnie to take me to the movies I wanted to see. It was still intoxicating to be able to see new releases when they came out instead of waiting months for them to reach Barrie. One I remember especially. I had studied Henry James's *Portrait of a Lady* in one of my courses, though I understood little of it. When *The Innocents* was released that year, a movie based on James's "The Turn of the Screw", I thought seeing it might help me understand James. The novella (and the movie) was billed as the first Freudian ghost story, and I hoped it wouldn't be too scary for Winnie. I counted on the fact that James was a highbrow author, and I thought Winnie might enjoy the setting in Victorian England. Not long into the movie, the suspenseful music and a glimpse of the black-clad ghost of the governess in a gazebo across a marshy pond did it. Winnie fled to the car, where I found her after the movie ended. It didn't help me with James, and I had to admit I was scared too.

I was more than surprised on the one occasion when I really did need Winnie. I was returning by train from a basketball game at McGill in Montreal. Something delayed the train, and we did not arrive back in Toronto until about two a.m. Women's residences in those days had an eleven o'clock curfew. At Margaret Addison Hall, where I shared a room, it was strictly enforced by a burly porter who locked the door and stood guard. This arrangement, which ironically often caused students to stay out all night even when they were only a few minutes late, was intended to ensure the girls' purity. There was certainly no possibility of getting into the residence at two a.m. I phoned Winnie from Union Station, expecting she would sleep through the ringing. She answered the phone, and — once she grasped what had happened — told me in a groggy voice to wait for her to pick me up. She was not at all angry, but simply worried that I was all right. I heard many comments, such as, "Those people in charge ought to be lined up and shot!" and "What was wrong with the engineer on the train? He should be fired!" and "I never heard of such a thing!" Yet she rose to the occasion.

By 1961, Winnie was still doing a little volunteer work for the Cancer Society. I think she sold daffodils for their annual drive to raise funds. Certainly she still answered the phone in the gift shop at Princess Margaret Lodge. This was as close as Winnie ever came to having a job. During the Second World War she had volunteered in one of the canteens serving Toronto soldiers. Mother said she flirted outrageously with them — especially members of the 48th Highlanders. To Winnie, they were collectively her personal guardians, since she was the "Daughter of the Regiment." I suppose it was in this role that she laid a wreath at the war memorial in Queen's Park on behalf of the 48th Highlanders on Remembrance Day for several years.

47

MY MOVE BACK
TO TORONTO, 1965

I left Toronto for the University of British Columbia with my first husband in the summer of 1962, and after graduating two years later I took my M.A. in Canadian literature at the University of New Brunswick in Fredericton. During these years, I hardly saw Winnie at all. In the summers, when I returned to my summer job teaching swimming and lifeguarding in Barrie, I heard about her from the points of view of my parents. I was far too busy with my university studies and my unsuccessful attempts to bring order to my wildly unruly personal life to think of much else.

When I returned to Toronto in the fall of 1965 after finishing my M.A., I was in a sort of limbo. My first husband and I had separated, amicably. He went to Queen's, while I entered the Ph.D. program at Toronto. I was not allowed to continue on in Canadian literature. I was told that there was not enough literature in this country worthy of Ph.D. study. Instead, I decided to turn to Victorian literature so I could understand my parents and Aunt Winnie better. I took an attic room and board with a widow and her daughter on Roxborough Avenue. It didn't occur to me to stay with Winnie because I had no idea where my personal life was headed. By then I was twenty-two, and I knew she would grill me with questions wherever I sat in her apartment.

I think the only date I went on that she really approved of was one that echoed her days as a debutante. A graduating law student invited me to the Law Society Ball at the King Edward Hotel. I squeezed myself into one of my mother's ball gowns, a white tulle strapless with a wide turquoise taffeta sash. I did not feel comfortable at this occasion. The King Edward ballroom overwhelmed me. This, I decided, was not a life I wanted. Winnie, of course, encouraged me. What was the orchestra like? Who were the other men I danced with? Would I bring the law student over for tea? Were there other social occasions he might ask me to?

Meanwhile, I was balancing dates with the law student (who later became a Canadian diplomat abroad) with return visits from my husband and illicit trysts with a married professor from my first year, who seemed disinclined to leave his family. Another side of my social life formed around the small English Graduate Committee of which I was a member. After meetings, we used to go to *The Roof* of the Park Plaza for drinks until late into the night.

One of these fellow students became a close friend. She was descended from the Bulls, one of the families that had crossed paths with Aunt Winnie socially in the 1920s. In fact one of her randy ancestors, Perkins Bull, was said to have chased Winnie around the block in Rosedale. Winnie approved. She was delighted when my friend invited her to a cocktail party in her apartment on Lowther Avenue. By then the Beatles were mid-career, and I recall that the music at this party in late August of 1964 was the newly released *Help!* Winnie arrived at this party "like a ship in full sail," as my friend said. She was wearing a billowing sapphire blue taffeta dress with a matching large, tilted hat worthy of Ascot. She was in her element, making small talk with the guests, smiling and tilting her head like the Queen Mother, and accepting her one drink. She inquired anxiously about what was in the canapés. Her voice, which carried well, could be heard from time to time asking various guests about the music. "Who is that alley cat?" she asked each of them in turn. By then I knew there was no point in getting Winnie to go to the Beatles movie, also called *Help!*, that had just been released. By now the whole western world had undergone a radical change, but Winnie hadn't changed at all. The guests at the party all loved her. To them she was an endearing eccentric, much talked about later.

At that stage, Winnie's main topic of conversation was the after-show party she had gone to in February 1964 for the cast of Richard Burton's Hamlet. Burton was staying at the King Edward Hotel with Elizabeth Taylor. Their scandalous relationship had begun on the set of Cleopatra in mid-1963. There was more than a trace of Toronto the Good left in the city, and large crowds protesting their adultery gathered around the hotel. Sir John Gielgud — who was directing the play for its two-week run before going to New York — was appalled. "Ghastly crowds of morons besiege the hotel," he wrote to his partner. It was dangerous for the couple to leave what was being called "their love nest." As soon as both their divorces were final, they stole away for the weekend to Montreal where they were married at the Ritz-Carlton Hotel by Leonard Mason, the same Unitarian minister who later married me and my third husband. It was Burton's second marriage, Elizabeth's fifth. At the start of the next performance of Hamlet, Burton quoted a line from the play to address the audience. It is a line directed at Ophelia, who soon after drowns herself: "I say, we will have no more marriages!" The audience cheered. Perhaps he might have considered Ophelia's fate and how ill-advised the date of their marriage had been, the fifteenth of March. A quote from another Shakespeare play correctly predicted disaster for Julius Caesar for that date: "Beware the Ides of March."

That Winnie had even the slightest connection to this worldwide scandal fascinated my friends, some of whom had seen Burton's minimalist Hamlet in which he was dressed in a trendy black turtleneck and black trousers. Winnie had met them both at the King Edward in a reception that was a far cry from the days when she used to foxtrot and waltz there with her beaux. Moreover, she knew where the couple had spent their secret honeymoon. They had rented a cottage from the Cassels family, whom Winnie had known in the '20s, on Kempenfelt Bay close to The Cabin near Shanty Bay. For once Winnie knew more than those she talked to. She said that she was unimpressed with Burton, and immune to his legendary animal magnetism. She was dazzled by Elizabeth Taylor, however. Above all she could not get over the enormous aquamarine earrings the star was wearing or the exquisite violet shade of her eyes. Of course, Winnie had not seen the play. Had she seen it, it would have bored her, and she probably would have left. As far as I know, she never saw any plays by Shakespeare. It's even possible she didn't know who Shakespeare was.

That year, Winnie continued her "work" at the Princess Margaret Lodge. She still visited the Kindersleys, travelling aboard one of the Cunard-White Star luxury liners. She had long since let The Cabin go, but she managed to get herself "by the lake" at the cottages of friends or at places like the expensive Bigwin Inn on Lake of Bays in Muskoka, a very expensive island resort that hosted the likes of Greta Garbo. (She joked about the name: "Big Win.") Later, there were summers when she rented the McKeiller cottage near Shanty Bay. I remember visiting her there. On one occasion she spotted a bat in the cottage, and my sister and I fled, one of us leaving the bathwater running. She appeared running through the door with a fish net upside down over her head. My sister and I, now grown women, collapsed into giggles. She continued to play bridge with her friends, though she reported to me that they were always getting angry with her: she still played the old 1920s auction bridge, whereas they had moved on to the bidding system popular since the late 1920s based on "contracts."

She claimed she couldn't understand it. She still woke her "great friends" with early phone calls. She continued to take drives — even on the highway — at no more than forty mph in her Chev Impala, and went shopping at Bloor and Bay. She still saved the bones from her roasts for a neighbour's dog, and gave them to the dog in person. She was still puzzled by Eric Aldwinkle's life. She once insisted I borrow her tiara for some occasion. This became a disaster when something happened to change the event, and the group I was with ended up at an ordinary movie. She still listed her name, address, and phone number under "Miss Winifred Cameron." She would not change it until logic prevailed after she got a series of phone calls from a heavy-breathing "motorcycle gang" who threatened to come over and tie her up in chains.

48

THE BANKRUPT, 1966

Aunt Winnie ran out of money in 1966, when she was sixty-five. She did not see it coming. She thought there would always be money to shop at Creeds, pay Dom and Tony's bills, get "by the lake" for the summer, and take trips south or abroad in the winter. It shocked her to the core. I was far removed from this inevitability, as I was enjoying the Summer of Love and the anti-war protests in San Francisco. I thought of myself then as in opposition to my family, so no letters or calls were exchanged. I was a groovy '60s rebel; they were part of the fuddy-duddy Establishment. I learned nothing of Winnie's disaster until later.

The first my parents learned about this crisis was from a hysterical phone call from Winnie. She complained in a high-pitched voice that the stores where she had credit were refusing to take her credit any longer. This did not surprise my father. He grasped immediately what had happened. He'd been expecting it for years. He hired a Barrie lawyer, Peter A. Mills, from Stewart, Esten, McTurk, Mills & Dick, to negotiate Winnie through what was traumatic to her and infuriating to him. My mother said sarcastically that only Creeds managed to get the money Winnie owed. The other creditors did not.

My father must have insisted that she finally get her birth certificate from Seattle. Or perhaps the lawyer needed it as part of his case for bankruptcy. Either way, in early December 1966 a copy of her birth certificate was sent to her from King County, Washington. The birth certificate, which is among the papers my mother gave me, shows that she was indeed born in Seattle on 2 February 1901, though only her surname is given. A few days later she had a neighbour and old friend, Marian Huff, who lived nearby at 52 Elm Avenue, submit an Affidavit for Correction of Birth Record. In it Marian wrote, "the true and correct name should be Winifred May Stuart Cameron." This affidavit was sent back to Seattle.

My parents saved copies of the legal letters from the lawyer. Perhaps they wanted me to condemn Winnie when I eventually got around to sorting through her papers. I did not condemn her; I loved her too much for that. Yet I admired my father for doing his duty in taking care of his spendthrift sister, despite his frugal nature. Her corrected birth certificate must have arrived from Seattle by early March 1968,

Winnie's first passport photo, May 2, 1975, after going bankrupt. Only then did she admit she was born in the United States.

for on 12 March 1968 the lawyer sent letters to her five creditors. Winnie owed Dom & Tony $241.29; Henry Birks & Sons $162.92; Bill Davis (Service Station & Garage) $197.54; Brown Brothers butchers $65.54; and Robert Simpson Company $811.73. The total was $2,160, give or take. Creditors were warned "there is really no hope of Miss Cameron being able to pay anything," and were also informed that "her brother in no way wishes to take responsibility for her debts." The letters mentioned that Winnie had no income but the Old Age Pension and was applying for welfare. Her furniture and clothes were covered under a warehouseman's lien.

The fact that Winnie had recently qualified for the government pension irritated my father into speaking out. "It's criminal that she gets the taxpayers' money," he said, "when she hasn't paid a cent into the pension — or anything else — all her life."

Bankruptcy was a concept she did not grasp. She felt betrayed by the businesses that had enjoyed her custom for so many years. She saw no reason why her money should have run out. She did not appreciate the fact that she now had a pension that she had never contributed to. Nor did she understand that my father's payment of a lawyer had freed her from most of her debt and retained her furniture and clothes.

Winnie blamed her father. "He did not leave me nearly enough money!" she stoutly maintained. My father blamed Winnie's financial advisor at the National Trust, Frank Hayes. My father probably had no idea that Winnie had been in love with Frank for years, and that conversations between them about money might have been affected by this. "She's been dipping into her capital for years," my father said. "That man should have advised her to live within her means. She had more than enough money to spend a comfortable life living off the interest." My mother blamed Winnie. "She had no more sense about money than a fly."

The train of events that followed was detested by all concerned. Forced to leave her apartment at 80 Elm Avenue, Winnie moved in with my parents in Barrie. Winnie called Barrie "that dump" more and more often. I missed those conversations, though all three told me of them later. Winnie was stunned and outraged that life as she knew it in Rosedale had come to an end. My father — skilled in evasion — was either at work or reading in the living room or his bedroom. It fell to my long-suffering mother to bear the brunt of Winnie's outpourings. Christmases had been hard, but the prospect of life with Winnie must have driven my mother to extreme desperation.

Winnie's car had been sold, along with some of her splendid mahogany furniture, as part of the assets that would partly offset her debts. She wept over the loss of her things, things she always said she was keeping for "you girls."

My parents undertook the massive enterprise of dismantling her Toronto apartment and moving her things to Barrie. Her clothes stuffed the small closet in my old bedroom, where Winnie was installed, and overflowed into other closets in the house. At some point, she got the flu. My mother waited on her, but was shocked and disgusted at having to clean the sheets on the occasions when Winnie could not make it to the bathroom. My father built a rickety shed attached to the old empty shed behind the garage to store her coats. There they would sit, damp in the summer humidity and inaccessible due to the snow in the winter. "She has over a hundred coats," he later said, shaking his head. Most of these were from Creeds or Simpson's, and the total cost must have been alarming. Certainly it was inconceivable for my father, who for years had had to be dragged to clothing stores by my mother. After each purchase he used to say, "This will see me out," even when he was only in his mid-fifties. By then, he had taken to retrieving items of his clothing thrown out by my mother who thought them unfit to wear, repeating "This will see me out!" Even his faded, moth-eaten turquoise and navy wool toque from Appleby School was still being salvaged. Mother was the opposite. Like Winnie, she had a fondness for fashion. She used to counsel us not to tell our father what she had bought on our shopping trips to

Toronto. This was futile; on the nights he did the monthly accounts at the kitchen counter, we would hear him calling, "Who bought a pair of brown shoes?" or, "Who's responsible for two umbrellas?" or, "Bertah, is this right? A dress costing $58.74?" He never reprimanded her or challenged costs. Since she had no idea how much he earned or had saved, as his bank accounts were in his name only, she had to gauge what she could get away with by instinct. It's possible her habit of sneaking in the things we bought in Toronto had more to do with suppressing our jubilation over our purchases. She always arrived home late from Toronto, often to find my father pacing up and down the dead-end street, looking anxious. He clearly felt abandoned.

At first, Winnie inveigled her "great friends" in Toronto to rescue her from "that dump." Whenever any of them went south, or went abroad to places she would never see again, they offered Winnie the chance to come by bus and housesit for them. I remember she stayed either with or for one of the debs from times lost, Marian Haas. I visited her there and met Marian. There was obvious tension between the two, and I gathered Winnie was not really welcome. After that,

Winnie, in her old opossum coat, house-sitting for the Walkers in Toronto, late '60s.

Winnie housesat for Denzil Walker and his sister, Phyllis, another deb from the 1920s. Perhaps one or both of them had lost their spouses. Possibly they had set up house together from the outset. The Walkers spent the legal limit of six months outside Canada in the Channel Islands to lower their taxes. They had a spacious house in Forest Hill, where Winnie paid their bills from their account and let their cleaning woman in and out. I visited her there more than once. She would begin to cry, and tell me how lonely she was. She would heat up a can of Campbell's tomato soup and butter some bread for our lunch. The sight of her sitting in that large living room, decorated in cool whites and neutrals, instead of the peach and turquoise she loved, was distressing. I gave her lots of hugs and reassurance. She told me of her troubles with the TTC. If she saw a "darkie" on the bus or subway, she would flee in fear. She still would not board a bus driven by a woman. She certainly had no money to go to Winston's or the Arcadian Court for lunch, or to shop along Bloor Street as she used to do. Instead of ordering her groceries almost daily by phone, she had to walk through winter weather in her now disreputable opossum coat and mink hat several blocks to Forest Hill Village and buy only what she could "haul back." She reminded me of Barry Lyndon, which I was then reading. It was a novel by Thackeray about the social and financial rise and fall of a good-natured character in the nineteenth century. I could never have discussed this with Winnie, who would have trotted out her usual platitudes — often misquoted — to justify why there was nothing she could do about her fate. It was plain to her: her father had not left her enough money. All the men her age had been killed in the war, so she couldn't marry. Since she didn't read and she no longer had us children to play cards with, she had only her needlepoint to resort to as a pastime. I profited from rose needlepoint dining room chair covers, which I eventually made into cushions that I still have. I also have a long turquoise bell pull that she made. It is meant for calling servants, and I don't know what to do with it.

In 1970 I remarried and moved to Toronto where my new husband had a job at York University. Winnie disliked my third husband because he was American and spoke with an upstate New York accent. She preferred my second husband because he was English and spoke "the Queen's English." She assailed me with tiresome questions about why we had divorced, why I liked an American, how the children would survive the upheaval. Overall, of course, she was glad that I was back in Toronto. Now when she was housesitting she could see me and my family. My second husband had treated her with amused detachment, except when she praised the monarchy, which he loathed. She was off to a much rockier start with my third husband. Just two months after we married in Montreal, we undertook a trip to Niger, West Africa with my children, aged seven and five. He was conducting research on slavery.

I invited Winnie over for tea before we left. We attempted to explain where we were headed. "What is the equator?" she interjected, then said, "I suppose there will be darkies there?" My exasperated husband — a Marxist and a specialist in black history — answered curtly, "Of course. We will be the only whites. Everyone else will be black." To which Winnie countered, with a look of horror, "As for black people, I loathe them every one!" This once-common view, which had produced thousands of black jockey garden statues (now repainted white) all over Ontario, pretty much terminated the conversation.

Shortly after we returned from what, for me, was five weeks of unmitigated hell, I invited Winnie over to Sunday lunch with my family. It was a rainy day when I picked her up, and I feared the worst.

I now can't remember what exactly Winnie did to provoke my husband. It could have been any of a number of things, from racist comments, to criticism of the food, to wearing her coat and hat to the table, to starting her meal before everyone else. I was so familiar by then with her quirks and rudeness that I easily overlooked them.

If anything, they were amusing to me. Not to my husband. I remember his standing up at the head of the table and yelling at her. Knowing her penchant for royalty, he shouted, "I expect you to have the manners of the Queen when you are at this table!" When she resisted and denied whatever problem it was, he went to the phone just around the corner in the kitchen and pretended to call the police. That did it. Winnie, extremely agitated, lurched up, grabbed her umbrella, and left. My two children were white-faced. I went after her in the car and drove her back to the Walkers'. She expostulated all the way with denials of rudeness, reminders that she had been presented at Buckingham Palace, and unflattering comments about my husband.

It was with this husband and our nine-year-old son that I finally visited Achnacarry Castle myself. We arrived impromptu after a picnic on the shore of Loch Lochy. There were Lochiel and his wife, Margot, he in his kilt and she in a wool dress. They were as friendly as Winnie had always told me they were. I was surprised and strangely moved to see the castle I had heard so much about the salmon stream surging past it, the dark — and, yes, dank — interior. It was almost like *Brigadoon*, a magical step from the present through the mist into the changeless past.

There were a few good times still left for Winnie. Her friends picked her up to play bridge, a somewhat dubious favour, since they then got upset that she still played auction bridge. Her "great friend" Bobbie Laidlaw, another 1920s character and a widowed multimillionaire, sometimes sent for Winnie in a chauffeured car to go with him to *Moongate*, his summer place at De Grassi Point. There he would entertain her "by the lake" in the manner to which she was no longer accustomed and send her back with a large box of the best chocolates. Though he was fifteen years older than Winnie, it was like having a beau for a few days.

49

THE
CASTLE

My parents must have thought it a supreme irony when they discovered an apartment in "that dump" Barrie for Winnie. The house
with eight apartments was called The Castle. The woman who had once
"felt like a duchess" at Buckingham Palace was now reduced — because
of her extravagance — to an old age pensioner dependent on her
brother for her rent. They probably saw it as resembling one of Aesop's
fables, or as a modern-day morality play. I saw it more as a tragedy.
A woman with more than one tragic flaw had been brought to her
knees from the highest rank of Toronto wealth and social power. The
city had changed from Toronto the Good to a metropolis filled with
lively entertainments and fewer churchgoers. Canada had moved
on from a British colony towards a more egalitarian, multicultural
nation. Even the western world had changed, from a fairly predictable group of countries where the military were widely honoured to
Marshall McLuhan's "global village," where anti-war sentiments and
anti-authority gestures prevailed.

Lount's Castle (1880), later apartments known as "The Castle," where Donald
supported Winnie from about 1979 on. Courtesy of the Simcoe County Archives.

Like Winnie, The Castle had seen better days. The original owner,
William Lount, had become a local judge in 1901, the year Winnie was
born. Lount was the nephew of the Reform MPP for Simcoe County,
Samuel Lount, who was hanged for treason for his role in the 1837
Rebellion. William Lount built The Castle (he had originally named
it The Oaks) as a summer place on a hill at the north end of town
overlooking Kempenfelt Bay. He must have had a grandiose vision
of himself, for this would be the only mansion of its kind ever built
in Barrie. Its Second Empire style echoed the lavish architecture in
Paris during Napoleon III's reign. The imposing red brick three-storey
building had a mansard roof with a flower pattern in slate, a tower, a
decorative chimney, turrets with intricate round windows, the tall
first-storey windows still seen in parts of Paris, and many ornate
dormer windows, all enhanced with wrought iron trim. On the former
farm of forty-five acres Lount also built another house, a red brick
carriage house with servants' quarters and a hay loft above.

The Castle was on its way down by 1950 when it was purchased by
the golf pro at a nearby course. He split the building into eight apartments, using the ballroom on the third floor for storage. Marble
fireplaces were incorporated into the apartments as shelves or parts

of desks. By the time Winnie took her cramped apartment on the ground floor, the original chandelier in the old ballroom had been replaced by a bald electric light bulb hanging on a wire. The acres of parkland surrounding Lount's Castle had been sold off over time and the outbuildings had been torn down, as the rapid expansion of Barrie swallowed up the north end once Highway 400 made the city a bedroom community for Toronto. By this time it was a city with a population of about 24,000.

I don't know how long Winnie stayed with my parents, or, rather, how long my mother tolerated her in the house before moving her out. By the time I was back in Barrie for a visit, she had been installed in The Castle. "I just couldn't take it," my mother pleaded to me, guilty with the thought that it might have been her duty to take care of her penniless sister-in-law. "She nearly ruined our marriage. Your father and I had to go out in the car to have a conversation."

I suppose it was my father who had filled out Winnie's application for Canadian citizenship, insisting she sign it while she still could. As a hospital administrator, he would have wanted to be sure her documents were ready in case she had to go into a provincial nursing home. She was seventy-three years old when she became the Canadian citizen she had always maintained she was. A year later, she was issued her first Canadian passport on 2 May 1975.

Before seeing Winnie at The Castle on one visit home, I drove downtown to do a few errands. Barrie had grown so much that I hardly recognized the town I grew up in. It now had a population of about 40,000. I was stopped at the main intersection known as the Five Points, when I noticed a street person shambling by. Though I could hardly believe it, it was Aunt Winnie. She was much thinner. Her clothes were shabby, and one of her stockings had slid down around her ankle. Her now-white hair was tangled. It was her carriage, her upright stance and air of entitlement, that had caught my eye. I leaned over, opened the passenger door, and called out to her. She stopped and looked around in a confused way, her eyes vague and unfocused, as Dollie's had been at Huntley Street. I yelled, "It's Pidge! Winnie, it's Pidge!" Still bewildered, she approached the car, then recognized me and smiled. I could see that she was missing some teeth. "Pidgie!" she exclaimed. "Well, I never heard of such a thing!" With cars honking behind me as the lights changed, I urged her to get in. She laboured to fold herself up enough to get into the seat, saying "Oh, *Bud*!"

When we arrived at The Castle on Valley Road — a building I had not been aware of when I grew up in Barrie — I couldn't imagine how Winnie had gotten herself downtown. Did she take a bus? Did she walk? It must have been two or three miles up the steep hill of Sunnybrook Road. I could see that downhill might not be such a bad walk, but how could she climb back up? Winnie, who had stopped and puffed, exclaiming "Oh, *Bud*!" even on short walks around level Rosedale?

Although I had picked Winnie up and dropped her off a few times at The Castle, I hadn't been inside before. Her apartment was even smaller than 80 Elm Avenue, yet there was much of the same old furniture. The rest, my mother told me, was in storage, another bill my father must have paid. "She just won't let go of her things," Mother said. "She identifies with those things. Her things are her." Amid the familiar furniture in unfamiliar places were boxes upon boxes of more things. "I try to unpack a box every month or so," Winnie said, as she lowered herself onto the sagging sofa on which I used to lie watching TV at Elm Avenue. "Well, dearie," she said, with tears in her eyes. "I hate this dump! There's nothing to do in Barrie. Without my car I can't go anywhere." My mother, predictably, said, "She has no one to blame but herself. We would have kept her here if she had even been polite. All she did was complain about everything. If I hear her say Barrie is a dump once more, I'll go mad. After all, we live here. And there's plenty to do here." Then she added, in one of her famous non sequiturs, "You know, she never even thanked your father for getting that lawyer. All she had to say was, 'He should be lined up and shot.'"

On another of my visits, Winnie surprised me. My parents had had her over for dinner on many occasions, driving her between The Castle and Mulcaster Street. On that occasion, I was sent (as the only one who could stand Winnie) to pick her up and meet the rest of the family and some friends at a Chinese restaurant on Dunlop Street next to the movie theatre. She did not like climbing up the narrow stairs to the restaurant on the second floor. Once there, we took our places with the others who had chosen a large, round table. She sat down and looked around for a few minutes. Then she suddenly got up and ordered me to drive her back to The Castle. At first, everyone thought it was the foreign food, or even the Chinese themselves. I knew it was not that because she had taken me so often to Lichee Gardens in Toronto. "I will not sit at a table with thirteen people around it!" she exclaimed, before heading down the stairs. When I returned after taking her home, the family were still laughing and shaking their heads. None of us knew she was superstitious about the number thirteen. It became yet another anecdote about "crazy" Aunt Winnie.

50

A VISIT TO
THE CASTLE

Eventually it became clear that Winnie was no longer able to live on her own at The Castle. I was now on my way to becoming a professor at the University of Toronto. I was writing as well as teaching, married with three children, and busy in a way that is indescribable. I had no time to visit Winnie or anyone else.

According to my parents Winnie sank deeper and deeper into some form of dementia. She lost track of whether it was day or night. This resulted in her phoning Mulcaster Street at odd times throughout the night. One of the cardinal rules in my family had always been that no one woke my mother before she was ready. She had a gift for sleep. When we moved from Dundonald Street to Mulcaster Street, the movers had taken everything from the place except my mother's bed. She slept through it all, but finally had to be wakened so they could complete the move. My father laughed with the movers. "She's a good sleeper, all right," he recalls saying.

That Winnie's phone calls in the middle of the night were

unwelcome was an understatement. It was a given that Mother would not put up with that for very long. Among the odd assortment of Winnie's papers that I was given are Bell Canada telephone bills from 12 November 1981 to 20 April 1982 indicating that Winnie not only phoned several times, but that she always called 411 information for my parents' number first. This would have upset my father as much as it upset my mother, since there was a charge for 411 calls. During those five months, she made forty-five 411 calls and six long distance calls to her "great friends" in Toronto at a total cost of $40.21. One of my parents — I suspect my father — must have kept these bills, since Winnie was too far gone by then to do so. Why did they keep them? Perhaps they wanted me — or anyone else who happened to go through Winnie's papers — to see that they were justified in what they eventually did.

Then came the complaints from the Barrie taxi companies. According to my mother, many of Winnie's telephone calls, 411 and otherwise, were for taxis "to take her nieces to the bus terminal or some other place." When taxis arrived, Winnie would come to the door with a pillowcase in each hand stuffed with things. "Here are my nieces," she'd say, handing them to the driver.

It was truly horrible, for my mother especially but also for my father, to obtain the necessary papers for Winnie's removal from The Castle. She refused to go willingly. My father must have handled most of it, since he was accustomed to a range of crises at the hospital, including being called in the middle of the night to subdue a naked man from the psychiatric ward who had broken into the fire box and stolen an axe. Mother recalls going to the apartment with my father and a doctor, who gave Winnie an injection to subdue her forceful struggles. She was then transported to the Collingwood Nursing Home, an Ontario long-term care facility, where my father had arranged for her to stay. Mother hated making any unpleasant decision that might result in blame. This was one she had dreaded for some time. She spoke later in anguish about how terrible it had been.

51

A LAST VISIT
TO WINNIE

I was the last one in the family to see Aunt Winnie alive. On one of my visits home, I got the address of the nursing home where my father had had her put a month or so earlier. I drove up to Collingwood to visit her. My parents were relieved, as they hated going there. It's possible my father never went. My mother certainly did, however. She also tracked Kate down in another Ontario nursing home and visited her.

When I got there, one of the staff showed me to her room, a small boxlike space. As she led me there, she said nothing. I suspected that Winnie was an unusually difficult patient. The staff member unlocked the door and opened it. Winnie was dressed surprisingly well and sat on a chair. She looked confused, almost dazed, staring at nothing in particular. Her once-clear blue eyes had turned milky and unfocused.

"Who is this?" she asked, looking right at me. "It's me, Pidge!" I said loudly, though I had no reason to think her hearing had gone. "Is that

Pidgie?" she said, peering into my face. When I took her small hands and reassured her that I was there, she looked terribly distressed and begged me to get her out of there. "I hate this dump!" she said, as if she thought she was still in Barrie.

She pulled her hands from mine and held them both out in front of her. "Would you please cut my nails, Pidgie?" she pleaded, almost whined. "Nobody here will do it."

That could not have been true, since her nails were not very long. "Sure." I said, "Just a minute. I'll see if I can find some scissors. You just wait here." I looked around the halls and found a staff member who gave me a small pair of nail scissors with blunt tips, asking that they be handled carefully and returned at once.

When I got back to Winnie's room, she was staring into nowhere again. "Who is this?" she asked, and we went through the whole conversation again. Once she realized it was me, she eagerly put out her hands so I could cut her nails. I felt the same tenderness I felt when I had cut my babies' little nails for the first time. Winnie was tearful. "Thank you so much, dearie," she said. "You can't imagine how much better that feels. Now you can take me home." Then her words became jumbled, interspersed with things from the past: Alex, "you girls," "by the lake," Barbara, Parklands.

Hoping that this meant she no longer realized where she was, I got up to leave. "Please, please don't go," she begged. Her eyes were fierce. "I'll come back soon," I said, giving her a long hug. I meant it. Yet somewhere, somehow, I knew it would be the last time I saw her.

It wasn't long after that that my mother phoned to say with a mixture of relief and guilt that Winnie had died on 21 July 1982 of bronchitis. She was eighty-one.

52

THE MAUSOLEUM,
PORT ELGIN

I attended Aunt Winnie's funeral on a clear summer day along with the rest of my family. No one else was there. It was held in Port Elgin, Ontario, where the Cameron family first arrived in Canada. The Cameron mausoleum was the largest of the few crypts in the Port Elgin cemetery. Inside the vault were several drawers in which various Cameron ancestors were "buried." My mother and sister had seen it when Dollie, wearing her diamond brooch, was put into her drawer in 1953. Winnie's interment was the first time I had seen it. I had never heard of most of the relatives in there. No doubt the stone mausoleum with its large door and enormous flat key was meant to inspire awe at one of Canada's "noble" Scottish families. Yet I found the whole idea of a mausoleum Gothic and somehow repugnant. I could imagine my claustrophobic father counting the drawers, making sure he would not be doubly enclosed in there.

The vault was erected by D.A.'s father, the Scot William Cameron,

Hugo Donald Cameron, with his grandfather Donald's bagpipes, a Captain in the
48th Highlanders, in front of the Cameron Mausoleum in Port Elgin Cemetery
on the occasion of Donald's burial, August 21, 1996. A Celtic cross is flanked by two
engravings of the clan Cameron crest. Donald was the first Cameron to be buried
beside the Mausoleum instead of inside it.

who had been in his drawer the longest. He died in Port Elgin in 1910.
His Scottish wife, Johanna Stark Cameron, would survive him for
forty-three years. She died only five months before her son D.A. was
set into his drawer. After William Cameron in 1910, Neil McGillivray,
the husband of Winnie's aunt Mary Jean Cameron — her father's
sister — died in Port Elgin in 1928. Mary Jean followed him four years
later.

The McGillivrays must have celebrated the Clan Cameron, for
it was Neil who commissioned three stained glass windows for Port
Elgin's Presbyterian church from Robert McCausland Ltd., Toronto,
in 1925, shortly after D.A.'s sudden death. McCausland's firm was an
important practitioner of stained glass; they had made the first stained

glass window in the country. Among the many works they had done all over Canada was an elaborate window depicting the proposal scene from Shakespeare's Henry V (now in the Royal Ontario Museum) for Timothy Eaton's house, and a religious window for the Massey family at St. Andrew's United Church in Toronto.

Neil wanted a three-part window for the Camerons, set in a wooden arch, that would depict the Ascension of Christ. McGillivray had specified "rich colours" for the window to shine like jewels in the strong south-facing light. The central window is dedicated to Johanna Cameron; the window to the left is for her husband, William; the one on her right commemorates her son, Donald Alexander. This arrangement may have signified Johanna's loss of her husband and her son within six months of each other. Perhaps it was meant to offer her comfort in the Christian promise of resurrection. It could also have affirmed Neil McGillivray's own hopes for the afterlife, since he was seventy-five at the time he commissioned the window and died only three years later to join his relations in the mausoleum in 1928.

The mausoleum door was opened twice four years later when both Mary Jane, McGillivray's wife, and Winnie's uncle Colin Stewart Cameron died in 1932. Colin, D.A.'s brother, had distinguished himself as a lawyer and KC, and had also served as Conservative MPP for Simcoe Grey in Ontario. It would be fourteen years before D.A.'s brother-in-law, James Walker Doherty, took his drawer in the mausoleum in 1946. Seven years later, it was Dollie's turn. In 1960, Emma Cameron Doherty, Winnie's aunt and the wife of James Doherty, joined her husband. Now — almost thirty years after her mother died — the mausoleum door swung open for Winnie.

I'm sure that we were told that Winnie got the last drawer. This would make a tidy ending to her story, but it's not true. Yet I think of her death as the end of an era for the Cameron family, a Scottish-Canadian version of Poe's *The Fall of the House of Usher*. Hers was actually the second-last of the eleven drawers in the mausoleum. The final drawer went to Joan Doherty, James's and Emma's daughter.

After Winnie died, her cousin Don Ireland, with whom my third husband and I used to play bridge, said with a twinkle in his blue eyes that she ought to have had a tombstone with this inscription:

> *Here lie the bones of Winifred Cameron,*
> *For her life held no terrors;*
> *A virgin born, a virgin died,*
> *No hits, no runs, no errors.*

Instead, Winnie's drawer had a metal plate with a simple inscription giving her name and the dates of her birth and death.

For Winnie's funeral, my father had chosen one of the least expensive coffins. It was not the fine casket Winnie might have expected. It was a pastel turquoise-blue made of something covered with fabric. Oddly enough, though he was being economical and saw no reason to "honour" her death with mahogany, she might have been pleased with the coffin. It was one of her two favourite colours and resembled a fancy box of chocolates, like the ones she enjoyed throughout her life.

She was dispatched matter-of-factly. I suppose there was a minister, but I don't remember. Winnie only attended churches for social reasons, such as weddings and teas. My parents were not religious either, though they sent us to Sunday school at the Collier Street United Church while they slept in, encouraged us as teenagers to sing in the choir, and signed me into the CGIT (Christian Girls in Training — for what I never knew). Mother was especially put off by the notion of communion. "Drinking blood and eating the body of Christ?" she'd exclaim. "That's barbaric!" Father no doubt had had his fill of enforced Anglican services at Appleby School in Oakville.

Afterwards, we stopped in at a nearby restaurant along the highway for lunch. There were no toasts, no fond remembrances, no tears. The conversation ran along the usual lines, with the occasional comment: "What a wasted life," (my father) or "Maybe there was more I could have done," (my mother) or "She was really crazy" (everyone but me). I knew that I was the only one who would miss her, who would think of her often, who would know that she had at least given me endless entertainment and a map for relaxing and for showing physical affection. I knew such thoughts would draw only laughter and sarcastic remarks. I kept them to myself.

❦

ACKNOWLEDGEMENTS

I am grateful for the help I have had with this project. Many friends have supported and encouraged me over the last two years, and I thank them warmly. One friend, Milica Kovacevich, not only helped with my research, but also shared her lively enthusiasm. Without her, I could not have enjoyed working on this book as much as I did. Rae Fleming, author of a biography of Sir William Mackenzie (*The Railway King of Canada*, 1991) and an expert on this period of Toronto's history, kindly read parts of the manuscript and offered corrections and comments. A special thank you to Don Foley of Foley's Photography Services, St. David's, for all his professional work on the photos for this book.

Most of this book has been written and revised at my local Starbucks on Lake Street in St. Catharines. The staff there was surprisingly encouraging, occasionally bringing me an extra latté as I worked. I thank them all for fostering a wonderful atmosphere.

My editor, Marc Côté, took the time to read a rough outline at the outset and gave me valuable guidance. He is the most effective editor I have worked with. I thank him for his belief in this project and for having a keen eye for what really matters.

I thank my Aunt Winnie for inspiring this book.